GW00707583

THE
ASHES

THE ASHES

A COMPLETE ILLUSTRATED HISTORY

Peter Arnold and Peter Wynne-Thomas

Foreword by Dickie Bird

Brian Trodd Publishing House Limited

First published in 1990 by
Brian Trodd Publishing House Limited
27 Swinton Street, London WC1X 9NW

ISBN 1 85361 128 X

Printed in Italy

Some material in this book was previously
published in *The Illustrated History of the Test Match*

Title page: Ian Botham clean bowled in
the Fourth Test at Old Trafford, 1989

Contents

THE UMPIRE'S OPINION

by Dickie Bird, M.B.E.

I was very pleased when the authors asked me to make a contribution to this book, because to me an Ashes Series is something special. I know it's been said before, but it really is true that there is more excitement and anticipation around the dressing rooms before an Ashes match than anywhere else.

I've been lucky enough to stand in many Ashes matches, and hope to stand in a few more yet. In fact sometimes I think I'm almost luckier than the players, because in nearly 20 years as an umpire I've seen many cricketing greats complete their careers. Lillee, Thompson, Marsh, Greg Chappell, Doug Walters: I've seen all these top Australian players as young men, and watched them through to their retirements.

Dennis Lillee, I think, is the best fast bowler I ever saw, and I would take a lot of convincing that he isn't the number one of all time. The best Australian batsman I've seen from my privileged position of 22 yards away is Greg Chappell. He was a very elegant stylist, with perfect timing. He never seemed to put much effort into his shots, but when he hit it sweetly the ball sped to the boundary.

If I had to pick a batsman from Ashes matches to bat for my life, however, I would choose my fellow Yorkshireman Geoffrey Boycott. He was a batsman to bat session after session. In fact when Geoffrey returned to Test cricket at Trent Bridge in 1977 he took 187 off the Australian bowlers for once out, and became only the second batsman ever to bat on every day of a five-day Test match. I had to give him a fresh guard every day, and I have to say it was a pleasure.

The most exciting Test I stood in was at Edgbaston in 1981 when Australia needed a mere 151 in the fourth innings to win, and passed 100 with only four men out. Ian Botham then came on to bowl and took five wickets for one run – Australia crashed to 121 all out in a breathless finish.

I thought Richie Benaud was the best Ashes captain I saw (although I didn't umpire in any of his Tests), but Ian Chappell, Ray Illingworth and Mike Brearley weren't far behind. I was very impressed with Allan Border in 1989. It seems to me that he has brought on his younger players excellently, and now he has the whole team pulling together. Winning the World Cup in India and Pakistan in 1987 is probably his greatest achievement.

The player I was most impressed with was Mark Taylor, the Aussie opening batsman, who scored 839 runs in the series. He hardly ever got hit on his pads, and I always think this is a good sign – and not only because it gives the umpire fewer awkard lbw decisions to make.

I look forward to enjoying many more Ashes series, either from the middle or the boundary.

Right: In 1859 the first-ever English touring team went to the United States and Canada. They played five matches and won all of them.

The Pre-Test Era

The original plans for a cricket team to travel abroad were made as early as 1789, when the great patron of Kent cricket, the Duke of Dorset, arranged for a side under the captaincy of the Surrey wicket-keeper, William Yalden, to go to France. The team arrived in Dover only to meet the Duke fleeing from the French Revolution. The proposed tour was immediately abandoned!

Instead of 'England v France' being the first cricket international, pride of place must go to another title, which to many readers appears almost as strange, 'United States v Canada', played in New York in September 1844.

The match was played almost yearly in the 1840s and 1850s and in 1859, the tenth in the series was regarded as a 'test' for players who would be opposing the England team which was touring the United States and Canada the following month.

This all-professional England side, under the leadership of the Notts captain, George Parr, was the first side from the British Isles to go overseas. Five matches were played, plus three exhibition games. The five proper matches were all Eleven v Twenty-Two, but despite these odds, the Englishmen were victorious in all.

Two years later, the catering firm of Spiers and Pond tried to persuade George Parr to take an English team to Australia.

He and his Notts colleagues all refused the terms offered, but the promoters pressed on with their plans and the Surrey cricketer, H.H. Stephenson, led this first team to the Antipodes. The side won six and lost two of their matches, but financially were most successful and when in 1863 a second opportunity arose for an Australian tour, George Parr quickly accepted the offer. His side returned home undefeated. All matches on these tours were against odds.

The next international exchange occurred in 1868 when a team of Australian aborigines, under the leadership of Charles Lawrence – who had gone to Australia with Stephenson's side and remained out there as coach – toured England. The side was not capable of playing English first-class counties, but opposed strong club sides and in addition to cricket gave exhibitions of boomerang throwing and other similar attractions. In the same year, Edgar Willsher took a second England side to America and again returned undefeated.

Four years later, the MCC sent an amateur side to America. All matches were against Twenty-Twos and seven of the eight were won, the other being drawn. The famous W.G.Grace captained the third English Team to Australia in 1873/74. The standard of cricket 'Down Under' was now beginning to improve and for two matches the odds were reduced to Eleven v Fifteen, whilst Eighteen of New South Wales actually beat the English Eleven by eight wickets, as did a similar number from Victoria.

American cricket was not making the same progress and, in 1874, the Americans took the courageous step of sending a Baseball Team to tour England – the Baseballers playing cricket matches against fairly good club teams, as well as giving exhibitions of baseball. The visit was not very successful.

James Lillywhite organized and captained the fourth English side to Australia in the autumn of 1876. The team were beaten by Fifteen of New South Wales in their second match and then by Fifteen of Victoria. This was followed by a crushing defeat in the return v Fifteen of New South Wales, who immediately challenged the tourists to an eleven-a-side game. The match was drawn, much in favour of Lillywhite's men, but it set the stage for the first proper eleven-a-side match between 'England' and Australia, which was played when the tourists returned from a visit, in mid-tour, to New Zealand. The match is regarded as the 'First Test'.

Subsequently other countries came into the Test match fold: South Africa (1988–89), West Indies (1928), New Zealand (1929–30), India (1932), Pakistan (1952–53) and Sri Lanka (1981–82). South Africa lost Test match status in 1969–70.

No series has, however, equalled the traditional magic of that between the 'old enemies', especially since the Ashes came into being in 1882–83. By the end of 1989 there had been 269 Test matches between the two countries.

It is with the first of these, in 1876–77, that this book begins.

England v Australia

1876–77: Australia sets the ball rolling

The first Test match was played on 15, 16, 17 and 19 March 1877. For the first time England toured Australia on their own initiative, i.e. the tour was based on a speculative venture by the British rather than on an invitation from Australian organizers.

James Lillywhite, the Sussex cricketer, arranged the tour, and naturally managed and captained the touring party of twelve players. He was also the selector, and the players were not necessarily England's best – in fact W.G. Grace did not go. The batting would be considered weak by the standards of the best in the country, because the Nottinghamshire players Richard Daft and Arthur Shrewsbury did not tour. The bowling was, however, representative, including the leading bowlers in the country in Alfred Shaw, Allen Hill, Tom Emmett and James Southerton.

Blackham, John McCarthy

Blackham was born on 11 May 1854 at North Fitzroy, Victoria, and having played for Victoria from 1874–75 made his Test debut in the first Test match of all in 1876–77. He was called the 'Prince of Wicket-keepers'. He developed the modern style of keeping, standing over the stumps and taking the ball and whipping off the bails in a single movement. He was on Australia's first eight tours to England, and was captain of the 1893 tourists. In 35 Tests he took 36 catches and made 24 stumpings. He also scored 800 runs, average 15.68. He died on 28 December 1932 in Melbourne.

The party also included the best wicket-keeper available in Ted Pooley of Surrey, but was to be deprived of his services for the first of all Test matches after he had been arrested in New Zealand. The New Zealand leg of the tour occurred after nine matches in Australia, during which the tourists had played odds matches and had actually been beaten by XV of Victoria and XV of New South Wales, in the latter instance by the convincing margin of 13 wickets. The tourists then had much the better of a draw with XI of New South Wales, who might well have been beaten by an innings had the match continued, before sailing from Sydney for New Zealand where they were to play eight more odds matches.

The New Zealand trip was full of adventure, at one time the cricketers being stuck in their horse-drawn coach in the middle of a swollen river and having not only to swim for it but to rescue the horses.

Pooley's personal misfortune was the result of his being much wiser in the ways of betting on cricket than the locals. All the matches were the subject of constant gambling, and on one of them Pooley bet a spectator that he could forecast the scores of all 22 batsmen on the opposing side. The poor man gave Pooley odds of £1 to 1s (20–1) and Pooley wrote down a duck for each player. It was a ploy well known to practised gamblers, as there was always a reasonable number of ducks, particularly in this kind of odds match. In this case there were 11, so Pooley required of his victim £11 minus 11s, or £10. 9s. The man refused to pay, there was a fight and some damage to

property, and this is why England's leading wicket-keeper was awaiting trial in New Zealand when his team-mates played in the first-ever Test in Australia.

As a postscript to this story, Pooley never did rejoin the touring party or play in a Test, and sadly spent many of his last years in the workhouse, but he did not feel too badly about New Zealand as the sporting public there, thinking he had been badly treated, raised a subscription for him which reached about £50.

On returning to Australia the party's 18th match of the tour was at Sydney against a Combined Australian XI, or in effect a combined Melbourne and Sydney XI, these being the rival centres of cricket in Australia at the time. This was the first meeting between England and Australia on level terms, and has been regarded since as the 'first Test match'. There was no such designation at the time. The term 'test match' had been used in cricket earlier than this, but it was not until subsequent years, when cricket's army of statisticians regularized records, that this match came to be the first 'official' Test.

The England team was in bad condition. Everybody was exhausted by the trials and tribulations of New Zealand – the journey from one match to another, in which the players had been forced to swim, also encountered a landslide, and had taken nearly four days. The deputy wicket-keeper, Henry Jupp, was suffering from inflammation of the eyes and a bout of insanity, and was not trusted behind the stumps, although he had to play, there now

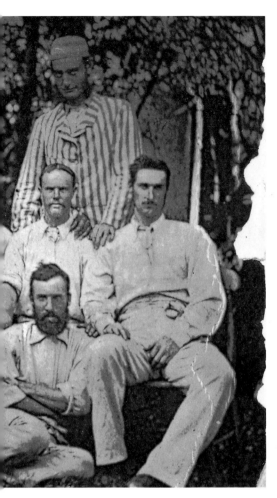

The Australian Test team in 1878-79

missed England for 196, William Midwinter taking 5–78.

England bowled better second time round, dismissing Australia for 104, but by scoring only 108 in the last innings themselves, were beaten by 45 runs.

It is interesting to note that Australia's highest scorers in each innings, Bannerman and Tom Horan, were born in Woolwich, England, and Middleton, Eire, respectively, while the leading wicket-takers, Midwinter and Tom Kendall, were born in Gloucestershire and Bedford, England. Midwinter later played Test cricket for England, one of a handful of players who have represented two countries. Nat Thompson was another Australian born in England. Of the rest Bransby Cooper was born in India, while the remaining five were born and bred in Australia.

Bannerman's innings is remarkable in that he scored 67.3 per cent of his side's first-innings total, and that in over 100 years and 1,000 Test matches since, that percentage has not been beaten.

James Southerton, from Petworth in Sussex, was 49 years old when he appeared in this match. He is not the oldest Test cricketer (Wilfred Rhodes was 52 when he played his last Test in 1930), but having been born on 16 November 1827 Southerton is the 'first-born' of all Test players.

After the tourists had played three up-country matches against sides of 22 players, a return match was played at Melbourne – the second Test. Australia were strengthened by the inclusion of Spofforth, Tom Kelly (another Irishman) and W.L. Murdoch, who was Australian, but like Midwinter later played for England, although in his case it was just one match at the end of his career, against South Africa.

The match was for the benefit of the English touring professionals, and drew about 15,000 spectators, a large number at the time, leading to those gamblers who had lost on betting on England in the first match claiming that it had been 'fixed' to attract a large crowd to the second, claims which

being only 11 players. Surprisingly he was England's top scorer with 63 after opening the batting. The man who kept wicket for England was the Notts batsman John Selby.

The Australian team, although not in the unfortunate state of the English, was also not quite representative of the best that could be fielded, lacking three of the best bowlers of the day in F.R. Spofforth, Francis Allan and Edwin Evans.

The match followed the day of the tourists' return, when many were still suffering from sea-sickness and not best pleased at having to field.

The first ball in Test cricket was bowled at 1.05 pm on 15 March 1877 by the Notts professional round-arm bowler Alfred Shaw, and Charles Bannerman of New South Wales faced it. The first run was scored by Bannerman off the second ball of the first over, overs at that time being of four balls each. Bannerman went on to score the first century in Test cricket, the only first-class century of his career. He was lucky to achieve this corner of fame in cricket's panorama. The England bowling and fielding was appalling and Bannerman was dropped by Tom Armitage, a simple catch being allowed to hit the fielder in what was probably already an upset stomach.

Apart from Bannerman, the Australian batting was not impressive, and when Bannerman was forced to retire hurt when a ball from George Ulyett split his finger, his 165 had come from a total of only 240 for seven. Australia totalled 245, and then dis-

---

AUSTRALIA V ENGLAND 1876–77

1st Test, Melbourne: Australia won by 45 runs

AUSTRALIA

C. Bannerman	retired hurt	165		b Ulyett	4
N. Thompson	b Hill	1		c Emmett b Shaw	7
T.P. Horan	c Hill b Shaw	12		c Selby b Hill	20
D.W. Gregory*	run out	1	(9)	b Shaw	3
B.B. Cooper	b Southerton	15		b Shaw	3
W.E. Midwinter	c Ulyett b Southerton	5		c Southerton b Ulyett	17
E.J. Gregory	c Greenwood b Lillywhite	0		c Emmett b Ulyett	11
J.M. Blackham†	b Southerton	17		lbw b Shaw	6
T.W. Garrett	not out	18	(4)	c Emmett b Shaw	0
T. Kendall	c Southerton b Shaw	3		not out	17
J.H. Hodges	b Shaw	0		b Lillywhite	8
Extras	(B 4, LB 2, W 2)	8		(B 5, LB 3)	8
Total		**245**			**104**

ENGLAND

H. Jupp	lbw b Garrett	63	(3)	lbw b Midwinter	4
J. Selby†	c Cooper b Hodges	7	(5)	c Horan b Hodges	38
H.R.J. Charlwood	c Blackham b Midwinter	36	(4)	b Kendall	13
G. Ulyett	lbw b Thompson	10	(6)	b Kendall	24
A. Greenwood	c E.J. Gregory b Midwinter	1	(2)	c Midwinter b Kendall	5
T. Armitage	c Blackham b Midwinter	9	(8)	c Blackham b Kendall	3
A. Shaw	b Midwinter	10		st Blackham b Kendall	2
T. Emmett	b Midwinter	8	(9)	b Kendall	9
A. Hill	not out	35	(1)	c Thompson b Kendall	0
James Lillywhite*	c and b Kendall	10		b Hodges	4
J. Southerton	c Cooper b Garrett	6		not out	1
Extras	(LB 1)	1		(B 4, LB 1)	5
Total		**196**			**108**

ENGLAND	O	M	R	W	O	M	R	W
Shaw	55.3	34	51	3	34	16	38	5
Hill	23	10	42	1	14	6	18	1
Ulyett	25	12	36	0	19	7	39	3
Southerton	37	17	61	3				
Armitage	3	0	15	0				
Lillywhite	14	5	19	1	1	0	1	1
Emmett	12	7	13	0				
AUSTRALIA								
Hodges	9	0	27	1	7	5	7	2
Garrett	18.1	10	22	2	2	0	9	0
Kendall	38	16	54	1	33.1	12	55	7
Midwinter	54	23	78	5	19	7	23	1
Thompson	17	10	14	1				
D.W. Gregory					5	1	9	0

FALL OF WICKETS

	A	E	A	E
Wkt	1st	1st	2nd	2nd
1st	2	23	7	0
2nd	40	79	27	7
3rd	41	98	31	20
4th	118	109	31	22
5th	142	121	35	62
6th	143	135	58	68
7th	197	145	71	92
8th	243	145	75	93
9th	245	168	75	100
10th	–	196	104	108

were intensified when England duly beat the home side by four wickets.

The England batting in this match was dominated by players from Yorkshire, who scored 329 of England's 383 runs (27 from Surrey, Sussex and Notts and 27 from extras). This percentage of 85.9, although helped by the fact that five of the original 12 tourists were from Yorkshire, is a record for a match in which so many wickets fell.

The tour was a financial success, and helped to establish what was still not yet regarded as 'Test cricket'.

1876–77 1st Series Aus 1, Eng 1

1 MELBOURNE Australia won by 45 runs

Australia 245 (C Bannerman 165) and 104 (A Shaw 5–38, G Ulyett 4–39)

England 196 (H Jupp 63, W E Midwinter 5–78) and 108 (T Kendall 7–55)

2 MELBOURNE England won by 4 wkts

Australia 122 (A Hill 4–27) and 259 (J Southerton 4–46, J Lillywhite 4–70)

England 261 (G Ulyett 52, T Kendall 4–82) and 122–6 (G Ulyett 63)

1878–79: Umpiring controversy, crowd invasion, captain assaulted

The Melbourne Cricket club invited a Middlesex amateur, I.D. Walker, to bring an amateur team to Australia in 1878–79. In order to improve the strength of the side, two professionals, George Ulyett and Tom Emmett were asked to join the tourists. In the event Walker was unable to go, and Lord Harris captained the party of 13 players.

The tour took in Australia, New Zealand and the USA, and consisted of 15 matches, the third of which, at East Melbourne, was labelled 'Gentlemen of England (with Ulyett and Emmett) v The Australian XI'. This rather strange collection has become accepted as the third Test match. While Australia fielded a stronger side than appeared two years earlier, the England side was not

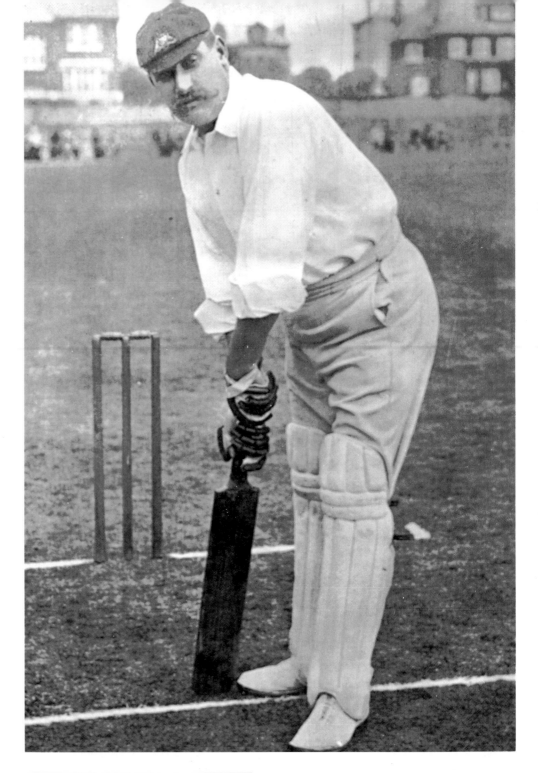

W.L. Murdoch who led the Australian tourists to England in 1880 for the first Test in England.

at all representative, including Leland Hone, an Irishman who never played county cricket and was taken to keep wicket, although he was not even a wicket-keeper. For six of the team, including F.A. MacKinnon, more splendidly titled The MacKinnon of MacKinnon, this would be the only Test they played, and it is perhaps unfortunate that this match, featuring a side which never claimed to be anything like 'England', should now be considered a Test match.

England batted first and were soon 26 for 7, with Spofforth taking the first Test hat-trick: Royle, MacKinnon and Emmett. There was a recovery, led by Harris (33) and Absolom (52) to 113, but Australia made 256, and after England's 160 needed only 18

Spofforth, Frederick Robert

Born on 9 September 1853 at Balmain, NSW, Spofforth first appeared for his state in 1874–75. Later he also played for Victoria. He played in the second of all Test matches. On his third tour of England he played in the first Test in that country and demolished England in the match that led to the 'Ashes' obituary notice. Spofforth was a right-arm fast bowler, who later became fast-medium, relying on his height of 6ft 2in and his guile rather than speed to bring wickets. His mastery over the best English batsmen was such that he became known as the 'Demon Bowler'. In 18 Tests he took 94 wickets, average 18.41. He died on 4 June 1926 at Long Ditton, Surrey.

Grace, William Gilbert

Grace was born on 18 July 1848 at Downend, Bristol. Taught cricket by his mother, he was an opening right-hand batsman, a medium-pace round-arm bowler and excellent field. He made his debut for Gloucestershire in 1870 and for England in 1880. He became the most famous cricketer of all time, and, with his black beard, the most recognizable. Two of his brothers, E.M. and G.F., also played for England and all three played in the first Test in England in 1880.

Grace created most of the first-class cricket records, but as he went to Australia only once, he appeared in only 22 Tests, in 13 of which he was captain. He scored 1,098 runs, average 32.29, and took nine wickets, average 26.22. He died at Mottingham, Kent, on 23 October 1915.

to win, and scored them without loss. Spofforth took 13 wickets in the match.

The tourists also played New South Wales and Victoria twice each on level terms, losing one and winning one with each state. It was in the second New South Wales match at Sydney that the crowd disapproved of a run-out decision against W.L. Murdoch and invaded the pitch. Lord Harris was struck with a whip or stick and had to be rescued by Hornby, a man known for his prowess with his fists. It was suggested that the umpire had bet heavily on a victory for the tourists. There was no further play that day, but eventually the tourists won by an innings.

1878–79 2nd Series Aust 1, Eng 0
1 **MELBOURNE** **Australia won by 10 wkts**
England 113 (C A Absolom 52, F R Spofforth 6–48) and 160 (F R Spofforth 7–62)
Australia 256 (A C Bannerman 73, T Emmett 7–68) and 19–0

1880: The first Test match in England a Graceful affair

An Australian party captained by W.L. Murdoch toured England in 1880. No matches were arranged against an England XI, the English still being unconvinced about the Aussies' ability at cricket, but C.W. Alcock, who was secretary of Surrey CCC, saw the possibilities of a game. Alcock had been instrumental in setting up the Football Association, of which he became secretary, and in organizing the first international soccer match between England and Scotland. Now he arranged for England to play Australia at the Oval on 6, 7 and 8 September 1880, days which had originally been reserved for a match with Sussex. This match has taken its place in history as the first Test in England.

The tourists were without their main bowler, Spofforth, who had damaged a finger. Fifteen players made their Test debuts in this match, eight of them for England. W.G. Grace made his Test debut, as did his two brothers E.M. and G.F., to provide the first instance of three brothers playing in the same Test (equalled only 12 years later by the Hearnes, who did not play all the same side, however).

England, captained by Lord Harris, batted first and W.G. scored the first English Test century. His 152 helped England to a total of 420, and with A.P. Lucas he added 120 for the second wicket, thus also establishing the first Test century partnership. Fred Morley of Notts took five Australian wickets for 56, and Australia, all out 149, were forced to follow on.

Murdoch, who had opened and scored a duck in the first innings, batted at number three and made 153 not out in the second. He became the first Test captain to score a century. Even so, with the eighth wicket down, Australia still needed 84 to avoid an innings defeat. However the last two wickets added 140, leaving England to get 57, and at 31 for 5 there might have been the makings of the first amazing reversal of fortunes in a

Test match, but England had altered the batting order, and now W.G. came in to see them home. His brother, G.F., who scored a pair but took a brilliant catch, caught a chill and died at Basingstoke exactly a fortnight after the match.

1881–82: More betting problems and another beating-up

In contrast to the previous tour, the 1881–82 English party to Australia was all-professional, and much stronger. The tour was still privately organized, with the Nottinghamshire professionals Alfred Shaw and Arthur Shrewsbury joining James Lillywhite of Sussex in a venture which arrived in Australia after touring America. The remaining players came from only four counties – two-thirds of the players came from Notts and Yorkshire.

Crowds were large, and 20,000 were at the second day of the second first-class game. This was against Victoria at Melbourne, and the home side had much the better of it for three innings, so that they needed only 94 to win when they began the fourth. At this stage, most of the tourists had £1 each on themselves at 30–1, and when Ted Peate took 6–30 to dismiss Victoria for 75, they collected. It then appeared that two English players, who had fielded badly (one dropped a catch) had been bribed with £100 to throw the match. Midwinter, who had been asked to join them, reported the matter and was later beaten up for his honesty.

The first Test was at Melbourne, beginning on 31 December 1881. Lillywhite, who had captained England in the first Test of all, was the English umpire. Alfred Shaw captained England, and Midwinter was in the side. Midwinter had played for Australia in the two Tests of 1876–77 and thus became the only player to play for both countries in Australia v England matches. Murdoch continued to captain Australia.

England made 294, with George Ulyett (87) and John Selby (55) adding 137 for the second wicket, a Test record stand. Australia passed this score by making 320, Tom Horan making 124. England batted solidly in the second innings for 308 leaving Australia to make 279 to win.

The match went into a fourth day (this was the first Test in which over 1,000 runs were scored) and the steamship waiting to take the tourists to New Zealand delayed its departure, but there was not time for a finish and the match was drawn at 127 for 3.

After playing various sides of 22 and 15 players, the tourists returned to Sydney for the second Test, this being the first Test to be played at Sydney. England fell before the bowling of George Palmer and Ted Evans,

who bowled all through the innings (58 and 57 four-ball overs respectively) to take 7–68 and 3–64. England were out for 133, but fought back to dismiss Australia for 197 and go ahead with all second innings wickets intact when Ulyett (67) and R.G. Barlow

England v Australia 1881–82 Averages					
Batting	I	No	Runs	HS	Avge
G. Ulyett (E)	8	0	438	149	54.75
P.S. McDonnell (A)	7	1	302	147	50.33
W.L. Murdoch (A)	7	1	215	85	35.83
T.P. Horan (A)	7	1	212	124	35.33
R.G. Barlow (E)	7	0	210	62	30.00
J. Selby (E)	8	1	202	70	28.85

Bowling	O	M	Runs	W	Avge	BB
T.W. Garrett (A)	213.3	76	367	18	20.38	6–78
W. Bates (E)	240.2	121	334	16	20.87	4–52
G.E. Palmer (A)	365.2	145	522	24	21.75	7–68
E. Peate (E)	232	117	256	11	23.37	5–43
W. Midwinter (E)	194	79	272	10	27.20	4–81

(62) made the first Test opening stand of a century (122). The later batting failed, however, and Australia needed only 168, which they scored for the loss of five wickets.

In the third Test, also at Sydney, England were dismissed for 188, despite Shrewsbury's 82. A.C. Bannerman (70) and Percy McDonnell (147) added a record Test stand of 199 for Australia's fourth wicket. The other nine batsmen managed only 29 between them. England failed again with 134, and Australia won comfortably by six wickets.

In the fourth and final Test at Melbourne Ulyett opened and scored 149 on the first day to record England's first century in Australia. The first innings scores were very even at 309 and 300, and England had made 234 for 2 in the second innings when the match was left drawn, there being no play on the fourth day. Strangely this was the last drawn Test match in Australia for over 60 years.

1882: The Ashes of English cricket taken to Australia

The only Test match played by the visiting Australians in 1882 provided England with the greatest cricketing shock in her history, and set up the Ashes series which has enthralled cricketers until this day.

Murdoch beat Hornby in the toss at the Oval, and Australia batted. Heavy rain had

made the pitch difficult, and they were rapidly 30 for six, and twenty minutes after lunch all out for 63, Peate and Barlow being the destroyers. The England batting was extremely strong, with only one player averaging less than 24, but Spofforth's dismissal of W.G. Grace for 4 gave the Aussies encouragement, and at the end of the day they had dismissed England for 101, with Spofforth taking seven for 46.

It poured overnight, to such an extent that when play resumed late next day, the conditions and wet ball were against the bowlers. Hugh Massie made the most of it by hitting out, scoring 55 runs in as many minutes in an opening stand of 66. When his brilliant innings was over, Australia slumped to 79 for five, but Murdoch held firm and by scoring 29 helped raise the total to 122. England needed just 85 to win.

Hornby and Barlow (of Francis Thompson's famous poem 'At Lord's') were dismissed by Spofforth with successive balls at 15, but Grace and Ulyett took the score past 50 and all seemed well. Then both were out: 53 for four.

Spofforth and Boyle continued to bowl splendidly, and wickets continued to fall:

1 THE OVAL   **Australia won by 7 runs**
Australia 63 (R G Barlow 5–19, E Peate 4–31) and 122 (H H
  Massie 55, E Peate 4–40)
England 101 (F R Spofforth 7–46) and 77 (F R Spofforth 7–44)

four fell between 70 and 75, leaving the last pair, Studd and Peate, to get ten to win. They could manage only two, and Australia won by seven runs. Spofforth's seven for 44 gave him match figures of 14 for 90 – he was truly the 'Demon' bowler. Grace described Blackham's wicket-keeping as perfection.

But the most famous comment has been credited to Reginald Shirley Brooks and appeared in the *Sporting Times* as an obituary notice, shown below.

IN AFFECTIONATE REMEMBRANCE

OF

ENGLISH CRICKET

WHICH DIED AT THE OVAL

ON

29th *August* 1882,

Deeply lamented by a large circle of sorrowing friends and acquaintances.

R. I. P.

N.B.—The body will be cremated, and the ashes taken to Australia.

1882–83: The Ashes assume substance and return to England

The 1882–83 tour of Australia was organized and managed by the Melbourne Cricket Club. The Hon Ivo Bligh, the Kent batsman, captained the party of eight amateurs and four professionals.

At a dinner before departure Bligh promised to bring back to England 'the Ashes of English cricket' of the famous obituary notice.

On the way out on the boat the team played a match at Colombo in Ceylon, which was to become a tradition lasting until air travel for Test teams replaced the steamer. Unfortunately 360 miles out of Colombo the boat collided with a sailing ship, and both returned to port. The party's only fast bowler, the Notts professional Fred Morley, broke a rib and was not much use on tour.

Having easily beaten Victoria and New South Wales, the tourists arrived at Sydney to begin the first of three matches billed as 'Mr Murdoch's XI v The Hon Ivo F.W. Bligh's Team'. Murdoch's XI was in effect the side which had won at the Oval, and this was the first 'Test' of the series.

With Morley in bed, the England team was the remainder. Australia scored 291, George Bonnor's hard-hitting 85 being the

highlight, while the best bowler was the seventh tried, the debutant C.F.H. Leslie, whose 3–31 remained his best effort in all first-class cricket. England could muster only 177, with Palmer taking seven for 65, and under the rules of the day were asked to follow on, making 169. Needing only 57 to win, Australia scored them easily. The match aroused great excitement and 54,000 watched the three days play.

The visitors played much better at Melbourne, and established some new Test records. Batting first, they made 294, and in Australia's innings Willie Bates of Yorkshire took England's first hat-trick in dismissing McDonnell, Giffen and Bonnor. He finished with seven for 28 as Australia were dismissed for 114 and made to follow on. Bates then returned 7–74 as Australia were put out again for 153. England thus achieved the first innings victory in Test cricket, while Bates, who scored 55 in England's knock, became the first player to score a half-century and take ten or more wickets in a match.

Both teams travelled straight to Sydney for the third and deciding match of the rubber. Bligh again won the toss and batted, and 20,000 spectators saw the beginning of play. England, at 75 for five, were not batting well, but E.F.S. Tylecote, the Kent wicket-keeper, scored 66, the first Test half-century by a keeper, and England reached 247. The opening batsman A.C. Bannerman did well for Australia, scoring 94, and at the end of the first day Australia were 133 for one, but on the second day they collapsed for 218. England then made only 123, with Spofforth taking seven for 44. Australia needed only 153 to win, but Dick Barlow returned even better figures of 7–40 as the home side were shot out for 83.

A curiosity of this match was that two pitches were prepared with the captains being able to choose on which pitch to bat. There was some criticism of Barlow from the Australians, who accused him of running on the pitch and spoiling it with his spikes. Bligh's defence was that Spofforth

was in the habit of doing exactly the same.

England had thus won the series 2–1, and some Melbourne ladies burned a bail, placed the ashes in a small urn and presented them to Bligh, as 'the Ashes of English cricket' which he had won back. The urn, with the embroidered velvet bag in which it was presented, remains in the Memorial Gallery at Lord's and is not sent back and forth between England and Australia, although the ownership of the Ashes has been hotly contested ever since.

Although England won the Ashes, a fourth match now designated a Test match was played at Sydney, between the tourists and a 'Combined Australian XI'. By now the small party was suffering further handicaps in the form of injuries and Australia won an interesting match by four wickets. There were some good performances, notably from Steel, who made 135 not out, and Blackham, who became the first wicket-keeper to score two half-centuries in a Test.

Two oddities in this match concerned the pitch, or rather pitches, because four were prepared, one for each innings, and Midwinter, who after two appearances for Australia and four for England, now reverted to Australia for the first of another six matches.

So Australia levelled the series and the tourists, nursing their aches and pains, finished with an innings defeat by Victoria. But by reclaiming the Ashes they had added interest to the whole series of England-Australia matches.

1882–83   6th Series   Aus 2, Eng 2
1 MELBOURNE   **Australia won by 9 wkts**
Australia 291 (G J Bonnor 85) and 58–1
England 177 (G E Palmer 7–65) and 169 (G Giffen 4–38)
2 MELBOURNE   **England won by an innings and 27 runs**
England 294 (W W Read 75, W Bates 55, C F H Leslie 54, G E
  Palmer 5–103, G Giffen 4–89)
Australia 114 (W Bates 7–28) and 153 (W Bates 7–74)
W Bates performed the hat-trick in the first innings
3 SYDNEY   **England won by 69 runs**
England 247 (W W Read 66, E F S Tylecote 66, F R Spofforth
  4–73) and 123 (F R Spofforth 7–44)
Australia 218 (A C Bannerman 94, F Morley 4–47) and 83 (R G
  Barlow 7–40)
4 SYDNEY   **Australia won by 4 wkts**
England 263 (A G Steel 135) and 197
Australia 262 (G J Bonnor 87, J McC Blackham 57) and 199–6
  (A C Bannerman 63, J McC Blackham 58)

1882–83 Averages					
Batting	I	No	Runs	HS	Avge
A.G. Steel (E)	7	1	274	135	45.66
A.C. Bannerman (A)	8	1	255	94	36.42
J.M. Blackham (A)	7	1	204	58	34.00
W.W. Read (E)	7	0	228	75	32.57
G.J. Bonnor (A)	7	0	217	87	31.00

Bowling	O	M	Runs	W	Avge	BB
W. Bates (E)	192.3	87	286	18	15.88	7–28
A.G. Steel (E)	130	49	195	11	17.72	3–27
G.E. Palmer (A)	270.1	114	397	21	18.90	7–65
R.G. Barlow (E)	244	124	343	16	21.43	7–40
F.R. Spofforth	244.1	93	408	18	22.66	7–44

ENGLAND V AUSTRALIA 1882
Only Test, The Oval: Australia won by seven runs

AUSTRALIA

A.C. Bannerman	c Grace b Peate	9	c Studd b Barnes	13
H.H. Massie	b Ulyett	1	b Steel	55
W.L. Murdoch*	b Peate	13	(4) run out	29
G.J. Bonnor	b Barlow	1	(3) b Ulyett	2
T.P. Horan	b Barlow	3	c Grace b Peate	2
G. Giffen	b Peate	2	c Grace b Peate	0
J.M. Blackham†	c Grace b Barlow	17	c Lyttelton b Peate	7
T.W. Garrett	c Read b Peate	10	(10) not out	2
H.F. Boyle	b Barlow	2	(11) b Steel	0
S.P. Jones	c Barnes b Barlow	0	(8) run out	6
F.R. Spofforth	not out	4	(9) b Peate	0
Extras	(B 1)	1	(B 6)	6
Total		**63**		**122**

ENGLAND

R.G. Barlow	c Bannerman b Spofforth	11	(3) b Spofforth	0
W.G. Grace	b Spofforth	4	(1) c Bannerman b Boyle	32
G. Ulyett	st Blackham b Spofforth	26	(4) c Blackham b Spofforth	11
A.P. Lucas	c Blackham b Boyle	9	(5) b Spofforth	5
Hon A. Lyttelton†	c Blackham b Spofforth	2	(6) b Spofforth	12
C.T. Studd	b Spofforth	0	(10) not out	0
J.M. Read	not out	19	(8) b Spofforth	0
W. Barnes	b Boyle	5	(9) c Murdoch b Boyle	2
A.G. Steel	b Garrett	14	(7) c and b Spofforth	0
A.N. Hornby*	b Spofforth	2	(2) b Spofforth	9
E. Peate	c Boyle b Spofforth	0	b Boyle	2
Extras	(B 6, LB 2, NB 1)	9	(B 3, NB 1)	4
Total		**101**		**77**

ENGLAND	O	M	R	W	O	M	R	W
Peate	38	24	31	4	21	9	40	4
Ulyett	9	5	11	1	6	2	10	1
Barlow	31	22	19	5	13	5	27	0
Steel	2	1	1	0	7	0	15	2
Barnes					12	5	15	1
Studd					4	1	9	0
AUSTRALIA								
Spofforth	36.3	18	46	7	28	15	44	7
Garrett	16	7	22	1	7	2	10	0
Boyle	19	7	24	2	20	11	19	3

FALL OF WICKETS				
	A	E	A	E
Wkt	1st	1st	2nd	2nd
1st	6	13	66	15
2nd	21	18	70	15
3rd	22	57	70	51
4th	26	59	79	53
5th	30	60	79	66
6th	30	63	99	70
7th	48	70	114	70
8th	53	96	117	75
9th	59	101	122	75
10th	63	101	122	77

1884: 'No play—rain' at Old Trafford and Lord's first Test

The Australian party which came to England in 1884 was a strong one, and for the first series of Tests in England the home country also put out strong teams – only three players made their Test debuts during the series.

Old Trafford staged the first Test on 10, 11 and 12 July, and amazingly there was no play on the first day because of rain. Old Trafford thereby began as it often seemed to continue in future years.

When play started, England batted first and were rapidly put out for 95, Spofforth and Boyle taking four for 42 and six for 42 respectively. Australia nearly doubled this with 182, but there was not quite time to complete a third innings by the end of the match, England being 180 for 9 at the close.

The second Test, on 21, 22 and 23 July was the first to be at Lord's, which thus became the third Test ground in England and the fifth in the world. At this stage England teams were picked by the authorities at the ground staging the match. There were four changes between Old Trafford and Lord's, and it is interesting to note that the captain and wicket-keeper at Old Trafford,

The Adelaide Oval became a Test match ground in 1884, joining Melbourne and Sydney in Australia and the Oval, Old Trafford and Lord's in England. This is the scene during the Test in January 1937.

the Lancashire players Hornby and Dick Pilling, were replaced at Lord's by Lord Harris and the Hon A. Lyttelton.

Australia batted first at Lord's and made 229, an odd feature being that the top scorer, H.J.H. Scott, was caught by his captain, Murdoch. W.G. Grace had injured a finger, and Murdoch, who had already been dismissed, fielded as substitute for him. Peate clean bowled four of the top five batsmen, establishing an English superiority early in the match. Steel scored 148 for England, and Ulyett took seven for 36 when Australia batted again, giving England victory by an innings and five runs.

Records were established at the Oval. Australia made 551, easily the highest innings total to date, and Murdoch, with 211, scored the first double century. Three of the first four' Australians made centuries, and Murdoch and Scott's stand of 207 for the third wicket was a Test match record. Australia reached 432, higher than any previous Test innings, before the fourth wicket fell.

The laws did not allow declarations in 1884, and Murdoch was forced to bat on. All eleven England players bowled (the first instance of such in a Test) and the most successful was the wicket-keeper, Alfred Lyttelton, who took four for 19 with lobs, claiming Midwinter caught behind the wicket by his substitute, W.G. Grace. England followed on, but there was no time for a result, and at 85 for two forced the draw. So England retained the hard-won Ashes in a strange and in many ways unsatisfactory first rubber in England.

1884–85: Captains, bowlers and umpires rebel, but an exciting series

The entrepreneurial team of Lillywhite, Shaw and Shrewsbury arranged their second tour to Australia in 1884–85, Lillywhite confining himself solely to umpiring this time, and Shaw being manager and occasional player in minor games. Shrewsbury was captain. It was the strongest side sent to Australia to date, with six of the players coming from Notts, four from Yorkshire, and one each from Lancashire and Surrey.

On the way, the team played a match in Suez, and on arrival at Adelaide learned that Fred Morley, the main victim of the boating accident off Ceylon on their previous tour, had died.

The eighth match played in Australia added the Adelaide Oval to the list of Test grounds. This first Test was labelled 'Murdoch's Australian Team v Alfred Shaw's Team', although in fact Shaw did not play and Shrewsbury was captain. The Australian team represented the 1884 tourists to England, although there were two enforced changes from the team at the Oval. There was no change in the excellence of McDonnell's batting, however, as he made 124 to register his second century in successive Test innings to become the first to achieve this feat. Australia's total of 243 was not good enough, however, England passing it with only two men out. Barnes' 134 was top score in a total of 369.

McDonnell was run out for 83 in Australia's second knock, but a total of 191 left only 65 for England to get. They got them for the loss of two wickets, the four batsmen to appear all being from Nottinghamshire.

Adelaide is regarded as one of the more beautiful Australian grounds, but this match, arranged by the South Australian Cricket Association, did not augur well. A violent dust storm on the second day caused the players to lie down to avoid suffocation, and the next day, luckily a Sunday, the ground was flooded.

There was an unfortunate squabble about

money, too. The English organizers, who were, it must be remembered, speculators hoping to make a profit, objected to the Australian players being paid the same fee as the English, this not having been the case in 1884, when the English had played for £10 a man and the Australian tourists had made a good profit. Murdoch, however, insisted that his team should receive the same as the English tourists, but most of the rest of Australia agreed with the tourists' view, with the result that when the second Test was played at Melbourne, none of the Australian 1884 tourists was picked. Nine of the team were making their Test debuts, one of the exceptions being the captain, Tom Horan. The changes meant that the wicket-keeper, Blackham, missed his first Test, having played in the first 17, the longest run of the 22 players who had played in the very first Test.

England were not surprisingly too strong for the Australians, scoring 401 (Briggs 121), forcing the follow-on, and needing to score only six runs for a ten-wicket victory.

For the third Test at Sydney, four of the 1884 Australians agreed to play, including Spofforth, who took ten wickets. H.H. Massie was the captain. England this time had the troubles, their best bowler Barnes, who had taken nine wickets in the previous Test, having an argument with Shrewsbury and refusing to bowl. It undoubtedly cost England the match. In a low-scoring game England needed 214 in the fourth innings, and despite a century stand for the seventh wicket between Flowers and Read, who each scored 56, they fell seven short.

Barnes bowled for England in the fourth Test, also at Sydney, when Blackham returned and captained the Australian side. England, having scored 269, were having the best of it until George Bonnor came to the wicket with Australia 119 for six. He scored the fastest Test century to date (100 minutes) and his 128 gave Australia a lead of 40. England were caught on a drying pitch and Palmer and Spofforth, bowling unchanged, dismissed them for 77, leading to an eight-wicket win for Australia.

This was the first Test series of five Tests, and the fifth assumed great significance as it would decide the rubber. It followed directly the Sydney Test and was played at Melbourne. Australia's captain changed for every Test in this series, Horan now being reinstated as skipper. In contrast, England played all five Tests with an unchanged side.

Australia's first-innings total of 163 would have been worse without a last-wicket stand of 64 between Trumble and Spofforth, who scored 50 at number eleven. Shrewsbury then made 105 not out as England compiled 386, and the match was virtually settled. Australia were hurried out for 125 and England won the series with an emphatic innings victory. An oddity was that Jarvis, the wicket-keeper, became the second Australian to field as a substitute for England and hold a catch (Spofforth). There were umpiring problems with umpire Hodges refusing to stand after tea on the third day because of the English play-

1884–85 Averages

Batting	I	No	Runs	HS	Avge	
W. Barnes (E)	8	1	369	134	52.71	
A. Shrewsbury (E)	9	3	301	105*	50.20	

Bowling	O	M	Runs	W	Avge	BB
W. Barnes (E)	206.2	97	292	19	15.36	6–31
F.R. Spofforth (A)	194.1	84	306	19	16.10	6–90
G. Ulyett (E)	178.2	86	295	14	21.07	4–52
R. Peel (E)	390.2	193	451	21	21.47	5–51
W. Attewell (E)	325.1	190	310	13	23.00	4–53

ers' criticism of him.

The tourists played a final match at Adelaide, and again were interrupted by a duststorm and violent rain. Other perils of touring were brought home when Briggs was reported killed after an accident when he was thrown from a horse and his pipe was rammed into the roof of his mouth – luckily he regained consciousness after four hours.

1886: Arthur Shrewsbury and W.G. swop the English innings record

It was a weak Australian party which toured England and played three Tests in 1886. Spofforth, Palmer and Garrett were all

Above: The 1886–87 English tourists in Australia.

The Australian tourists in 1886. Left to right, back: McIlwraith, Trumble, Jarvis, Bruce, Jones, Palmer, Spofforth. Front: Major B.J. Wardill (manager), Blackham, Evans, Scott, Bonnor, Garrett, Giffen.

nearing the ends of their Test careers. H.J.H. Scott captained the tourists, and A.G. Steel led England in all three Tests.

In the first Test at Old Trafford, Hornby and Pilling were recalled to the colours, but in the event Hornby could not play – he and Barnes, another who cried off, were replaced by Barlow and Briggs, two other Lancastrians. Australia made 205, of which Sam Jones made 87, a total England bettered by only 18. Barlow took seven for 44 in helping dismiss Australia a second time for only 123, but England did not find the 106 runs needed easy to get, winning only by four wickets.

At Lord's Briggs and Barlow retained their places, but Pilling was replaced by Tylecote. Shrewsbury batted brilliantly on a wicket made awkward by rain, and compiled England's highest score to date with 164. The total of 353 was too much for Australia, who were dismissed for 121, Briggs taking five for 29, and forced to follow on. Briggs did even better this time with six for 45, and Australia were beaten by an innings and 106 runs.

W.G. Grace opened the England innings at the Oval and soon regained his highest Test score for England record, making 170, which was also the size of the opening partnership between him and W.H. Scotton, a record opening for either side. Scotton made only 34 of them, having spent over an hour on 24. George Lohmann, in his first series, took seven Australian wickets for 36, bowling throughout the innings with Briggs, and Australia made only 68. The batting order was revised for the follow-on, and 149 was a more respectable score, but not enough to avoid defeat by an innings and 217. Lohmann and Briggs took eight wickets between them in this innings. It was an easy retention of the Ashes for England.

1886 9th Series Eng 3, Aus 0
1 OLD TRAFFORD **England won by 4 wkts**
Australia 205 (S P Jones 87, G Ulyett 4–46) and 123 (R G Barlow 7–44)
England 223 (W W Read 51, F R Spofforth 4–82) and 107–6
2 LORD'S **England won by an innings and 106 runs**
England 353 (A Shrewsbury 164, W Barnes 58, F R Spofforth 4–73)
England 121 (J Briggs 5–29) and 126 (J Briggs 6–45)
3 THE OVAL **England won by an innings and 217 runs**
England 434 (W G Grace 170, W W Read 94, J Briggs 53, F R Spofforth 4–65)
Australia 68 (G A Lohmann 7–36) and 149 (G A Lohmann 5–68)

1886 Averages

Batting	I	No	Runs	HS	Avge
A. Shrewsbury (E)	4	0	243	164	60.75
W.G. Grace (E)	4	0	200	170	50.00

Bowling	O	M	Runs	W	Avge	BB
J. Briggs (E)	134.1	75	132	17	7.76	6–45
R.G. Barlow (E)	120	70	95	10	9.50	7–44
G.A. Lohmann (E)	116.2	55	191	13	14.69	7–36
F.R. Spofforth (A)	168.3	73	260	14	18.57	4–65

1886–87: England win again, but Australia's new boys shine

The third Lillywhite/Shaw/Shrewsbury party to tour Australia, with its usual dependence on Nottinghamshire, included only eleven players.

Australia produced two brilliant new Test bowlers for the combined Australia XI which played Shaw's Team in the first Test at Sydney, J.J. Ferris and C.T.B. Turner. They were the only bowlers required for the first innings. Percy McDonnell, captaining Australia for the first time, put England in – the first occasion this happened in a Test, and with such spectacular results that England were shot out for what remains their lowest Test total, 45. It might have been worse – Lohmann made 17 at number eight, coming in at 17 for six.

Australia did not bat too well in their turn, making only 119. England made good the arrears with only one man out but then lost six wickets in adding 23, only a wagging tail bringing their score to 184 in a fluctuating match. Australia sadly fell 14 runs short of their target, being out for 97, Barnes taking six for 28. McDonnell's brave decision had not paid.

McDonnell and Barnes, both argumentative characters came to blows and Barnes got the worst of it, for a punch intended for the Aussie skipper's face missed and hit a brick wall, putting Barnes out of action for most of the rest of the tour. While mentioning law and order, a curiosity of the match was that Charles Bannerman, who played in the first Test of all, made his Test umpiring debut in a match in which his brother, A.C., was playing.

When the Second Test came round, also at Sydney, Reg Wood, born in Cheshire but living in Australia and working on the Melbourne ground, was co-opted to take Barnes' place in what for him was, not surprisingly, his only Test.

England batted first again, and were again dismissed for a low score, 151, with Turner and Ferris sharing the wickets. Lohmann, however, bowled brilliantly and took eight wickets for 35, the most wickets anybody had taken in a Test innings to date. Australia were out for 84. Australia, following England's 154, needed 222 in the fourth innings, but fell 72 short. Wood, England's 'substitute', scored six in each innings.

England had retained the Ashes, and had now won six Tests consecutively, but Turner and Ferris, the Australian bowlers in their debut series, had taken 35 of the 40 English wickets.

1886–87 10th Series Eng 2, Aus 0
1 SYDNEY **England won by 13 runs**
England 45 (C T B Turner 6–15, J J Ferris 4–27) and 184 (J J Ferris 5–76)
Australia 119 and 97 (W Barnes 6–28)
2 SYDNEY **England won by 71 runs**
England 151 (J J Ferris 5–71, C T B Turner 5–41) and 154 (J J Ferris 4–69, C T B Turner 4–52)
Australia 84 (G A Lohmann 8–35) and 150 (W Bates 4–26)

1887–88: Discord as two parties tour Australia

The manager of the 1886 Australian tourists to England, Major Wardill, indicated that the Melbourne Club would invite a team to Australia in 1887–88. The Hon M.B. Hawke (later Lord Hawke) captained a party raised by G.F. Vernon, consisting of six professionals from Yorkshire, Surrey and Notts, and seven amateurs, including Hawke and Vernon. The Lillywhite, Shaw and Shrewsbury combination would not give up their by now established tour and organized a rival party. Supported by the New South Wales Association and captained by C.A. Smith (later C. Aubrey Smith, the Hollywood film actor) it consisted of eight professionals (another five from Yorkshire, Surrey and Notts) and four amateurs.

The parties arrived at Adelaide on the same boat, but went their different ways, only to join together when Vernon's team had played 21 games and Shrewsbury's 16. The occasion was the Combined England Team v Combined Australia, at Sydney, now regarded as the only Test of the tour.

The England side contained seven of Shrewsbury's men (six professional) and four of Vernon's (two professional), one of whom, W.W. Read, was captain.

It should have been the most representative match to date between the countries, but several Australians refused to play, and the England bowlers, in particular, were too good. Put in by McDonnell on a dead pitch, England made 113, but Lohmann and Peel bowled throughout to dismiss Australia for 42. Set a target of 209, Australia were dismissed largely by the same bowlers for 82. Turner and Ferris took 18 wickets for Australia to maintain their run.

1887–88 11th Series Eng 1, Aus 0
1 SYDNEY **England won by 126 runs**
England 113 (C T B Turner 5–44, J J Ferris 4–60) and 137 (C T B Turner 7–43)
Australia 42 (R Peel 5–18, G A Lohmann 5–17) and 82 (R Peel 5–40, G A Lohmann 4–35)

1888: Rain causes collapses for both sides

The 1888 Australians had played a match against Vernon's side and two against Shrewsbury's side in Australia, losing them all, so prospects did not look good when P.S. McDonnell opened his side's batting at Lord's. England had now won seven Tests consecutively.

Play began late because of heavy rain. Australia were dismissed for 116, but this turned out to be a winning score. They captured three England wickets overnight, and then on a muddy pitch the next day 27 wickets fell for 157 in little more than three hours: England 53, Australia 60, England 62. Australia won by 61 runs, Turner and Ferris doing the damage.

At the Oval, the Surrey selectors chose five Surrey men (two more than at Lord's), and Grace took over the captaincy from Steel. Australia made only 80, and when England replied with 317, were dismissed again for 100 and an innings defeat.

All was to play for at Old Trafford, hosting the final Test. True to tradition, Pilling was back as wicket-keeper and there was a downpour before the start.

England made 172, and like Australia's 116 in the first Test it proved to be a big score. Two Australian wickets were down overnight, but the remaining 18 fell before lunch on the second day, setting up several records: the most wickets to fall before lunch in a Test, the shortest innings in a Test (69 minutes) and the shortest Test in England (6 hours, 34 minutes

1888 12th Series Eng 2, Aus 1
1 LORD'S **Australia won by 61 runs**
Australia 116 (R Peel 4–36) and 60 (R Peel 4–14, G A Lohmann 4–33)
England 53 (C T B Turner 5–27) and 62 (C T B Turner 5–36, J J Ferris 5–26)
2 THE OVAL **England won by an innings and 137 runs**
Australia 80 (J Briggs 5–25) and 100 (W Barnes 5–32, R Peel 4–49)
England 317 (R Abel 70, W Barnes 62, G A Lohmann 62, C T B Turner 6–112)
3 OLD TRAFFORD **England won by an innings and 21 runs**
England 172 (C T B Turner 5–86)
Australia 81 (R Peel 7–31) and 70 (R Peel 4–37)

1888 Averages
Batting: No one qualifies

Bowling	O	M	Runs	W	Avge	BB
R. Peel (E)	110.2	48	181	24	7.54	7–31
J. Briggs (E)	84.1	42	94	12	7.83	5–25
C.T.B. Turner (A)	164	62	261	21	12.42	6–112
G.A. Lohmann (E)	94.3	50	144	11	13.09	4–33
J.J. Ferris (A)	119.2	59	167	11	15.18	5–26

of play). Peel did most damage with nine pre-lunch wickets (11 in all).

The figures of Turner and Ferris remained astonishing – since their joint debuts in Test cricket they had taken 85 of 96 wickets taken by Australian bowlers.

1890: Records for debutants beginning short careers

Australia brought a strong team to England under Murdoch in 1890, and John Lyons began the tour confidently enough by having his half-century on the board only 36 minutes after the start of the first Test at Lord's. Australia, however, subsided to 132. England began much worse, with W.G. Grace out without a run on the board, but prospered to 174 despite Lyons claiming five wickets – the first Australian bowler other than Turner or Ferris to obtain more than two for six Tests. A debutant, John Barrett, opened in Australia's second knock and carried his bat for 67 not out, the first instance in Test matches. Australia's 176 left England to get 136, and W.G. was still there

Turner, Charles Thomas Biass
Turner was born at Bathurst, NSW, on 16 November 1862, appearing first for New South Wales in 1882–83. He was a right-arm medium fast bowler, and made his debut for Australia in 1886–87. His Test career was highly successful, and he led the Australian bowling on his three tours to England. In 17 Tests he took 101 wickets, average 16.53. All his wickets were against England, and of those with 100 wickets in Ashes Tests, his average is the best. He died on 1 January 1944 at Manly, NSW.

when the seven-wicket win was achieved.

The second Test was at the Oval, and Yorkshire refused to release Peel and Ulyett, two stalwarts, for the match, so Stoddart decided he, too, would miss the Test to play against them for Middlesex.

Rain delayed the start, and Australia were soon out for 92 on a difficult wicket, Fred Martin of Kent, making his debut, taking six for 50. England did little better with only 100, and Australia lost two more quick second-innings wickets on the first day. Australia did reach 102, the highest innings of the match, on the second day, however, and Turner and Ferris caused England to struggle to get the 95 needed, taking eight wickets in the process. The match was won on an overthrow by Barrett, the record-maker of the first Test. Sadly, because of his profession as a doctor, he did not play Test cricket again. Martin took six wickets in the second innings – his 12 in a match on his debut was a record which lasted for 82 years, but strangely, he, too, was to play in only two Tests. Even more oddly, his record was beaten by Bob Massie in 1972, with 16 wickets on his debut at Lord's – he, too, had a very short Test career, appearing in only two series.

The third Test at Old Trafford was washed out without a ball being bowled. Barrett was thus deprived of another Test, but not Martin – after his 12-wicket debut he was not picked.

1890 13th Series Eng 2, Aus 0
1 LORD'S England won by 7 wkts
Australia 132 (J J Lyons 55, W Attewell 4–42) and 176 (J E Barrett 67)
England 173 (G Ulyett 74, J J Lyons 5–30) and 137–3 (W G Grace 75)
2 THE OVAL England won by 2 wkts
Australia 92 (F Martin 6–50) and 102 (F Martin 6–52)
England 100 (J J Ferris 4–25) and 95–8 (J J Ferris 5–49)
(The match arranged to be played at Old Trafford was abandoned without a ball being bowled)

1891–92: The recovery of Australia and Australian cricket

Because the dual tour of Australia in 1887–88 had been disastrous financially, nobody cared to risk another. Cricket began to fall in popularity in Australia. Lord Sheffield, a great patron of Sussex cricket, then came to the rescue by organizing a tour for 1891–92, with W.G. Grace as captain. (Sheffield later presented the Sheffield Shield for inter-state cricket in Australia.) Shrewsbury and Gunn of the old order declined the terms, but it was a strong side which included four Surrey professionals.

Blackham, the wicket-keeper, captained the Combined Australia side which began the first of three Tests by batting at Melbourne on New Year's Day. Australia's 240 was passed by England's 264, Grace scoring 50 in his first Test in Australia. Over 20,000 watched the first two days and over 10,000 the next two in what was a good

match. Scoring 286, Australia left England needing 213. Grace and Stoddart soon had 60 on the board, but then both were out, and England collapsed, to manage only 158.

England were unlucky in the second Test at Sydney. Lohmann captured eight Australian wickets for the second time in his career as the home team were dismissed for 145. Bobby Abel then became the first English batsman to carry his bat through a Test innings with 132 not out in a total of 307. But excellent batting by Lyons (134) and a stubborn innings by Bannerman (91 in 448 minutes) turned certain defeat into chance of victory, with England set 230 to win. Rain did not help the cause, and Australia were victorious amid enthusiastic scenes at a great recovery.

A perfect wicket at the Adelaide Oval enabled England to reach 490 for 9 on the second day before a rainstorm stopped play for the day. Australia had no chance on the damaged pitch, especially against Briggs, who took 12 wickets, and were beaten by an innings.

1891–92 14th Series Aus 2, Eng 1
1 MELBOURNE Australia won by 54 runs
Australia 240 (W Bruce 57, J W Sharpe 6–84) and 236 (J J Lyons 51)
England 264 (W G Grace 50, G Bean 50, R W McLeod 5–55) and 158 (C T B Turner 5–51)
2 SYDNEY Australia won by 72 runs
Australia 145 (G A Lohman 8–58) and 391 (J J Lyons 134, A C Bannerman 91, W Bruce 72, J Briggs 4–69)
England 307 (R Abel 132, G Giffen 4–88) and 157 (A E Stoddart 69, G Giffen 6–72, C T B Turner 4–46)
3 ADELAIDE England won by an innings and 230 runs
England 499 (A E Stoddart 134, R Peel 83, W G Grace 58, J M Read 57)
Australia 100 (J Briggs 6–49) and 169 (J Briggs 6–87)

1891–92 Averages

Batting	I	No	Runs	HS	Avge
R. Abel (E)	5	1	217	132*	54.25
A.E. Stoddart (E)	5	0	565	134	53.00
J.J. Lyons (A)	6	0	287	134	47.83
W. Bruce (A)	6	0	226	72	37.66
A.C. Bannerman (A)	6	0	202	91	33.66

Bowling	O	M	Runs	W	Avge	BB
J. Briggs (E)	116.3	31	268	17	15.76	6–49
G.A. Lohmann (E)	188.3	71	289	16	18.06	8–58
C.T.B. Turner (A)	155.2	52	338	16	21.12	5–51
R.W. McLeod (A)	110.4	37	227	10	22.70	5–55
G.Giffen (A)	130.3	35	397	15	26.46	6–72

1893: Newcomers appear with centuries and wickets

Debutants and an old-stager made the biggest impressions on the first Test at Lord's. Arthur Shrewsbury, opening for England, made 106 in the first innings and 81 in the second, passing 1,000 runs in Tests, the first player to achieve this aggregate. F.S. Jackson, one of four English debutants, made 91, helping Shrewsbury to add 137 in the first innings, in which England totalled 334.

When Australia batted, it was the turn of another England debutant to make a name for himself, Bill Lockwood, with six for 101. Australia's only newcomer, Harry Graham, did best of all, making his maiden first-class century when coming in at 75 for five. The match petered out as rain interfered, but Stoddart, captain because Grace was unavailable through injury, did just have time to become the first captain to use the Law allowing declarations in a Test match.

The Surrey player, J.M. Read, who retired early for professional reasons, was awarded the Oval Test as a benefit match, although his Test career had ended with the previous Test. Jackson made a century with the last man at the wicket, and England batted solidly for 483. Australia collapsed before Lockwood and Briggs, who repeated their nine wickets in the second innings, but this time Australia batted with determination to 349. It did not avoid the innings defeat, but A.C. Bannerman had the consolation of becoming the second player, and first Australian, to 1,000 Test runs.

At Old Trafford, Tom Richardson, the Surrey fast bowler, was a notable newcomer, and he took ten wickets, five in each innings. With a deficit of 37 on first innings, Australia were heading for defeat at 200 for nine, but Turner and Blackham put on 36 and used up time for the last wicket, which saved the game, England, with the series won, not attempting the eventual target of 198 in 135 minutes. Dr Grace belied his reputation for bad sportsmanship by putting back Turner's dislocated finger during the match-saving stand.

1893 15th Series Eng 1, Aus 0, Drawn 2
1 LORD'S **Match Drawn**
England 334 (A Shrewsbury 106, F S Jackson 91, C T B Turner 6–67) and 234–8 dec (A Shrewsbury 81, W Gunn 77, G Giffen 5–43)
Australia 269 (H Graham 107, S E Gregory 57, W H Lockwood 6–101)
2 THE OVAL **England won by an innings and 43 runs**
England 483 (F S Jackson 103, A E Stoddart 83, W G Grace 68, A Shrewsbury 66, A Ward 55, W W Read 52, G Giffen 7–128)
Australia 91 (J Briggs 5–34, W H Lockwood 4–37) and 349 (G H S Trott 92, A C Bannerman 55, G Giffen 53, J Briggs 5–114, W H Lockwood 4–96)
3 OLD TRAFFORD **Match Drawn**
Australia 204 (W Bruce 68, T Richardson 5–49, J Briggs 4–81) and 236 (A C Bannerman 60, T Richardson 5–107)
England 243 (W Gunn 102, G Giffen 4–113) and 118–4

1893 Averages

Batting

	I	No	Runs	HS	Avge
A. Shrewsbury (E)	5	1	284	106	71.00
W. Gunn (E)	5	1	208	102*	52.00

Bowling

	O	M	Runs	W	Avge	BB
W.H. Lockwood (E)	93	27	234	14	15.28	6–101
T. Richardson (E)	57.4	20	156	10	15.60	5–49
J. Briggs (E)	120.1	40	293	16	18.31	5–34
G. Giffen (A)	171.4	59	342	16	21.37	7–128
C.T.B. Turner (A)	170	72	315	11	28.63	6–67

1894–95: Twists of fortune finally point England's way in five exciting Tests

The growing importance of Test cricket was evidenced by the fact that in 1894–95 the Melbourne and Sydney authorities agreed to promote jointly an English touring team. The opposite side of the coin was that five of England's best players declined the tour, so the side was not representative, particularly in batting.

Peel, Robert

Peel was born on 12 February 1857 at Cherwell, Leeds, and first played for Yorkshire in 1882. He was a slow left-arm bowler, whose success quickly led to an England place in 1884–85. He played in 20 Tests, 14 of them on his four tours to Australia. His Test career was cut short when Lord Hawke sacked him from the Yorkshire side in 1897 for his inebriate habits. All his 102 Test wickets were Australian, taken at an average of 16.81, the best average of any Englishman with 100 Australian wickets. He died on 12 August 1941 at Leeds, Yorkshire.

At Sydney, Australia were 21 for three, but climbed to 586, with Giffen making 161 and Syd George 201, while captain Blackham, far from declaring, made 74 at number ten, helping Gregory add 154. England batted well without a really big individual effort, and compiled 325, being forced to follow on. This time Albert Ward added 117 to his first-innings 75 (top scorer in each innings) and 437 was amassed. Australia needed only 177 to win and at the end of the fifth day were 113 for two. For the first time a Test went into a sixth day, and it was a fatal day for Australia. The rains came after the fifth day, and on the last morning Peel and Briggs wrapped up eight wickets for 53, the last five falling for only eight runs. England had won an exciting, if lucky, victory after following on 261 behind – the next Test victory after a follow-on would not occur for about 87 years.

The next Test, at Melbourne, was almost as remarkable. The only debutant was Arthur Coningham, whose first ball in Test cricket dismissed A.C. MacLaren. It was also the first ball of the Test – registering two 'firsts' in Test match history. This, oddly, was Coningham's only Test.

England stumbled on an awkward wicket to 75 all out, fought back to dismiss Australia for 123, then, as the wicket eased, scored 475, with every batsman reaching double figures and Stoddart getting an English record Test score of 173. Australia began well, with 191 on the board before the second wicket fell, but reached only 333 to lose by 94. Giffen, who had taken over the captaincy from Blackham, had scored 277 and taken 14 wickets in the first two Tests without being on the winning side. Giffen's time came in the third Test at Adelaide. First he scored 58 to help Australia to 238, then took five wickets as England were put out for 124. Iredale made 140 in Australia's second knock and Albert Trott took eight for 43 to give Australia a big win by 382 runs. Trott, whose first Test this was, also took part in last-wicket stands of 81 and 64, scoring 110 runs without being out. One excuse given for the poor English performance was the extraordinary heat, which reached 155F.

At Sydney, Stoddart put Australia in on a glue pot, and they were soon 51 for six, but then Graham, brought back into the side, scored a century which won the match. He thus made a century on his first appearance in both England and Australia, but he only played in two more Tests. He was helped in this match by Trott, who, promoted to number nine, helped add 112, and made 85, again not out. England were dismissed rapidly for an overwhelming Australian win which levelled the rubber.

During this match Johnny Briggs became the first to take 100 Test wickets, but only because Australia batted first. Turner achieved the feat in the English first innings.

All was to be decided at Melbourne, and public interest was at its greatest for the big match. Australia batted solidly all down the order on a good wicket to total 414, the England bowlers at last dismissing A.E. Trott. MacLaren made 120 for England be-

---

1894–95 16th Series Eng 3, Aus 2
1 SYDNEY **England won by 10 runs**
Australia 586 (S E Gregory 201, G Giffen 161, F A Iredale 81, J McC Blackham 74, T Richardson 5–181) and 166 (J Darling 53, R Peel 6–67)
England 325 (A Ward 75, J Briggs 57, G Giffen 4–75) and 437 (A Ward 117, J T Brown 53, G Giffen 4–164)
2 MELBOURNE **England won by 94 runs**
England 75 (C T B Turner 5–32) and 475 (A E Stoddart 173, R Peel 53, G Giffen 6–155)
Australia 123 (T Richardson 5–57) and 333 (F A Iredale 68, G H S Trott 95, W Bruce 54, R Peel 4–77)
3 ADELAIDE **Australia won by 382 runs**
Australia 238 (G Giffen 58, T Richardson 5–75) and 411 (F A Iredale 140, W Bruce 80, A E Trott 72, R Peel 4–96)
England 124 (G Giffen 5–76, S T Callaway 5–37) and 143 (A E Trott 8–43)
4 SYDNEY **Australia won by an innings and 147 runs**
Australia 284 (H Graham 105, A E Trott 85, J Briggs 4–65)
England 65 and 72 (G Giffen 5–26, C T B Turner 4–33)
5 MELBOURNE **England won by 6 wkts**
Australia 414 (J Darling 74, S E Gregory 70, G Giffen 57, J J Lyons 55, R Peel 4–114) and 267 (G Giffen 51, J Darling 50, T Richardson 6–104)
England 385 (A C MacLaren 120, R Peel 73, A E Stoddart 68, G H S Trott 4–71, G Giffen 4–130) and 298–4 (J T Brown 140, A Ward 93)

Giffen, George

Born on 27 March 1859 at Adelaide, Giffen was the nearest Australian counterpart to W.G. Grace. He was a hard-hitting right-hand middle-order batsman and a medium-slow bowler. He first appeared for South Australia in 1877–78 and for Australia in 1881–82. He made five tours to England. In 31 Tests, in four of which he was captain, he scored 1,238 runs, average 23.35, and took 103 wickets, average 27.09. He died on 29 November 1927 at Adelaide.

1894–95 Averages

Batting	I	No	Runs	HS	Avge
G. Giffen (A)	9	0	475	161	52.88
J.T. Brown (E)	10	2	343	140	42.87
A. Ward (E)	10	0	419	117	41.00
S.E. Gregory (A)	9	0	362	201	40.22
A.E. Stoddart (E)	10	1	352	173	39.11
F.A. Iredale (A)	9	0	337	140	38.44
G.H.S. Trott (A)	9	0	264	95	29.33
J. Darling (A)	9	0	258	74	28.66

Bowling	O	M	Runs	W	Avge	BB
C.T.B. Turner (A)	187.1	76	349	18	19.38	5–32
G. Giffen (A)	343.2	111	820	34	24.11	6–155
G.H.S. Trott (A)	102.4	17	296	12	24.66	4–71
T. Richardson (E)	309.1	63	849	32	26.53	6–104
R. Peel (E)	325.1	77	721	27	26.70	6–67
J. Briggs (E)	150.3	29	435	15	29.00	4–65

fore being out 'hit wicket' – at 385 England were 29 behind. Richardson (6–104) bowled well when Australia went in again, but everybody got double figures except A.E. Trott (0), and 267 left England needing 297 for the Ashes.

Two men were out for 28, but John Brown then played an exhilarating innings, passing 50 in 28 minutes and 100 in 95, both new Test records, and adding 210 with Ward before being out for 140. Ward was

out for 93 but England won a famous victory by six wickets. Giffen scored 573 runs and took 34 wickets in the series – a great all-round performance in a series-losing team. It was A.E. Trott's third and last match for Australia – he later played twice for England against South Africa.

1896: Clem Hill and Ranji enter the lists

Australia took a strong team under G.H.S. Trott to England for the 1896 series. Clem Hill made his debut in the first Test at Lord's, as did two outstanding wicket-keepers, A.F.A. Lilley for England and J.J. Kelly for Australia.

Australia were dismissed by the Surrey pair of Richardson and Lohmann, playing his last Test, for 53. A huge crowd of 30,000 saw England take a big lead on the first day, with captain Grace completing his 1,000 runs in Tests. However, Trott and Gregory fought back and added a record Test partnership of 221 after three second-innings wickets had fallen for 62.

Australia had 347, but England needed only 109 to win by six wickets.

Old Trafford witnessed a very exciting match. Australia made 412, with Iredale making a century, and then removed England for 231, forcing the follow-on. Ranjitsinhji, making his debut, followed his first innings 62 with a brilliant 154 not out, scoring the last 113 before lunch on the third day. With 305, England set Australia to get 125 to win, which they achieved, but only after losing seven wickets for 100. Richardson took 13 of the 17 Australian wickets. George Giffen became the first to 1,000 runs and 100 wickets in Tests.

Five players, four of them from Surrey, disputed the fees for the deciding match at the Oval, and Gunn and Lohmann refused to play. Rain prevented play for most of the first day, and gave the spinners the opportunity to skittle the opposition from the second. England made 145, and Australia collapsed from 75 without loss to 119 all out. England then made only 84, but Australia made their lowest total in England

---

AUSTRALIA V ENGLAND 1894–95
1st Test, Sydney: England won by ten runs

AUSTRALIA

J.J. Lyons	b Richardson	1	b Richardson	25
G.H.S. Trott	b Richardson	12	c Gay b Peel	8
G. Giffen	c Ford b Brockwell	161	lbw b Briggs	41
J. Darling	b Richardson	0	c Brockwell b Peel	53
F.A. Iredale	c Stoddart b Ford	81	(6) c and b Briggs	5
S.E. Gregory	c Peel b Stoddart	201	(5) c Gay b Peel	16
J.C. Reedman	c Ford b Peel	17	st Gay b Peel	4
C.E. McLeod	b Richardson	15	not out	2
C.T.B. Turner	c Gay b Peel	1	c Briggs b Peel	2
J.M. Blackham*†	b Richardson	74	(11) c and b Peel	2
E. Jones	not out	11	(10) c MacLaren b Briggs	1
Extras	(B 8, LB 3, W 1)	12	(B 2, LB 1, NB 4)	7
Total		**586**		**166**

ENGLAND

A.C. MacLaren	c Reedman b Turner	4	b Giffen	20
A. Ward	c Iredale b Turner	75	b Giffen	117
A.E. Stoddart*	c Jones b Giffen	12	c Giffen b Turner	36
J.T. Brown	run out	22	c Jones b Giffen	53
W. Brockwell	c Blackham b Jones	49	b Jones	37
R. Peel	c Gregory b Giffen	4	b Giffen	17
F.G.J. Ford	st Blackham b Giffen	30	c and b McLeod	48
J. Briggs	b Giffen	57	b McLeod	42
W.H. Lockwood	c Giffen b Trott	18	b Trott	29
L.H. Gay†	c Gregory b Reedman	33	b Trott	4
T. Richardson	not out	0	not out	12
Extras	(B 17, LB 3, W 1)	21	(B 14, LB 8)	22
Total		**325**		**437**

ENGLAND	O	M	R	W	O	M	R	W
Richardson	55.3	13	181	5	11	3	27	1
Peel	53	14	140	2	30	9	67	6
Briggs	25	4	96	0	11	2	25	3
Brockwell	22	7	78	1				
Lockwood	3	2	1	0	16	3	40	0
Ford	11	2	47	1				
Stoddart	3	0	31	1				

AUSTRALIA	O	M	R	W	O	M	R	W
Turner	44	16	89	2	35	14	78	1
Jones	18	6	44	1	19	0	57	1
Giffen	43	17	75	4	75	25	164	4
McLeod	14	2	25	0	30	6	67	2
Trott	15	4	59	1	12.4	3	22	2
Reedman	3.3	1	12	1	6	1	12	0
Lyons	2	2	0	0	2	0	12	0
Iredale					2	1	3	0

FALL OF WICKETS

	A	E	E	A
Wkt	1st	1st	2nd	2nd
1st	10	14	44	26
2nd	21	43	115	45
3rd	21	78	217	130
4th	192	149	245	135
5th	331	155	290	147
6th	379	211	296	158
7th	400	211	385	159
8th	409	252	398	161
9th	563	325	420	162
10th	586	325	437	166

to date with 44, a score which relied on 16 from number eleven McKibbin. In fact at 25 for nine, Australia had lost 19 wickets while scoring 69. Peel, in his last Test, and J.T. Hearne, did the damage, while Trumble took 12 wickets for Australia.

1896 Averages

Batting	I	No	Runs	HS	Avge	
K.S. Ranjitsinhji (E)	4	1	235	154*	78.33	
G.H.S. Trott (A)	6	0	206	143	34.33	
Bowling	O	M	Runs	W	Avge	BB
J.T. Hearne (E)	127.1	56	211	15	14.06	6–41
T.R. McKibbin (A)	69.3	20	162	11	14.72	3–35
T. Richardson (E)	175	58	439	24	18.29	7–168
H. Trumble (A)	170.1	58	339	18	18.38	6–30

1897–98: Australia regain Ashes with convincing win over Stoddart's team

After the great success of the previous tour, A.E. Stoddart took another side to Australia at the invitation of the Sydney and Melbourne authorities.

Stoddart did not play in the first Test at Sydney because his mother had died, and MacLaren was the England captain. The Sydney authorities put the match back by a day because they considered the pitch unfit, which caused controversy. It helped England because it gave Ranjitsinhji, who had been ill, time to recover. Coming in at number seven, he scored a rapid 175, England's highest so far, and England reached 551. MacLaren also scored a century. Australia were dismissed for 237 and then 408, despite Darling's century. Charles McLeod, the Australian all-rounder batting at number three in the second innings, was run out by Derbyshire's wicket-keeper, Bill Storer, when he left his crease after being bowled by a no-ball, his deafness having led him not to hear the call. England easily scored the 95 needed to win.

At Melbourne, McLeod, who opened, scored 112, and was then bowled ironically by Storer, forced into use as England's seventh bowler as Australia compiled 520. England got the worst of the wicket in this match and were beaten by an innings and 55. Monty Noble made his debut for Australia and took six second-innings wickets. Ernest Jones, Australia's fast bowler, was the first player to be no-balled for throwing in a Test match.

The wicket was perfect at Adelaide but England, with Stoddart returned as captain, were again outplayed. Darling made 178, and Australia's total was higher than at Melbourne: 573. England followed on nearly 300 behind, and when a second-wicket stand of 142 between MacLaren, like Darling scoring his second century of the series, and Ranjitsinhji was broken, England collapsed to another innings defeat.

England, and especially Hearne, began well at Melbourne in the fourth Test, where they needed a win to even the rubber, and Australia were reduced to 58 for six. But Clem Hill, still two months short of 21, with tail-end support played one of the great Test innings of 188, hoisting Australia's total to

323. For the third time running, at 174, England followed on, but at least this time set Australia a target: 115. Australia won by eight wickets.

With the Ashes lost, Stoddart dropped himself from the fifth Test at Sydney, and MacLaren once more took over. England batted well to make 335, and Richardson, in his last Test, bowled superbly for his best analysis, 8–94, and England led by 96. The second-innings batting was poor, however, and Australia were given a chance with a target of 275. Darling then made his third hundred of the series in only 91 minutes and went on to 160, helping Australia to win by six wickets.

It was an emphatic series win and led to a period of Australian excellence.

The England team at Trent Bridge in 1899. Left to right, back: Barlow (umpire), Hayward, Hirst, Gunn, Hearne, Storer, Brockwell, Titchmarsh (umpire). Seated: Fry, Ranjitsinhji, Grace, Jackson. Front: Rhodes, Tyldesley.

The Australians in England in 1899. Left to right, back: Trumper, Laver, Trumble, Howell, McLeod, Noble. Seated: Johns, Jones, Darling, Kelly, Worrall, Iredale. Front: Hill, Gregory.

1897–98   18th Series   Aus 4, Eng 1

1 SYDNEY   England won by 9 wkts
England 551 (K S Ranjitsinhji 175, A C MacLaren 109, T W Hayward 72, G H Hirst 62) and 96–1 (A C MacLaren 50)
Australia 237 (H Trumble 70, C E McLeod 50, J T Hearne 5–42) and 408 (J Darling 101, C Hill 96, J T Hearne 4–99)

2 MELBOURNE   Australia won by an innings and 55 runs
Australia 520 (C E McLeod 112, F A Iredale 89, G H S Trott 79, S E Gregory 71, C Hill 58)
England 315 (K S Ranjitsinhji 71, W Storer 51, H Trumble 4–54) and 150 (M A Noble 6–49) H Trumble 4–53)

3 ADELAIDE   Australia won by an innings and 13 runs
Australia 573 (J Darling 178, F A Iredale 84, C Hill 81, S E Gregory 52, T Richardson 4–164)
England 278 (G H Hirst 85, T W Hayward 70, W P Howell 4–70) and 282 (A C MacLaren 124, K S Ranjitsinhji 77, C E McLeod 5–65, M A Noble 5–84)

4 MELBOURNE   Australia won by 8 wkts
Australia 323 (C Hill 188, J T Hearne 6–98) and 115–2 (C E McLeod 64)
England 174 (E Jones 4–56) and 263 (K S Ranjitsinhji 55)

5 SYDNEY   Australia won by 6 wkts
England 335 (A C Maclaren 65, N F Druce 64, E Jones 6–82) and 178 (H Trumble 4–37)
Australia 239 (C E McLeod 64, T Richardson 8–94) and 276–4 (J Darling 160, J Worrall 62)

1897–98 Averages

Batting	I	No	Runs	HS	Avge
J. Darling (A)	8	0	537	178	67.12
C.E. McLeod (A)	8	2	352	112	58.66
C. Hill (A)	8	0	452	188	56.50
A.C. MacLaren (E)	10	1	488	124	54.22
K.S. Ranjitsinhji (E)	10	1	457	175	50.77
S.E. Gregory (A)	8	2	264	71	44.00
T.W. Hayward (E)	9	0	336	72	37.33
N.F. Druce (E)	9	0	252	64	28.00

Bowling	O	M	Runs	W	Avge	BB
M.A. Noble (A)	150.5	33	385	19	20.29	6–49
E. Jones (A)	198.2	32	553	22	25.13	6–82
J.T. Hearne (E)	217	66	538	20	26.90	6–98
H. Trumble (A)	232.3	57	535	19	28.15	4–37
T. Richardson (E)	255.3	50	776	22	35.27	8–94

1899: Australia have Trumper and the luck and register a narrow victory

The side which Australia sent to England in 1899 under Joe Darling was regarded as one of the strongest seen, and is still acknowledged as outstanding. England, too, had some good players, and the series of the 'Golden Age' of cricket were brilliantly fought.

The first Test was the first at Trent Bridge, England's fourth Test ground, and Wilfred Rhodes made his debut. He was to become the oldest player in Test cricket, and by coincidence this match was the last of W.G. Grace, who, at nearly 51, established the record Rhodes was to beat. Australia, too, had a great debutant: Victor Trumper. Australia made 252 (Trumper b Hearne 0), but England could manage only 193. Australia declared their second innings at 230 for eight, setting England 290, and captured four quick wickets, but 93 not out from Ranjitsinhji ensured the draw.

At Lord's England, with MacLaren back as captain, were restricted to 206, thanks to Jones, who took seven for 88, and Australia took a big lead by scoring 421. Trumper, who was only 21, made 135 not out, and Hill, now just turned 22, also scored 135. England were dismissed for 240 and Australia won by ten wickets.

1899 19th Series   Aus 1, Eng 0, Drawn 4

1 TRENT BRIDGE   Match drawn

Australia 252 (C Hill 52, W Rhodes 4–58, J T Hearne 4–71) and 230–8 dec (C Hill 80)

England 193 (F S Fry 50, E Jones 5–88) and 155–7 (K S Ranjitsinhji 93)

2 LORD'S   Australia won by 10 wkts

England 206 (F S Jackson 73, G L Jessop 51, E Jones 7–88) and 240 (A C MacLaren 88, T W Hayward 77)

Australia 421 (C Hill 135, V T Trumper 135, M A Noble 54) and 28–0

3 HEADINGLEY   Match Drawn

Australia 172 (J Worrall 76, H I Young 4–30) and 224 (H Trumble 56, J T Hearne 4–50)

England 220 (A F A Lilley 55, H Trumble 5–60) and 19–0

4 OLD TRAFFORD   Match Drawn

England 372 (T W Hayward 130, A F A Lilley 58) and 94–3

Australia 196 (M A Noble 60, W M Bradley 5–67, H I Young 4–79) and 346–7 dec (M A Noble 89, V T Trumper 63, J Worrall 53)

5 THE OVAL   Match Drawn

England 576 (T W Hayward 137, F S Jackson 118, C B Fry 60, K S Ranjitsinhji 54, E Jones 4–164)

Australia 352 (S E Gregory 117, J Worrall 55, J Darling 71, W H Lockwood 7–71) and 254–5 (C E McLeod 77, J Worrall 75, M A Noble 69)

1899 Averages

Batting	I	No	Runs	HS	Avge
T.W. Hayward (E)	7	1	413	137	68.83
C. Hill (A)	5	0	301	135	60.20
M.A. Noble (A)	9	2	367	89	52.42
K.S. Ranjitsinhji (E)	8	2	278	93	46.33
J. Worrall (A)	8	1	318	76	45.42
Hon F.S. Jackson (E)	8	1	303	118	43.28

Bowling	O	M	Runs	W	Avge	BB
H.I. Young (Eng)	110.1	39	262	12	21.83	4–30
J.T. Hearne (E)	199.3	87	321	13	24.69	4–50
H. Trumble (A)	192.3	78	375	15	25.00	5–60
E. Jones (A)	255.1	73	657	26	25.26	7–88
W. Rhodes (E)	146.2	41	341	13	26.23	4–56
M.A. Noble (A)	170	73	406	13	31.23	3–82

Headingley joined the Test match circuit for the third Test, and Australia were dismissed for 172. Johnny Briggs, who took three wickets, had an epileptic fit on the first night and was sent to Cheadle Asylum. He returned to cricket, but not to Tests, but was to die in the Asylum less than three years later. England established a lead of 48, and dismissing Australia for 224 were on the way to victory at 19 without loss at the end of the second day, but rain washed out the last day, and Australia's 1–0 lead was preserved.

At Old Trafford, 130 from Tom Hayward helped England to 372, and then good bowling by Walter Bradley, in his first Test, and H.I. Young, in his second, dismissed Australia for 196, forcing them to follow on. Noble, 60 not out in the first innings, continued batting and made 89, thus uniquely scoring two separate 50s on the same day. Altogether he batted 510 minutes, saving the match. Australia made a declaration and the match was drawn. MacLaren had not wished to enforce the follow-on, which at that time was compulsory when a side was 120 behind, and the match provoked the change whereby the follow-on is at the discretion of the side in the lead.

England's last chance to level the series was at the Oval, and Hayward and Jackson began with a record Test opening stand of 185. England went impressively on to 576. Lockwood took seven for 71 as Australia were finally got out for 352, but McLeod,

Worrall and Noble made sure there would be no quick dismissal in the second innings and the match was drawn.

1901–02: Barnes makes an impact, but Australia win well

The MCC agreed to make the arrangements to send a side to Australia in 1901–02, but then withdrew, finding it impossible to raise a representative side. The Yorkshire committee refused to allow Rhodes and Hirst, the best bowlers of the summer, to go. A.C. MacLaren was asked to get a side together, and although he took some good players, it was clear that the side would struggle against the strong Australians.

As it happened, England began well, MacLaren, who went on to his fourth Test century, and Hayward scoring 154 for the first wicket at Sydney. The revelation of the match, was, however, Sydney Barnes, most of whose cricket had been for Rishton and Burnley in the Lancashire League. The unknown bowler took five wickets and Australia were dismissed for 168, followed on nearly 300 behind and were finally beaten by an innings and 124 runs.

At Melbourne MacLaren won the toss and put Australia in on a sticky wicket. Barnes took Trumper's wicket with the second ball, and he and Blythe shot out Australia for 112. However Noble (7–17) and Trumble did better, and England were dismissed for 61. But the first day was still possibly England's as Barnes had four more wickets as Australia collapsed again to 48 for five. However the best batsmen had been held back. Clem Hill made 99, and became the first to be dismissed at this score, and Reg Duff, batting number ten, made a century on his debut. He and Warwick Armstrong, also playing his first Test, added 120 for the tenth wicket, the first century last-wicket stand. Australia reached 353 and dismissed England for 175, Trumble's hat-trick at the end restricting Noble to 13 wickets in the match.

England were unlucky to lose the third Test at Adelaide. They made 388 with Braund getting a century, and dismissed Australia for 321, despite Barnes, who had taken 19 wickets in the first two Tests, having to retire with an injured knee after only seven overs. He took no further part in the series. Trumble bowled well in the second innings but Australia needed 315 to

ENGLAND V AUSTRALIA 1902
4th Test, Old Trafford: Australia won by three runs

AUSTRALIA

V.T. Trumper	c Lilley b Rhodes	104	c Braund b Lockwood	4
R.A. Duff	c Lilley b Lockwood	54	b Lockwood	3
C. Hill	c Rhodes b Lockwood	65	b Lockwood	0
M.A. Noble	c and b Rhodes	2	(6) c Lilley b Lockwood	4
S.E. Gregory	c Lilley b Rhodes	3	lbw b Tate	24
J. Darling*	c MacLaren b Rhodes	51	(4) c Palairet b Rhodes	37
A.J.Y. Hopkins	c Palairet b Lockwood	0	c Tate b Lockwood	2
W.W. Armstrong	b Lockwood	5	b Rhodes	3
J.J. Kelly†	not out	4	not out	2
H. Trumble	c Tate b Lockwood	0	lbw b Tate	4
J.V. Saunders	b Lockwood	3	c Tyldesley b Rhodes	0
Extras	(B 5, LB 2, W 1)	8	(B 1, LB 1, NB 1)	3
Total		**299**		**86**

ENGLAND

L.C.H. Palairet	c Noble b Saunders	6	b Saunders	17
R. Abel	c Armstrong b Saunders	6	(5) b Trumble	21
J.T. Tyldesley	c Hopkins b Saunders	22	c Armstrong b Saunders	16
A.C. MacLaren*	b Trumble	1	(2) c Duff b Trumble	35
K.S. Ranjitsinhji	lbw b Trumble	2	(4) lbw b Trumble	4
Hon F.S. Jackson	c Duff b Trumble	128	c Gregory b Saunders	7
L.C. Braund	b Noble	65	st Kelly b Trumble	3
A.F.A. Lilley†	b Noble	7	c Hill b Trumble	4
W.H. Lockwood	run out	7	b Trumble	0
W. Rhodes	c and b Trumble	5	not out	4
F.W. Tate	not out	5	b Saunders	4
Extras	(B 6, LB 2)	8	(B 5)	5
Total		**262**		**120**

ENGLAND	O	M	R	W	O	M	R	W
Rhodes	25	3	104	4	14.4	5	26	3
Jackson	11	0	58	0				
Tate	11	1	44	0	5	3	7	2
Braund	9	0	37	0	11	3	22	0
Lockwood	20.1	5	48	6	17	5	28	5

AUSTRALIA	O	M	R	W	O	M	R	W
Trumble	43	16	75	4	25	9	53	6
Saunders	34	5	104	3	19.4	4	52	4
Noble	24	8	47	2	5	3	10	0
Trumper	6	4	6	0				
Armstrong	5	2	19	0				
Hopkins	2	0	3	0				

FALL OF WICKETS

Wkt	A 1st	E 1st	A 2nd	E 2nd
1st	135	12	7	44
2nd	175	13	9	68
3rd	179	14	10	72
4th	183	30	64	92
5th	256	44	74	97
6th	256	185	76	107
7th	288	203	77	109
8th	292	214	79	109
9th	292	235	85	116
10th	299	262	86	120

win. Unfortunately, with Barnes in bed, Blythe injured his finger, and Australia became the first side to score 300 in the fourth innings to win a Test. A curiosity was that Hill followed his 99 on the previous Test with innings of 98 and 97.

After one innings each at Sydney, England had a lead of 18 runs, but their batting in the second innings against Noble and J.V. Sanders, making his debut, was appalling and they were dismissed for 99. Australia clinched the rubber with a seven-wicket win.

The fifth Test at Melbourne was evenly fought. England led again on first innings, and needing 211 were 87 for three overnight, and they fell 33 short of their target.

Noble and Trumble took 60 wickets between them in the series, exploiting their new mastery of swing bowling. Trumble captained Australia in the last two Tests.

1901-02 20th Series Aus 4, Eng 1

1 SYDNEY **England won by an innings and 124 runs**
England 464 (A C MacLaren 116, A F A Lilley 84, T W Hayward 69, L C Braund 58, C E McLeod 4–84)
Australia 168 (S F Barnes 5–65) and 172 (L C Braund 5–61, C Blythe 4–30)

2 MELBOURNE **Australia won by 229 runs**
Australia 112 (S F Barnes 6–42, C Blythe 4–64) and 353 (R A Duff 104, C Hill 99, S F Barnes 7–121)
England 61 (M A Noble 7–17) and 175 (J T Tyldesley 66, M A Noble 6–60, H Trumble 4–49)

3 ADELAIDE **Australia won by 4 wkts**
England 388 (L C Braund 103, T W Hayward 90, W G Quaife 68, A C MacLaren 67) and 247 (H Trumble 6–74)
Australia 321 (C Hill 98, V T Trumper 65, S E Gregory 55, J R Gunn 5–76) and 315–6 (C Hill 97, J Darling 69, H Trumble 62)

4 SYDNEY **Australia won by 7 wkts**
England 317 (A C MacLaren 92, J T Tyldesley 79, J V Saunders 4–119) and 99 (M A Noble 5–54, J V Saunders 5–43)
Australia 299 (M A Noble 56, W W Armstrong 55, G L Jessop 4–68, L C Braund 4–118) and 121–3 (R A Duff 51)

5 MELBOURNE **Australia won by 32 runs**
Australia 144 (T W Hayward 4–22, J R Gunn 4–38) and 255 (C Hill 87, L C Braund 5–95)
England 189 (H Trumble 5–62) and 178 (M A Noble 6–98)

1901–2 Averages

Batting	I	No	Runs	HS	Avge	
C. Hill (A)	10	0	521	99	52.10	
A.C. MacLaren (E)	9	0	412	116	45.77	
R.A. Duff (A)	8	1	311	104	44.42	
L.C. Braund (E)	9	2	256	103*	36.57	
T.W. Hayward (E)	9	0	305	90	33.88	
S.E. Gregory (A)	10	1	269	55	29.88	

Bowling	O	M	Runs	W	Avge	BB
S.F. Barnes (E)	138.2	33	323	19	17.00	7–21
M.A. Noble (A)	230	68	608	32	19.00	7–17
H. Trumble (A)	267.2	93	561	28	20.03	6–74
J.R. Gunn (E)	144.3	52	360	17	21.17	5–76
C. Blythe (E)	175	63	470	18	26.11	4–30
L.C. Braund (E)	258.1	76	738	21	35.14	5–61

1902: Australia win the battle of the two great sides

The 1902 season is often thought of as one where each country had one of its strongest sides. It produced some exhilarating cricket and two of the closest finishes in Tests.

Unfortunately the first two Tests were spoiled by rain. At Edgbaston, which joined the list of Test grounds, Australia were caught on a sticky wicket and dismissed for their record low score, 36 (Rhodes 7–17) after a big England score, but the rain prevented a finish.

Trumper, Victor Thomas
Trumper was born on 2 November 1877 at Darlinghurst, NSW. He was a brilliant opening right-hand batsman, and a medium-pace bowler. He played for New South Wales from 1894–95 and Australia from 1899. Trumper was a natural batsman, who played with such grace and artistry combined with such modesty and lack of concern for statistics that he became a legendary figure even among the giants of the 'golden age'. In 48 Tests he scored 3,163 runs, average 39.04. He also took eight wickets at 39.62. He died young, at Darlinghurst on 28 June 1915, of Bright's disease.

At Lord's there was only 105 minutes play, but Hopkins caused a flutter by removing Fry and Ranjitsinhji before a run was on the board.

The third Test was at Bramall Lane, Sheffield, a new Test venue staging its only Test. Barnes returned to the England attack for his only Test of the series and took six for 49, but Australia gained a lead of 49, and then Trumper hit a rapid 62 and Hill 119 to set England 339 to win, but Trumble and Noble shared the wickets as Australia won by 143.

Old Trafford proved to be a decisive match, and poor Fred Tate is famous for his part in it. On the first morning MacLaren asked his bowlers to keep Trumper quiet till lunch, by when the sun would have had time to work on the rain-affected wicket. But Trumper was 103 not out at lunch and Australia 173–1. It was the first of only three centuries scored before lunch on the first day in Tests. Jackson (128) and Braund (65) added 141 for England's sixth wicket, but at 262 all out England trailed by 37.

Australia were then out for 86, but Fred Tate dropped Darling at a crucial stage, and Darling made top score of 37. England required 124 and were proceeding satisfactorily at 92 for three, but then wickets began to fall to Trumble and Saunders. Hill made a wondrous running and diving catch on the boundary to dismiss Lilley and when Tate joined Rhodes for the last wicket eight

were still required. Tate scored four and was bowled. It was his one and only Test. Later his son Maurice retrieved the family reputation.

The fifth Test at the Oval saw one of the great recoveries and innings of Test cricket. Australia batted and reached 324, thanks to some strong lower-order run-making, and then Trumble, who had made 64 not out at number nine, took eight for 65 to dismiss England for 183. As the wicket began to deteriorate, Australia made 121, and England, needing 263, were 48 for five when Gilbert Jessop joined Jackson.

Jessop then played perhaps the most exciting innings in Test cricket, scoring a century in 75 minutes. Only one Test

Trumble, Hugh
Trumble was born on 12 May 1867 at Abbotsford, Victoria, and played for Victoria from 1887–88. A tall off-break bowler, he bowled at medium pace and with such control that he gave the batsman no rest. He made his Test debut in 1890 in England, and made five tours to England. All his 141 Test wickets were English, a record number for the Ashes series until passed by Lillee. His wickets cost 21.78 runs each. He also scored 851 runs, average 19.79. He became secretary of Melbourne Cricket Club. He died on 14 August 1938 at Hawthorn, Victoria.

century has been scored faster, and in much different circumstances. Jackson, then Hirst, supported him, and when he was dismissed for 104 out of 139, England were 187 for 7.

There was still a long way to go for victory but Hirst kept going, and 15 were needed when Rhodes joined him for the last wicket. According to one of Neville Cardus' romances, they decided to 'make them in singles'. Although this was invention, make them they did for a legendary win.

1902   21st Series   Aus 2, Eng 1, Drawn 2

1 EDGBASTON   Match Drawn
England 376–9 dec (J T Tyldesley 138, F S Jackson 53, W H Lockwood 52)
Australia 36 (W Rhodes 7–17) and 46–2

2 LORD'S   Match Drawn
England 102–2 (F S Jackson 55)
Australia did not bat

3 BRAMALL LANE, SHEFFIELD   Australia won by 143 runs
Australia 194 (S F Barnes 6–49) and 289 (C Hill 119, V T Trumper 62, W Rhodes 5–63)
England 145 (J V Saunders 5–50, M A Noble 5–51) and 195 (A C MacLaren 63, G L Jessop 55, M A Noble 6–52, H Trumble 4–49)

4 OLD TRAFFORD   Australia won by 3 runs
Australia 299 (V T Trumper 104, C Hill 65, R A Duff 54, J Darling 51, W H Lockwood 6–48, W Rhodes 4–104) and 86 (W H Lockwood 5–28)
England 262 (F S Jackson 128, L C Braund 65, H Trumble 4–75) and 120 (H Trumble 6–53, J V Saunders 4–52)

5 THE OVAL   England won by 1 wkt
Australia 324 (H Trumble 64, M A Noble 52, G H Hirst 5–77) and 121 (W H Lockwood 5–45)
England 183 (H Trumble 8–65) and 263–9 G L Jessop 104, G H Hirst 58, H Trumble 4–108, J V Saunders 4–105)

1902 Averages

Batting	I	No	Runs	HS	Avge
Hon F.S. Jackson	8	1	308	128	44.42
C. Hill (A)	8	1	258	119	36.85

Bowling	O	M	Runs	W	Avge	BB
W.H. Lockwood (E)	81.1	18	206	17	12.11	6–48
H. Trumble (A)	172.4	55	371	26	14.26	8–65
W. Rhodes (E)	140.5	38	336	22	15.27	7–17
M.A. Noble (A)	127	41	307	14	21.92	6–52
J.V. Saunders (A)	131.1	23	473	18	26.27	5–50

1903–04: Foster's great innings and the new Bosies regain the Ashes

MacLaren was asked by the Australian authorities to bring a team in 1903–04 but declined when Barnes and Lockwood refused to go. MCC stepped in and for the first time were responsible for the touring side. They announced Pelham Warner as captain. Most of the best English amateur batsmen declined to go. Noble captained Australia.

Noble made 133 on the first Test at Sydney, but was eclipsed by R.E. Foster, whose 287 was the highest Test score to date. It remains the highest English Test innings in Australia, and the highest score by a Test batsman on his debut. He added 130 with Rhodes for the last wicket, the highest last-wicket Ashes stand. England led by nearly 300, but Trumper, too, played a magnificent innings, reaching 100 in 94 minutes, and continuing to 185 not out. England needed 194 and got them for five wickets. A total of 1,541 runs were scored, but E.G. Arnold bowled the great Trumper with his first ball in Test cricket.

1903-04   22nd Series   Eng 3, Aus 2

1 SYDNEY   England won by 5 wkts
Australia 285 (M A Noble 133, E G Arnold 4–76) and 485 (V T Trumper 185, R A Duff 84, C Hill 51, W Rhodes 5–94)
England 577 (R E Foster 287, L C Braund 102, J T Tyldesley 53) and 194–5 (T W Hayward 91, G H Hirst 60)

2 MELBOURNE   England won by 185 runs
England 315 (J T Tyldesley 97, P F Warner 68, T W Hayward 58, H Trumble 4–107) and 103 (J T Tyldesley 62, H Trumble 5–34)
Australia 122 (V T Trumper 74, W Rhodes 7–56) and 111 (W Rhodes 8–68)

3 ADELAIDE   Australia won by 216 runs
Australia 388 (V T Trumper 113, C Hill 88, R A Duff 79, M A Noble 59) and 351 (S E Gregory 112, M A Noble 65, V T Trumper 59, B J T Bosanquet 4–73)
England 245 (G H Hirst 58) and 278 (P F Warner 79, T W Hayward 67, A J Hopkins 4–81)

4 SYDNEY   England won by 157 runs
England 249 (A E Knight 70, M A Noble 7–100) and 210 (T W Hayward 52)
Australia 131 (E G Arnold 4–28, W Rhodes 4–33) and 171 (M A Noble 53, B J T Bosanquet 6–51)

5 MELBOURNE   Australia won by 218 runs
Australia 247 (V T Trumper 88, L C Braund 8–81) and 133 (G H Hirst 5–48)
England 61 (A Cotter 6–40, M A Noble 4–19) and 101 (H Trumble 7–28)

1903–4 Averages

Batting	I	No	Runs	HS	Avge
V.T. Trumper (A)	10	1	574	185*	63.77
R.E. Foster (E)	9	1	486	287	60.75
M.A. Noble (A)	10	3	417	133	59.57
T.W. Hayward (E)	9	0	321	91	36.66
R.A. Duff (A)	10	0	277	97	27.70
J.T. Tyldesley (E)	10	0	277	97	27.70
C. Hill (A)	10	0	276	88	27.60

Bowling	O	M	Runs	W	Avge	BB
W. Rhodes (E)	172	36	488	31	15.74	8–68
H. Trumble (A)	199.4	60	398	24	16.58	7–28
M.A. Noble (A)	136.1	41	330	16	20.62	7–100
W.P. Howell (A)	137.5	51	296	14	21.14	4–43
B.J.T. Bosanquet (E)	104.1	7	403	16	25.18	6–51
E.G. Arnold (E)	158.3	32	475	18	26.38	4–28
L.C. Braund (E)	129.3	30	359	13	27.61	8–81
G.H. Hirst (E)	163.2	29	451	15	30.06	5–48

Foster retired ill on 49 not out in the second Test at Melbourne, but England were then 221 for two, runs which proved doubly valuable when rain interfered on the second day. The last three innings only just passed 100, and England were fortunate winners. The catching on both sides was described as appalling, and Rhodes is said to have had eight catches dropped despite ending with figures of 15 for 124.

Australia won the third Test at Adelaide when Trumper, Hill and Gregory all mastered the faster wicket better than the English and Australia won by 216. Hill passed 2,000 runs in Tests and Trumper scored his fourth century against England – both records.

The fourth Test at Sydney was again several times interrupted by rain, and on the second day, with about 30,000 present, the crowd began some intensive barracking and bottle-throwing. There had earlier been

---

ENGLAND V AUSTRALIA 1902
5th Test, The Oval: England won by one wicket

AUSTRALIA

V.T. Trumper	b Hirst	42	run out	2
R.A. Duff	c Lilley b Hirst	23	b Lockwood	6
C. Hill	b Hirst	11	c MacLaren b Hirst	34
J. Darling*	c Lilley b Hirst	3	c MacLaren b Lockwood	15
M.A. Noble	c and b Jackson	52	b Braund	13
S.E. Gregory	b Hirst	23	b Braund	9
W.W. Armstrong	b Jackson	17	b Lockwood	21
A.J.Y. Hopkins	c MacLaren b Lockwood	40	c Lilley b Lockwood	3
H. Trumble	not out	64	(10) not out	7
J.J. Kelly†	c Rhodes b Braund	39	(11) lbw b Lockwood	0
J.V. Saunders	lbw b Braund	0	(9) c Tyldesley b Rhodes	2
Extras	(B 5, LB 3, NB 2)	10	(B 7, LB 2)	9
Total		**324**		**121**

ENGLAND

A.C. MacLaren*	c Armstrong b Trumble	10	b Saunders	2
L.C.H. Palairet	b Trumble	20	b Saunders	6
J.T. Tyldesley	b Trumble	33	b Saunders	0
T.W. Hayward	b Trumble	0	c Kelly b Saunders	7
Hon F.S. Jackson	c Armstrong b Saunders	2	c and b Trumble	49
L.C. Braund	c Hill b Trumble	22	c Kelly b Trumble	2
G.L. Jessop	b Trumble	13	c Noble b Armstrong	104
G.H. Hirst	c and b Trumble	43	not out	58
W.H. Lockwood	c Noble b Saunders	25	lbw b Trumble	2
A.F.A. Lilley†	c Trumper b Trumble	0	c Darling b Trumble	16
W. Rhodes	not out	0	not out	6
Extras	(B 13, LB 2)	15	(B 5, LB 6)	11
Total		**183**	(9 wickets)	**263**

ENGLAND	O	M	R	W	O	M	R	W
Lockwood	24	2	85	1	20	6	45	5
Rhodes	28	9	46	0	22	7	38	1
Hirst	29	5	77	5	5	1	7	1
Braund	16.5	5	29	2	9	1	15	2
Jackson	20	4	66	2	4	3	7	0
Jessop	6	2	11	0				

AUSTRALIA	O	M	R	W	O	M	R	W
Trumble	31	13	65	8	33.5	4	108	4
Saunders	23	7	79	2	24	3	105	4
Noble	7	3	24	0	5	0	11	0
Armstrong					4	0	28	1

FALL OF WICKETS

	A	E	A	E
Wkt	1st	1st	2nd	2nd
1st	47	31	6	5
2nd	63	36	9	5
3rd	69	62	31	10
4th	82	67	71	31
5th	126	67	75	48
6th	174	83	91	157
7th	175	137	99	187
8th	256	179	114	214
9th	324	183	115	248
10th	324	183	121	—

The Australians of 1902. Left to right, back: Howell, Armstrong, Jones, Trumble, Major B.J. Wardill (manager), Hopkins, Gregory, Hill. Seated: Trumper, Saunders, Darling, Noble, Kelly. Front: Carter, Duff.

Armstrong, Warwick Windridge

Born in Kyneton, Victoria, on 22 May 1879, Armstrong was a good right-hand batsman and a bowler who began for Victoria in 1895–99 at fast-medium but in 1905 switched to leg-breaks. He played 50 times for Australia from 1901–02, captaining them from 1920–21. As captain he led his country to eight successive wins over England. He scored 2,863 Test runs, average 38.66, and took 87 wickets at 33.59. Always tall, by the end of his career he weighed over 20 stone and was known as 'The Big Ship'. He died on 13 July 1947 at Darling Point, NSW.

trouble at Sydney in the first Test when Hill had been adjudged run out and Warner had considered withdrawing his team from the match.

Knight made 70 in 260 minutes in a low-scoring match and Bosanquet, in his first series, sealed England's Ashes-winning victory with a spell of five for 12 with his googlies in the second innings.

Rain spoiled the fifth Test at Melbourne, where this time Australia had the same luck that England had had two months earlier. Batting first they made 247, while neither side could make more than 133 after the rains came. Trumble, in his last first-class match, took his second Test hat-trick.

1905: England keep the Ashes without alarms

Jackson was captain for the Australian tour of 1905, winning all five tosses, while Darling once again led the visitors.

The first Test was at Trent Bridge, and although Jackson reduced Australia from 129 for one to 130 for four in one over, Australia passed England's 196 to lead by 25. Then MacLaren made a record fifth Test century and England could declare at 426 for five. Trumper was unable to bat because of a back strain, and Bosanquet took eight for 105, England winning by 213 runs.

1905 23rd Series   Eng 2, Aus 0, Drawn 3

1 TRENT BRIDGE   England won by 213 runs
England 196 (J T Tyldesley 56, F Laver 7–64) and 426–5 dec (A C MacLaren 140, F S Jackson 82, J T Tyldesley 61)
Australia 221 (C Hill 54, M A Noble 50, F S Jackson 5–52) and 188 (S E Gregory 51, B J T Bosanquet 8–107)

2 LORD'S   Match Drawn
England 282 (C B Fry 73, A C MacLaren 56) and 151–5 (A C MacLaren 79)
Australia 181 (F S Jackson 4–50)

3 HEADINGLEY   Match Drawn
England 301 (F S Jackson 144, and 295–5 dec (J T Tyldesley 100, T W Hayward 60, W W Armstrong 5–122)
Australia 195 (W W Armstrong 66, A Warren 5–57) and 224–7 (M A Noble 62)

4 OLD TRAFFORD   England won by an innings and 80 runs
England 446 (F S Jackson 113, T W Hayward 82, R H Spooner 52, C E McLeod 5–125)
Australia 197 (J Darling 73, W Brearley 4–72) and 169 (R A Duff 60, W Brearley 4–54)

5 THE OVAL   Match Drawn
England 430 (C B Fry 144, F S Jackson 76, T W Hayward 59, A Cotter 7–148) and 261–6 dec (J T Tyldesley 112, R H Spooner 79)
Australia 363 (R A Duff 146, J Darling 57, W Brearley 5–110) and 124–4

1905 Averages

Batting	I	No	Runs	HS	Avge
Hon F.S. Jackson (E)	9	2	492	144*	70.28
C.B. Fry (E)	7	1	348	144	58.00
J.T. Tyldesley (E)	9	1	424	112*	53.00
A.C. MacLaren (E)	7	0	303	140	43.28
R.A. Duff (A)	8	0	335	146	41.87
T.W. Hayward (E)	9	0	305	82	33.88
W.W. Armstrong (A)	9	1	252	66	31.50

Bowling	O	M	Runs	W	Avge	BB
Hon F.S. Jackson (E)	67.5	8	201	13	15.46	5–52
W. Brearley (E)	73.1	16	277	14	19.78	5–110
F. Laver (A)	189.3	55	510	16	31.87	7–64
A. Cotter (A)	127	13	427	13	32.84	7–148
W.W. Armstrong (A)	280.3	94	538	16	33.62	5–122

Prolonged rain ruined the second Test at Lord's (as it had in 1902), England having the better of draws here and at Headingley, where Jackson and Tyldesley made centuries and Arnold Warren of Derbyshire took six wickets, including Trumper twice, in his only Test.

At Old Trafford England made 446 by solid batting, including another century from Jackson, and won by an innings when Walter Brearley, on his debut, took four wickets in each innings.

Centuries from Fry, Tyldesley and Duff and fine bowling from Cotter could not produce a result at the Oval, and England retained the Ashes 2–0. The disappointing form of Hill, Trumper and Noble and the return of the best English batsmen made the series a little one-sided.

Barnes, Sydney Francis

Regarded by his contemporaries as the greatest of all bowlers, he bowled right-arm, varied his pace each side of medium and could turn the ball both ways. He was a master on any type of wicket. Born on 19 April 1873 in Smethwick, Staffordshire, he was an aloof character and did not care for county cricket, preferring League cricket, although he did play for Lancashire and Warwickshire. However, he was chosen by MacLaren to tour Australia in 1901–02, when he made his Test debut. He played in 27 Tests, although only ten at home, where those in authority were wary of his forbidding ways. He took 189 wickets, then a record, at only 16.43 each. On the South African tour of 1913–14 he took 49 wickets, still a record for one series, in only four Tests. He died on Boxing Day 1967.

Right: A page from the scorebook of the 1905 Test at Trent Bridge.

Below right: The 1905 Australians. Left to right, top: Newland, Duff, Hill, Cotter, Laver. Middle: Gregory, Gehrs, Darling, Noble, Kelly. Bottom: Armstrong, Hopkins, McLeod, Trumper, Howell.

1907–08: The third innings provides the big totals throughout

Squabbles among the Australian authorities made a 1906–07 tour of Australia difficult to arrange – when they were settled MCC said it was too late and sent a team to New Zealand instead.

The Australian tour took place in 1907–08 under A.O. Jones of Notts, but many players declined the invitation, and it was not a representative side which sailed.

Jones was taken ill early in the tour and F.L. Fane of Essex captained the side in the first Test at Sydney. Noble captained Australia. Jack Hobbs, on his first tour, was England's 12th man.

George Gunn of Notts, who was not a member of the party but in Australia for his health, played for England and made 119 on his debut. Australia, scoring 300, led by 27 on the first innings, and when England also scored exactly 300 on their second knock, with Gunn again top scorer, Australia needed 274 to win, a hard task. At 124 for six they faced defeat, but wicket-keeper

Hanson Carter (born in Halifax, Yorkshire) came in and made 61. An unbroken ninth-wicket stand of 56 by Hazlitt and Cotter then saw Australia home by two wickets.

Rolls were reversed in the second Test at Melbourne. Australia made 266, but Hobbs, on his debut, made 83 and K.L. Hutchings, in his second Test, 126, and England reached 382. Australia batted better to make 397, setting England to make 282. At 209 for eight it seemed lost, but Barnes added 34 with Humphries and 39 unbeaten with Fielder to win by one wicket. Hazlitt's throw missed the wicket as the winning single was made.

There was a dramatic change of fortune in the third Test at Adelaide. England led by 78 on the first innings, and with Australia at 180 for seven in the second, appeared to have the match won. But Hill, who had flu and was unable to field, then came in at number nine in very severe heat to join debutant Roger Hartigan. They were both dropped early on, but added 243, Hill getting 160 and Hartigan 116. Saunders and O'Connor then shared the wickets as Eng-

1907–08   24th Series   Aus 4, Eng 1

1 SYDNEY   Australia won by 2 wkts

England 273 (G Gunn 119, A Cotter 6–101) and 300 (G Gunn 74, J Hardstaff 63, J V Saunders 4–68)

Australia 300 (C Hill 87, A Fielder 6–82) and 275–8 (H Carter 61)

2 MELBOURNE   England won by 1 wkt

Australia 266 (M A Noble 61, J N Crawford 5–79) and 397 (W W Armstrong 77, C G Macartney 54, M A Noble 64, V T Trumper 63, H Carter 53, S F Barnes 5–72)

England 382 (K L Hutchings 126, J B Hobbs 83, A Cotter 5–142) and 282–9 (F L Fane 50)

3 ADELAIDE   Australia won by 245 runs

Australia 285 (C G Macartney 75, A Fielder 4–80) and 506 (C Hill 160, R J Hartigan 116, M A Noble 65)

England 363 (G Gunn 65, J N Crawford 62, J Hardstaff 61) and 183 (J Hardstaff 72, J V Saunders 5–65, J D A O'Connor 5–40)

4 MELBOURNE   Australia won by 308 runs

Australia 214 (V S Ransford 51, J N Crawford 5–48, A Fielder 4–54) and 385 (W W Armstrong 133, H Carter 66, V S Ransford 54, A Fielder 4–91)

England 105 (J B Hobbs 57, J V Saunders 5–28) and 186 (J V Saunders 4–76)

5 SYDNEY   Australia won by 49 runs

Australia 137 (S F Barnes 7–60) and 422 (V T Trumper 166, S E Gregory 56, J N Crawford 5–141, W Rhodes 4–102)

England 281 (G Gunn 122, J B Hobbs 72) and 229 (W Rhodes 69, J V Saunders 5–82)

1907–8 Averages

Batting	I	No	Runs	HS	Avge
G. Gunn (E)	10	1	462	122*	51.33
W.W. Armstrong (A)	10	1	410	133*	45.55
J.B. Hobbs (E)	8	1	302	83	43.14
H. Carter (A)	10	3	300	66	42.85
M.A. Noble (A)	10	0	396	65	39.60
C. Hill (A)	10	0	360	160	36.00
V.T. Trumper (A)	10	0	338	166	33.80
V.S. Ransford (A)	10	1	288	54	32.00
J. Hardstaff, sr (E)	10	0	311	72	31.10
C.G. Macartney (A)	10	0	273	75	27.30
K.L. Hutchings (E)	10	0	273	126	27.30

Bowling	O	M	Runs	W	Avge	BB
J.V. Saunders (A)	267.1	52	716	31	23.09	5–28
J.N. Crawford (E)	237.4	36	742	30	24.73	5–48
J.D.A. O'Connor (A)	107	21	300	12	25.00	5–40
A. Fielder (E)	218.3	31	627	25	25.08	6–82
W.W. Armstrong (A)	180.1	63	361	14	25.78	3–53
S.F. Barnes (E)	273.2	74	626	24	26.08	6–82
A. Cotter (A)	108.5	8	426	14	30.42	6–101

land were beaten by 183.

It was England's last chance of retaining the Ashes, as rain conspired against them at Melbourne. Jones returned as captain, and Fielder and Crawford did well to dismiss Australia for 214. England then batted on a pitch ruined by rain, and could make only 105, with Hobbs making a brilliant 57. The England bowlers did not take full advantage of the pitch. Australia were 77 for five, but as conditions improved went on to 385, with Warwick Armstrong getting 133 not out. Needing 495, England were well beaten by 308 runs.

The fifth Test followed a similar course to the third. England, with Gunn making 122 not out, established a lead of 144, but Australia again made a big score in the third innings. This time it was Trumper who turned the match with 166 in 241 minutes. England fell 50 runs short of the 279 needed and Australia regained the Ashes 4–1.

1909: Australia retain the Ashes after losing first Test

Noble led Australia to England in 1909, and met a much stronger England side led by MacLaren.

The first Test at Edgbaston was a fairly short affair, the left-arm bowlers Hirst and Blythe getting all the Australian wickets as they were shot out for 74 and 151. England needed 105 to win, and Hobbs and Fry, both out first ball in the first innings, knocked them off without loss.

An innings of 143 not out by Ransford, who was dropped three times, established an Australian lead of 81 at Lord's, and then excellent bowling by Armstrong meant that only 41 were required to win.

Barnes returned to the England side at Headingley, but Macartney, with 11 wickets, was the dominant bowler of the match. Jessop was unfit to bat for England in either innings, and after a level first innings England collapsed for 87 in the second to lose by 126 runs.

Barnes and Blythe did well to dismiss Australia for 147 at Old Trafford, but Frank Laver produced what remains the best analysis by a tourist in a Test in England:

Hill, Clement

Hill was born on 18 March 1877 at Adelaide, South Australia, and made his debut for his state in 1892–93. A brilliant left-hand middle-order batsman, he made his first Test appearance in England on the 1896 tour. He was one of Australia's leading players of the 'golden age', playing in 49 Tests and scoring 3,412 runs, average 39.21. He is also remembered for a famous diving catch in front of the pavilion at Old Trafford in 1902 which helped win the match for Australia by three runs. He died on 5 September 1945 in Melbourne.

1909   25th Series   Aus 2 Eng 1, Drawn 2

1 EDGBASTON   England won by 10 wkts

Australia 74 (C Blythe 6–44, G H Hirst 4–28) and 151 (C Blythe 5–58, G H Hirst 5–58)

England 121 (W W Armstrong 5–27) and 105–0 (J B Hobbs 62)

2 LORD'S   Australia won by 9 wkts

England 269 (J H King 60, A Cotter 4–80) and 121 (W W Armstrong 6–35)

Australia 350 (V S Ransford 143, A E Relf 5–85) and 41–1

3 HEADINGLEY   Australia won by 126 runs

Australia 188 (W Rhodes 4–38) and 207 (S F Barnes 6–63)

England 182 (J Sharp 61, J T Tyldesley 55, C G Macartney 7–58) and 87 (A Cotter 5–38, C G Macartney 4–27)

4 OLD TRAFFORD   Match Drawn

Australia 147 (S F Barnes 5–56, C Blythe 5–63) and 279–9 dec (V S Ransford 54, C G Macartney 51, W Rhodes 5–83)

England 119 (F Laver 8–31) and 108–3 (R H Spooner 58)

5 THE OVAL   Match Drawn

Australia 325 (W Bardsley 136, V T Trumper 73, C G Macartney 50, D W Carr 5–146) and 339–5 dec (W Bardsley 130, S E Gregory 74, M A Noble 55)

England 352 (J Sharp 105, W Rhodes 66, C B Fry 62, K L Hutchings 59, A Cotter 6–95) and 104–3 (W Rhodes 54)

1909 Averages

Batting	I	No	Runs	HS	Avge
V.S. Ransford (A)	9	3	353	143*	58.83
W. Bardsley (A)	10	0	396	136	39.60

Bowling	O	M	Runs	W	Avge	BB
C. Blythe (E)	91.3	19	242	18	13.44	6–44
F. Laver (A)	108.2	38	189	14	13.50	8–31
C.G. Macartney (A)	127.2	33	258	16	16.12	7–58
S.F. Barnes (E)	155.3	52	340	17	20.00	6–63
W.W. Armstrong (A)	140.2	51	293	14	20.92	6–35
A. Cotter (A)	122.4	10	365	17	21.47	6–95
G.H. Hirst (E)	143.4	27	348	16	21.75	5–58

Ranjitsinhji, Kumar Shri

Ranji, as he was popularly known, was born at Sarodar, India, on 10 September 1872. Later he was to become His Highness Shri Sir Ranjitsinhji Vibhaji, Jam Sahib of Nawanagar. He studied at Cambridge University and played for Sussex from 1895. He was a magical right-hand batsman who revolutionized techniques, developing the leg-glance into an art in an age of front-foot driving. The most prolific batsman of his day, he made his debut for England in 1896, and in 15 Tests scored 989 runs, average 44.95. He died on 2 April 1933 at Jamnagar, India.

eight for 31 as England were out for 119. Australia declared on the second innings, but there was no prospect of a result.

The feature of the Oval Test was the batting of Warren Bardsley, who scored 136 and 130 to become the first to score a century in each innings of a Test. Jack Sharp, the Everton footballer, scored a century for England but a high-scoring match was drawn and Australia kept the Ashes 2–1. Noble won the toss in all five Tests.

1911–12: Hill and Trumper retire in a losing series; Hobbs takes over

A strong team went to Australia in 1911–12, captained again by Warner, after Fry had finally declined to go. In the event Warner became ill before the first Test, and J.W.H.T. Douglas was captain in all five.

In the first at Sydney, he was criticized for not opening the bowling with Barnes. Australia made 447 (Trumper 113) and led by 129, eventually winning a high-scoring game by 146 runs, the googly bowler H.V. Hordern taking 12 wickets.

The Test at Melbourne opened sensationally, with Barnes, given the new ball, having four wickets for one run after

1911–12 26th Series Eng 4, Aus 1

1 SYDNEY Australia won by 146 runs
Australia 447 (V T Trumper 113, R B Minnett 90, W W Armstrong 60) and 308 (C Kelleway 70, C Hill 65, F R Foster 5–92, J W H T Douglas 4–50)
England 318 (J W Hearne 76, J B Hobbs 63, F R Foster 56, H V Hordern 5–85) and 291 (G Gunn 62, H V Hordern 7–90)

2 MELBOURNE England won by 8 wkts
Australia 184 (S F Barnes 5–44) and 299 (W W Armstrong 90, F R Foster 6–91)
England 265 (J W Hearne 114, W Rhodes 61, A Cotter 4–73, H V Hordern 4–66) and 219–2 (J B Hobbs 126)

3 ADELAIDE England won by 7 wkts
Australia 133 (F R Foster 5–36) and 476 (C Hill 98, H Carter 72, W Bardsley 63, T J Matthews 53, S F Barnes 5–105)
England 501 (J B Hobbs 187, F R Foster 71, W Rhodes 59, A Cotter 4–125) and 112–3 (W Rhodes 57)

4 MELBOURNE England won by an innings and 225 runs
Australia 191 (R B Minnett 56, S F Barnes 5–74, F R Foster 4–77) and 173 (J W H T Douglas 5–46)
England 589 (W Rhodes 179, J B Hobbs 178, G Gunn 75, F E Woolley 56, F R Foster 50)

5 SYDNEY England won by 70 runs
England 324 (F E Woolley 133, G Gunn 52, H V Hordern 5–95) and 214 (G Gunn 61, H V Hordern 5–66)
Australia 176 and 292 (R B Minnett 61, V T Trumper 50, F R Foster 4–43, S F Barnes 4–106)

1911–12 Averages

Batting	I	No	Runs	HS	Avge
J.B. Hobbs (E)	9	1	662	187	82.75
W. Rhodes (E)	9	1	463	179	57.87
F.E. Woolley (E)	7	1	289	133*	48.16
G. Gunn (E)	9	0	381	75	42.33
J.W. Hearne (E)	9	1	281	114	35.12
W.W. Armstrong (A)	10	0	324	90	32.40
V.S. Ransford (A)	10	2	252	43	31.50
R.B. Minnett (A)	10	0	305	90	30.50
V.T. Trumper (A)	10	1	269	113	29.88
C. Hill (A)	10	0	274	98	27.40

Bowling	O	M	Runs	W	Avge	BB
F.R. Foster (E)	275.4	58	692	32	21.62	6–91
S.F. Barnes (E)	297	64	778	34	22.88	5–44
J.W.H.T. Douglas (E)	139.5	30	355	15	23.66	5–46
Dr H.V. Hordern (A)	277.2	43	780	32	24.37	7–90
A. Cotter (A)	166	26	548	12	45.66	4–73

five overs, and five for six after 11. Australia recovered to 184, but J.W. Hearne scored a century (at just under 21 the youngest Englishman to do so until Compton). England needed 219 and scored them easily with Hobbs making his first hundred against Australia.

Australia were shot out for 133 at Adelaide by Foster and Barnes, and Hobbs and Rhodes put on 147 for England's first wicket, Hobbs going on to 187, and England to 501. Although Australia made 476 in the second innings, with Hill making 98 (his fifth Test score between 96 and 99), England won easily.

Australia were put in at Melbourne, and Barnes and Foster dismissed them for 191. Hobbs and Rhodes scored 323 for the first wicket, still a record in Ashes history. England scored 589 and won easily by an innings.

THE AUSTRALIAN TEAM, 1909.
Back Row:— W. J. Whitty, A. Cotter, Roger Hartigan, V. Ransford, Warren Bardsley, H. Carter.
Second Row:— P. A. M'Alister, V. Trumper, A. J. Hopkins, M. A. Noble, Frank Laver, W. W. Armstrong, J. A. O'Conn..
Front Row:— S. Gregory, Macartney, W. Carkeek.

Right: A menu decoration for a celebration dinner given to the England touring team on their return from Australia in 1912.

Left, below: The 1909 Australians. Left to right, back: Whitty, Cotter, Hartigan, Ransford, Bardsley, Carter. Middle: McAlister, Trumper, Hopkins, Noble, Laver, Armstrong, O'Connor. Front: Gregory, Macartney, Carkeek.

THE COURT OF KING CRICKET

At Sydney England batted first and Woolley made 133 not out from 324. Australia needed 363 in the second innings to win but fell 71 short.

Barnes' 34 wickets in the rubber was an English record but Foster (32 wickets and 226 runs) did even better. The last Test marked the end of the Test careers of Hill and Trumper, the only cricketers at the time to have scored over 3,000 Test runs.

1911–12   26th Series   Eng 4, Aus 1

1 SYDNEY   Australia won by 146 runs

Australia 447 (V T Trumper 113, R B Minnett 90, W W Armstrong 60) and 308 (C Kelleway 70, C Hill 65, F R Foster 5–92, J W H T Douglas 4–50)

England 318 (J W Hearne 76, J B Hobbs 63, F R Foster 56, H V Hordern 5–85) and 291 (G Gunn 62, H V Hordern 7–90)

2 MELBOURNE   England won by 8 wkts

Australia 184 (S F Barnes 5–44) and 299 (W W Armstrong 90, F R Foster 6–91)

England 265 (J W Hearne 114, W Rhodes 61, A Cotter 4–73, H V Hordern 4–66) and 219–2 (J B Hobbs 126)

3 ADELAIDE   England won by 7 wkts

Australia 133 (F R Foster 5–36) and 476 (C Hill 98, H Carter 72, W Bardsley 63, T J Matthews 53, S F Barnes 5–105)

England 501 (J B Hobbs 187, F R Foster 71, W Rhodes 59, A Cotter 4–125) and 112–3 (W Rhodes 57)

4 MELBOURNE   England won by an innings and 225 runs

Australia 191 (R B Minnett 56, S F Barnes 5–74, F R Foster 4–77) and 173 (J W H T Douglas 5–46)

England 589 (W Rhodes 179, J B Hobbs 178, G Gunn 75, F E Woolley 56, F R Foster 50)

5 SYDNEY   England won by 70 runs

England 324 (F E Woolley 133, G Gunn 52, H V Hordern 5–95) and 214 (G Gunn 61, H V Hordern 5–66)

Australia 176 and 292 (R B Minnett 61, V T Trumper 50, F R Foster 4–43, S F Barnes 4–106)

1911–12 Averages

Batting	I	No	Runs	HS	Avge
J.B. Hobbs (E)	9	1	662	187	82.75
W. Rhodes (E)	9	1	463	179	57.87
F.E. Woolley (E)	7	1	289	133*	48.16
G. Gunn (E)	9	0	381	75	42.33
J.W. Hearne (E)	9	1	281	114	35.12
W.W. Armstrong (A)	10	0	324	90	32.40
V.S. Ransford (A)	10	2	252	43	31.50
R.B. Minnett (A)	10	0	305	90	30.50
V.T. Trumper (A)	10	1	269	113	29.88
C. Hill (A)	10	0	274	98	27.40

Bowling	O	M	Runs	W	Avge	BB
F.R. Foster (E)	275.4	58	692	32	21.62	6–91
S.F. Barnes (E)	297	64	778	34	22.88	5–44
J.W.H.T. Douglas (E)	139.5	30	355	15	23.66	5–46
Dr H.V. Hordern (A)	277.2	43	780	32	24.37	7–90
A. Cotter (A)	166	26	548	12	45.66	4–73

1912: A disappointing Triangular Tournament is won by England and the rain

In 1912 a triangular tournament was played in England in which Australia and South Africa played the host country and each other three times each. The whole project was ruined by rain.

Bitter squabbles between players, selectors and the Australian Board were weakening Australian cricket at this time. Jealousies had led to a fist fight between Peter McAlister, a selector, and Clem Hill, captain and selector in 1911–12. The two had already been appointed selectors for the 1912 party, where the biggest problem concerned whether the players would be allowed their own manager, Frank Laver. The Board, apparently not satisfied with the book-keeping of the 1905 tour, when Laver kept an account book for the players but vice-captain McAlister had failed to do so for the Board, decreed they would not. Hill, Trumper, Armstrong, Cotter, Carter and Ransford declined to tour. The 1912 Australian party was thus something of a second eleven.

In the first England v Australia Test, at Lord's, England declared after Hobbs had

---

1912   27th Series   Eng 1, Aus 0, Drawn 2

1 LORD'S   Match Drawn

England 310–7 dec (J B Hobbs 107, W Rhodes 59)

Australia 282–7 (C G Macartney 99, C Kelleway 61)

2 OLD TRAFFORD   Match Drawn

England 203 (W Rhodes 92, G R Hazlitt 4–77, W J Whitty 4–43)

Australia 14–0

3 THE OVAL   England won by 244 runs

England 245 (J B Hobbs 66, F E Woolley 62, R B Minnett 4–34, W J Whitty 4–69) and 175 (C B Fry 79, G R Hazlitt 7–25)

Australia 111 (S F Barnes 5–30, F E Woolley 5–29) and 65 (H Dean 4–19, F E Woolley 5–20)

1912 Averages

Batting	I	No	Runs	HS	Avge
J.B. Hobbs (E)	4	0	224	107	56.00
W. Rhodes (E)	4	0	204	92	51.00

Bowling	O	M	Runs	W	Avge	BB
F.E. Wolley (E)	23.2	7	55	10	5.50	5–20
G.R. Hazlitt (A)	113.3	36	218	12	18.16	7–25
W.J. Whitty (A)	110	42	252	12	21.00	4–43

Tate, Maurice William

Born on 30 May 1895 at Brighton, Tate was the son of a Test cricketer. He made his debut for Sussex in 1912 as an off-break bowler. Ten years later he changed to right-arm fast-medium and became one of the best bowlers in the world. He was a pioneer of the use of the seam. He was also a hard-hitting middle-order batsman. He first played for England in 1924, and in 39 Tests scored 1,198 runs, average 25.48, and took 155 wickets, average 26.16. He achieved 1,000 runs and 200 wickets in a season three times, a record, and is one of nine players with 2,000 wickets and 20,000 runs in a career. He died on 18 May 1956 at Wadhurst.

made a century, but Australia could not complete an innings – Macartney made 99.

It was worse at Old Trafford, only five hours play being possible.

Before the ninth and final match of the tournament it was decided that the winners would be champions and the match would be played to a finish. England, after Hobbs and Rhodes had put on 107, made only 245, but Barnes and Woolley dismissed Australia for 111. G.R. Hazlitt got seven English second-innings wickets for 25, but the wicket by now was so bad that there was no chance of Australia scoring 310, and Woolley for the second time took five wickets as they were dismissed for 65.

England were thus Champions of a tournament so disappointing that nothing like it was attempted again until the World Cup was instituted in 1975.

1920–21: Australia win all five Tests in a series of 14 centuries

Exactly half of the players in the first post-war Ashes match were making their debuts. MCC had declined to tour the previous year, but this time sent a party under Douglas, Spooner having been forced to drop out.

England did well to dismiss Australia for 267 at Sydney but then collapsed to 190 all out themselves. Centuries by Herbie Collins, in his first Test, and captain Armstrong, paved the way for an Australian total of 581, and England were heavily beaten by 377.

At Melbourne, it was the turn of C.E. Pellew and J.M. Gregory to score centuries, and Australia totalled 499. Gregory then took seven English wickets, and despite Hobbs' 122, England were made to follow-on on a rain-ruined pitch, and lost by an innings and 91.

Collins scored his second century at Adelaide, 162 out of 354, but C.A.G. Russell made 135 not out and England led by 92. Australia then made the highest score to date, 582, with Kelleway, Armstrong and Pellew making hundreds. Hobbs scored the sixth century of the match, but England,

despite scoring 370, were beaten by 119. The 1,753 runs scored remains an Ashes record; 302 were scored off Arthur Mailey, who took five wickets in each innings.

J.W.H. Makepeace, the second Everton footballer to score a century against Australia, made 117 out of 284 in the fourth Test, but Armstrong made his third century of the series and Australia led by 105. Mailey's nine wickets (9–121) in the second innings remains an Australian record in Tests. Australia needed 211 and scored them for the loss of two wickets.

Macartney made his highest Test score at Sydney of 170 in 244 minutes, giving Australia a lead which left them only 93 to get in the second innings and complete the only 5–0 'whitewash' between the two countries. Mailey's 39 wickets in the series remains an Australian record for a five-Test rubber.

1920–21 28th Series Aus 5, Eng 0

1 SYDNEY Australia won by 377 runs
Australia 267 (H L Collins 70) and 581 (W W Armstrong 158, H L Collins 104, C Kelleway 78, C G Macartney 69, W Bardsley 57, J M Taylor 51)
England 190 (F E Woolley 52) and 281 (J B Hobbs 59, J W Hearne 57, E H Hendren 56)

2 MELBOURNE Australia won by an innings and 91 runs
Australia 499 (C E Pellew 116, J M Gregory 100, J M Taylor 68, H L Collins 64, W Bardsley 51)
England 251 (J B Hobbs 122, E H Hendren 67, J M Gregory 7–69) and 157 (F E Woolley 50, W W Armstrong 4–26)

3 ADELAIDE Australia won by 119 runs
Australia 354 (H L Collins 162, W A S Oldfield 50, C H Parkin 5–60) and 582 (C Kelleway 147, W W Armstrong 121, C E Pellew 104, J M Gregory 78, H Howell 4–115)
England 447 (C A G Russell 135, F E Woolley 79, J W H Makepeace 60, J W H T Douglas 60, A A Mailey 5–160) and 370 (J B Hobbs 123, C A G Russell 59, E H Hendren 51, A A Mailey 5–142)

4 MELBOURNE Australia won by 8 wkts
England 284 (J W H Makepeace 117, J W H T Douglas 50, A A Mailey 4–115) and 315 (W Rhodes 73, J W H T Douglas 60, P G H Fender 59, J W H Makepeace 54, A A Mailey 9–121)
Australia 389 (W W Armstrong 123, J M Gregory 77, H L Collins 59, W Bardsley 56, P G H Fender 5–122) and 211–2 (J M Gregory 76, J Ryder 52)

5 SYDNEY Australia won by 9 wkts
England 204 (F E Woolley 53, C Kelleway 4–27) and 280 (J W H T Douglas 68, A A Mailey 5–119)
Australia 392 (C G Macartney 170, J M Gregory 93, P G H Fender 5–90) and 93–1 (W Bardsley 50)

1921: Armstrong reads a paper to see who is playing for England

Armstrong captained the party to England in 1921. Hobbs was injured or ill for the whole series; although he appeared at Headingley he retired with appendicitis while fielding and did not bat. England were still in a state of post-war flux and no fewer than 16 players made their debuts during the series.

At Headingley, Gregory and McDonald, Australia's fast-bowling partnership, captured nine wickets as England were dismissed for 112, and seven more in the second innings, when Ernest Tyldesley played a bumper from Gregory onto his wicket via his face. Australia won by 10 wickets.

Noble, Montague Alfred

Noble was born on 28 January 1873 in Sydney, NSW, and made his debut for that state in 1893–94. A defensive middle-order right-hand batsman, and medium-paced off-break bowler, he was also a brilliant field at point. He first appeared for Australia in 1897–98, and became captain in 1903–04. In 42 Tests he scored 1,997 runs, average 30.25 and took 121 wickets, average 25.00. On retirement he wrote some notable books on cricket. He died on 22 June 1940 at Randwick, NSW.

The treatment continued at Lord's. Thirteen wickets for the fast-bowling pair led to a comfortable eight-wicket victory for Australia.

Australia batted first at Headingley and Macartney made the first century of the series. Australia totalled 407. The Hon Lionel Tennyson captained England, Douglas having led the side to seven successive defeats against Australia. He kept his place, and took over the captaincy when Tennyson injured his hand fielding. Tennyson showed spirit in scoring 63 virtually one-handed in England's 259. He also made 36 in the second innings but could not prevent a 219-run defeat.

Rain washed out the first day at Old Trafford, a Test interesting mostly for a breach in the rules. With Russell scoring 101, Tennyson attempted to declare on the second day, but Armstrong pointed out that under two-day rules this was not permissible unless 100 minutes batting were possible for the other side. After a 25-minute delay England resumed and Armstrong bowled consecutive overs; having bowled the last before the break, he bowled the first afterwards. England were well on top but the match was destined to be a draw.

At the Oval, Sandham was England's 30th player of the rubber, a record. Mead scored 182 not out, including 109 before lunch on the second day. England declared, led by 14, but could only bat out time. Armstrong read a paper in the outfield to demonstrate the pointlessness of it.

1920–21 Averages

Batting	I	No	Runs	HS	Avge
C.G. Macartney (A)	4	1	260	170	86.66
W.W. Armstrong (A)	7	1	464	158	77.33
J.M. Gregory (A)	8	2	442	100	73.66
H.L. Collins (A)	9	0	557	162	61.88
C.E. Pellew (A)	6	0	319	116	53.16
J.B. Hobbs (E)	10	0	505	123	50.50
C. Kelleway (A)	7	0	330	147	47.14
J.W.H.T. Douglas (E)	10	1	354	68	39.33
W. Bardsley (A)	9	1	311	57	38.87
C.A.G. Russell (E)	8	1	258	135*	36.85
J.W.H. Makepeace (E)	8	0	279	117	34.87
E.H. Hendren (E)	10	0	319	67	31.90
F.E. Woolley (E)	10	0	285	79	28.50

Bowling	O	M	Runs	W	Avge	BB
C. Kelleway (A)	146.5	32	315	15	21.00	4–27
J.M. Gregory (A)	208.1	30	556	23	24.17	7–69
A.A. Mailey (A)	243.5	27	946	36	26.27	9–121
P.G.H. Fender (E)	100.2	7	410	12	34.16	5–90
C.H. Parkin (E)	212.2	28	670	16	41.87	5–60

1924–25: Hobbs and Sutcliffe join forces, but Australia win again

The England party under A.E.R. Gilligan included seven of the players who had lost 5–0 four years earlier.

Centuries by the captain, H.L. Collins, and W.H. Ponsford, on his debut, got Australia away to a good start of 450 in the first Test at Sydney. Hobbs and Sutcliffe opened the England innings for the first time together, and put on 157, but the rest of the side, except Hendren, batted poorly. With a lead of 152, Australia added 452, J.M. Taylor scoring a century and adding 127 for the last wicket with Mailey, still Australia's highest against England. Hobbs and Sutcliffe opened with another three-figure stand (each scored a century and a fifty in the match), Woolley scored 123, and England's 411 was a fourth-innings record, but they lost by 193.

At Melbourne Ponsford became the first to score a century in each of his first two Tests; V.Y. Richardson scored another, and Australia made a record Test score of 600. Hobbs (154) and Sutcliffe (176) then batted all the third day, the first such instance in Tests, and put on 283, but again the rest of the batting failed and England made 479. Set to get 372 they fell 82 short, despite a third century in three innings by Sutcliffe. Tate had 20 wickets in the first two Tests.

Injuries possibly cost England the third Test. With Australia 22 for three, Tate and Gilligan had to retire, and at 119 for six Freeman followed. Ryder then made 201

Hobbs, John Berry

Hobbs was born in Cambridge on 16 December 1882, and played for Surrey from 1905. He was a brilliant opening right-hand batsman, and an excellent field, especially at cover. He was called 'The Master', and is regarded by some as the world's greatest batsman, although his figures were later well beaten by Bradman. Hobbs was an attractive, artistic batsman, whose best innings were often played on difficult wickets. He was highly admired in Australia, where he made five successful tours. His totals of first-class runs, 61,760, and centuries, 199, are unsurpassed. His Test debut was in 1907–08, and he played in 61 Tests, scoring 5,410 runs, average 56.95. With Sutcliffe, he made 15 opening stands of 100 for England. He was knighted in 1953, and died on 21 December 1963 at Brighton.

not out and Australia recovered to 489. England kept Hobbs (119) and Sutcliffe back to numbers five and six and made 365. Having dismissed Australia for 250 with the help of a little rain, England needed 375 and made a great effort, finishing only 12 short of victory.

At Melbourne, England won the toss for the only time in the series. Hobbs and Sutcliffe opened with 126, Sutcliffe became the first batsman to score four centuries in a series and England made 548. Australia were beaten by an innings and 29 runs, their first defeat in 17 Tests.

Clarrie Grimmett made his debut for Australia at Sydney, and took 11 wickets in a 307-run Australian victory. Sutcliffe's and Tate's aggregates of 734 runs and 38 wickets were records for a series.

The Australians in 1921. Left to right, standing: Bardsley, Ryder, Hendry, Gregory, Mayne, Andrews, S. Smith jun (manager). Seated: Mailey, MacDonald, Collins, Armstrong, Macartney, Carter, Taylor. Front: Pellew, Oldfield.

1924–25 30th Series Aus 4, Eng 1

1 SYDNEY **Australia won by 193 runs**

Australia 450 (H L Collins 114, W H Ponsford 110, M W Tate 6–130) and 452 (J M Taylor 108, A J Richardson 98, H L Collins 60, M W Tate 5–98)

England 298 (J B Hobbs 115, H Sutcliffe 59, E H Hendren 74, J M Gregory 5–111, A A Mailey 4–129) and 411 (F E Woolley 123, H Sutcliffe 115, J B Hobbs 57, A P Freeman 50)

2 MELBOURNE **Australia won by 81 runs**

Australia 600 (V Y Richardson 138, W H Ponsford 128, A E V Hartkopf 80, J M Taylor 72) and 250 (J M Taylor 90, M W Tate 6–99, F E Woolley 4–84)

England 479 (H Sutcliffe 176, J B Hobbs 154) and 290 (H Sutcliffe 127, F E Woolley 50, A A Mailey 5–92, J M Gregory 4–87)

3 ADELAIDE **Australia won by 11 runs**

Australia 489 (J Ryder 201, A J Richardson 69, T J E Andrews 72, R Kilner 4–127) and 250 (J Ryder 88, R Kilner 4–51, F E Woolley 4–77)

England 365 (J B Hobbs 119, E H Hendren 92) and 363 (W W Whysall 75, H Sutcliffe 59, A P F Chapman 58)

4 MELBOURNE **England won by an innings and 29 runs**

England 548 (H Sutcliffe 143, W W Whysall 76, R Kilner 74, J B Hobbs 66, E H Hendren 65, A A Mailey 4–186)

Australia 269 (J M Taylor 86) and 250 (J M Taylor 68, M W Tate 5–75)

5 SYDNEY **Australia won by 307 runs**

Australia 295 (W H Ponsford 80, M W Tate 4–92, R Kilner 4–97) and 325 (T J E Andrews 80, C Kelleway 73, W A S Oldfield 65, M W Tate 5–115)

England 167 (C V Grimmett 5–45) and 146 (C V Grimmett 6–37)

1924–25 Averages

Batting	I	No	Runs	HS	Avge
H. Sutcliffe (E)	9	0	734	176	81.55
J. Ryder (A)	6	1	363	201*	72.60
J.B. Hobbs (E)	9	0	573	154	63.66
J.M. Taylor (A)	10	0	541	108	54.10
W.H. Ponsford (A)	10	0	468	128	46.80
W.A.S. Oldfield (A)	10	3	291	65	41.57
E.H. Hendren (E)	9	1	314	92*	39.25
F.E. Woolley (E)	9	0	325	123	36.11
H.L. Collins (A)	10	0	294	114	29.40
C. Kelleway (A)	10	1	252	73	28.00

Bowling	O	M	Runs	W	Avge	BB
M.W. Tate (E)	315	62	881	38	23.18	6–99
R. Kilner (E)	179.1	35	399	17	23.47	4–51
C. Kelleway (A)	171	39	413	14	29.50	3–57
J.M. Gregory (A)	207.5	22	816	22	37.09	5–111
A.A. Mailey (A)	239	21	999	24	41.62	5–92

1926: England regain the Ashes at last

Collins led the Australians to England in 1926, but was not called upon for many decisions in the first Test at Trent Bridge, only 50 minutes play being possible.

At Lord's Bardsley carried his bat through the Australian innings of 383, making 193 not out. Hobbs (119) and Sutcliffe (82) put on 182, Hendren made 127 not out, and England captain A.W. Carr declared at 475 for three. But Macartney made 133 not out and the match was drawn. Hobbs became the first to

1926 31st Series Eng 1, Aus 0, Drawn 4

1 TRENT BRIDGE **Match Drawn**

England 32–0 Australia did not bat

2 LORD'S **Match Drawn**

Australia 383 (W Bardsley 193, R Kilner 4–70) and 194–5 (C G Macartney 133)

England 475–3 dec (E H Hendren 127, J B Hobbs 119, F E Woolley 87, H Sutcliffe 82, A P F Chapman 50)

3 HEADINGLEY **Match Drawn**

Australia 494 (C G Macartney 151, W M Woodfull 141, A J Richardson 100, M W Tate 4–99)

England 294 (G G Macaulay 76, C V Grimmett 5–88) and 254–3 (H Sutcliffe 94, J B Hobbs 88)

4 OLD TRAFFORD **Match Drawn**

Australia 335 (W M Woodfull 117, C G Macartney 109, C F Root 4–84)

England 305–5 (G E Tyldesley 81, J B Hobbs 74, F E Woolley 58)

5 THE OVAL **England won by 289 runs**

England 280 (H Sutcliffe 76, A A Mailey 6–138) and 436 (H Sutcliffe 161, J B Hobbs 100)

Australia 302 (J M Gregory 73, H L Collins 61) and 125 (W Rhodes 4–44)

The England tourists in Australia, 1924–25. Left to right, back: Bryan, Tyldesley, Tate, F.C. Toone (manager), Whysall, Chapman, Sandham.

pass 4,000 runs in Tests.

Bardsley captained Australia at Headingley because Collins was ill, but was out without a run on the board. Macartney then arrived to make a century before lunch. With Woodfull and A.J. Richardson also scoring centuries Australia reached 494, and dismissed England for 294. Hobbs and Sutcliffe, with a 156 opening stand, ensured the draw.

At Old Trafford, rain ruined the first day, and then Macartney and Woodfull scored their third and second centuries of the series respectively, but there was no time for England to complete their innings.

The Oval Test was to be played to a finish, and England replaced Carr as captain with A.P.F. Chapman. Rhodes was recalled at 45 years old after a five-year break, and

1926 Averages

Batting	I	No	Runs	HS	Avge
C.G. Macartney (A)	6	1	473	151	94.60
J.B. Hobbs (E)	7	1	486	119	81.00
H. Sutcliffe (E)	7	1	472	161	78.66
W.M. Woodfull (A)	6	0	306	141	51.00

Bowling	O	M	Runs	W	Avge	BB
M.W. Tate (E)	208.3	64	388	13	29.84	5–88
C.V. Grimmett (A)	204	59	414	13	31.84	5–88
A.A. Mailey (A)	172.4	25	592	14	42.28	6–138

Woolley was chosen for his 52nd consecutive Test match, dating back to 1909.

England made 298, Maily claiming six for 138, and Australia recovered from 122 for

Middle: Hearne, Strudwick, Douglas, Gilligan, Hobbs, Woolley. Front: Kilner, Hendren, Freeman, Sutcliffe, Howell.

The most successful of all Test opening partnerships, Jack Hobbs and Herbert Sutcliffe. In the 1924–25 and 1926 series, Hobbs averaged 63.66 and 81.00, Sutcliffe 81.55 and 78.66.

cord crowd of 58,456 turned up to watch Hobbs bat on the second day, and they gave him a tremendous ovation. It was Hammond who scored most of England's runs, however, in a record Test total of 636: he made 251. Woodfull and Hendry made centuries second time round for Australia, but England needed only 15 to win, and the bowlers were sent in to get them.

Australia needed to win at Melbourne, and began with 397, with Ryder and Kippax scoring centuries and adding 161 together. Hammond, however, became the first player to score a double-century in successive Test innings, and England led by 20 runs. Australia set a target of 332, with Woodfull and Bradman (at 20 years 129 days old) getting centuries. The odds were heavily in Australia's favour when England began, for rain had made the wicket almost unplayable, but Hobbs and Sutcliffe produced some of the

six to 302, a lead of 22. England were ahead by the end of the second day, but then came a storm. The batting of Hobbs and Sutcliff on a sticky wicket on the third day has become legendary. Their first-wicket stand realized 172; both made centuries and Sutcliffe went on to 161. The partnership won the match. Australia were set 415 and were shot out for 125.

1928–29: Hammond's triumphant tour and England win easily

Chapman continued as England captain for the tour to Australia in 1928–29. Ryder captained Australia.

Brisbane made its debut as a Test venue for the first Test, and Bradman made his first appearance for Australia. Most of the English players scored runs, Hendren's 169 being the main score of the side's 521. Larwood, on his first visit to Australia, then achieved his best Test analysis, 6–32, on a perfect batting pitch. Australia made 122. England declared at 342 for eight (Oldfield did not allow a bye in 863 runs). It was a wise decision not to enforce the follow-on, because after Larwood had taken two quick wickets in the fourth innings, overnight rain led Australia to be dismissed for 66, and a record victory for England in terms of runs alone by 675 runs.

Bradman was dropped for the second Test at Sydney, where Australia made 253. A re-

1928–29 Averages					
Batting	**I**	**No**	**Runs**	**HS**	**Avge**
W.R. Hammond (E)	9	1	905	251	113.12
A. Jackson (A)	4	0	276	164	69.00
D.G. Bradman (A)	8	1	468	123	66.85
J. Ryder (A)	10	1	492	112	54.66
W.M. Woodfull (A)	10	1	491	111	54.55
E.H. Hendren (E)	9	0	472	169	52.44
H. Sutcliffe (E)	7	0	355	135	50.71
J.B. Hobbs (E)	9	0	451	142	50.11
D.R. Jardine (E)	9	1	341	98	42.62
A.F. Kippax (A)	10	1	311	100	31.10

Bowling	**O**	**M**	**Runs**	**W**	**Avge**	**BB**
G. Geary (E)	240.3	70	477	19	25.10	5–35
J.C. White (E)	405.5	134	760	25	30.10	5–35
D.D. Blackie (A)	210	52	444	14	31.71	6–94
H. Larwood (E)	258.7	41	728	18	40.44	6–32
M.W. Tate (E)	371	122	693	17	40.76	4–77
C.V. Grimmett (A)	398.2	95	1024	23	44.52	6–131

best batting ever seen in the circumstances. Playing a dead bat to everything that needed to be played, they put on 105 and stayed while the wicket eased. Sutcliffe completed his fourth century at Melbourne and England won by three wickets.

At Adelaide Hammond scored 119 not out and England reached 334. Then Archie Jackson, opening for Australia on his debut, scored 164 at 19 years 152 days old, the youngest to score an Ashes century. It helped Australia to a 35-run lead. Hammond (177) then completed his second century of the match and his fourth of the rubber (equalling Sutcliffe's record), and with Jardine (98) put on 262 for the third wicket. Australia needed 349 to win, and batting solidly, failed by only 13 runs. J.C. White took eight for 126.

In the last Test at Melbourne, Hobbs, at 46 years 82 days, became the oldest to score a Test century (142), and Leyland scored 137 in his first match against Australia. England, without Sutcliffe, made 519. Woodfull and Bradman made centuries for Australia, who ended only 28 behind. Good bowling by T.W. Wall, on his debut, helped get England out for 257, and, needing 286, Australia won by five wickets. Hammond's aggregate of 905 runs (av 113.12) for the series was a record, and in his second innings Hobbs became the first to pass 5,000 runs in Tests.

1930: Farewell to Hobbs, and the rise of Bradman

Chapman retained the captaincy of England when W.M. Woodfull's Australians arrived in England in 1930. At Trent Bridge England led by 126 in a low-scoring first innings, and then, thanks to Hobbs' second 70, made 302, setting Australia 429 to win. With Bradman and McCabe batting well at 229 for three, a Notts groundstaff substitute, S.H. Copley, made a brilliant catch to dismiss McCabe for 49. Bradman made 131 in his first Test in England but England won by 93.

At Lord's Duleepsinhji's 173 helped England to 425, but Australia replied with 729 for six declared, the highest score made at Lord's. Bradman contributed 254 (the highest Test score at Lord's) and Kippax 155. Chapman's century could not save England from a seven-wicket defeat.

Bradman broke more records at Headingley. He made 309 on the first day (still a record for one day in a Test), including 105 before lunch. His final score of 334 was the highest individual Test score. Australia made 566, but Hammond scored a century and the match was drawn.

There was little play at Old Trafford after the first two days. Hobbs and Sutcliffe made their last (eleventh) century opening stand against Australia.

The final Test at the Oval was a timeless Test to decide the rubber. R.E.S. Wyatt took over the England captaincy and helped Sutcliffe (161) add 170 for the sixth wicket.

The England tourists in Australia, 1928–29. Left to right, back: Duckworth, Ames, Mead, Tate, Hendren, Geary. Middle: Leyland, Staples, Hammond, F.C. Toone (manager), Sutcliffe, Larwood, Freeman. Front: Tyldesley, White, Chapman, Jardine, Hobbs.

Jack Hobbs sweeps high to leg in the Test at Trent Bridge in 1930. Hobbs made 78 and 74.

England made 405, but Australia passed this total with only three wickets down, Bradman (232) and Ponsford (110) doing most damage. With a deficit of 290, England made only 251 (Hornibrook 7–92), and Australia won back the Ashes.

Hobbs' Test career ended with a record 5,410 runs, while Bradman's stormed ahead with a record series aggregate of 974, average 139.14.

1930 33rd Series Aus 2, Eng 1, Drawn 2

1 TRENT BRIDGE **England won by 93 runs**
England 270 (J B Hobbs 78, A P F Chapman 52, R W V Robins
  50, C V Grimmett 5–107) and 302 (J B Hobbs 74, E H
  Hendren 72, H Sutcliffe 58, C V Grimmett 5–94)
Australia 144 (A F Kippax 64, R W V Robins 4–51) and 335 (D
  G Bradman 131)

2 LORD'S **Australia won by 7 wkts**
England 425 (K S Duleepsinhji 173, M W Tate 54, A G Fairfax
  4–101) and 375 (A P F Chapman 121, G O B Allen 57, C V
  Grimmett 6–167)
Australia 729–6 dec (D G Bradman 254, W M Woodfull 155, A F
  Kippax 83, W H Ponsford 81) and 72–3

3 HEADINGLEY **Match Drawn**
Australia 566 (D G Bradman 334, A F Kippax 77, W M Woodfull
  50, M W Tate 5–124)
England 391 (W R Hammond 113, C V Grimmett 5–135) and
  95–3

4 OLD TRAFFORD **Match Drawn**
Australia 345 (W H Ponsford 83, W M Woodfull 54, A F Kippax
  51, C V Grimmett 50)
England 251–8 (H Sutcliffe 74, K S Duleepsinhji 54, S J McCabe
  4–41)

5 THE OVAL **Australia won by an innings and 39 runs**
England 405 (H Sutcliffe 161, R E S Wyatt 64, K S Duleepsinhji
  50, C V Grimmett 4–135) and 251 (W R Hammond 60, H
  Sutcliffe 54, P M Hornibrook 7–92)
Australia 695 (D G Bradman 232, W H Ponsford 110, A Jackson
  73, W M Woodfull 54, S J McCabe 54, A G Fairfax 53, I A R
  Peebles 6–204)

1930 Averages

Batting	I	No	Runs	HS	Avge
D.G. Bradman (A)	7	0	974	334	139.14
H. Sutcliffe (E)	7	2	436	161	87.20
K.S. Duleepsinhji (E)	7	0	416	173	59.42
W.M. Woodfull (A)	7	1	345	155	57.50
W.H. Ponsford (A)	6	0	330	110	55.00
A.F. Kippax (A)	7	1	329	83	54.83
A.P.F. Chapman (E)	6	0	259	1231	43.16
W.R. Hammond (E)	9	0	306	113	34.00
J.B. Hobbs (E)	9	0	301	78	33.44

Bowling	O	M	Runs	W	Avge	BB
A.G. Fairfax (A)	134.2	34	335	12	27.91	4–101
C.V. Grimmett (A)	349.4	78	925	29	31.89	6–167
P.M. Hornibrook (A)	196.1	50	471	13	36.23	7–92
M.W. Tate (E)	280.1	82	574	15	38.26	5–124
T.W. Wall (A)	229.4	44	593	13	45.61	3–67

ENGLAND V AUSTRALIA 1930
3rd Test, Headingley: Match Drawn

AUSTRALIA

W.M. Woodfull*	b Hammond	50
A.A. Jackson	c Larwood b Tate	1
D.G. Bradman	c Duckworth b Tate	334
A.F. Kippax	c Chapman b Tate	77
S.J. McCabe	b Larwood	30
V.Y. Richardson	c Larwood b Tate	1
E.L. a'Beckett	c Chapman b Geary	29
W.A.S. Oldfield†	c Hobbs b Tate	2
C.V. Grimmett	c Duckworth b Tyldesley	24
T.W. Wall	b Tyldesley	3
P.M. Hornibrook	not out	1
Extras	(B 5, LB 8, W 1)	14
Total		**566**

ENGLAND

J.B. Hobbs	c A'Beckett b Grimmett	29	run out	13
H. Sutcliffe	c Hornibrook b Grimmett	32	not out	28
W.R. Hammond	c Oldfield b McCabe	113	c Oldfield b Grimmett	35
K.S. Duleepsinhji	b Hornibrook	35	c Grimmett b Hornibrook	10
M. Leyland	c Kippax b Wall	44	not out	1
G. Geary	run out	0		
G. Duckworth†	c Oldfield b A'Beckett	33		
A.P.F. Chapman*	b Grimmett	45		
M.W. Tate	c Jackson b Grimmett	22		
H. Larwood	not out	10		
R.K. Tyldesley	c Hornibrook b Grimmett	6	(LB 8)	8
Extras	(B 9, LB 10, NB 3)	22		
Total		**391**	**(3 wickets)**	**95**

ENGLAND	O	M	R	W	O	M	R	W
Larwood	33	3	139	1				
Tate	39	9	124	5				
Geary	35	10	95	1				
Tyldesley	33	5	104	2				
Hammond	17	3	46	1				
Leyland	11	0	44	0				
AUSTRALIA								
Wall	40	12	70	1	10	3	20	0
A'Beckett	28	8	47	1	11	4	19	0
Grimmett	56.2	16	135	5	17	3	33	1
Hornibrook	41	7	94	1	11.5	5	14	1
McCabe	10	4	23	1	2	1	1	0

FALL OF WICKETS

	A	E	E
Wkt	1st	1st	2nd
1st	2	53	24
2nd	194	64	72
3rd	423	123	94
4th	486	206	–
5th	491	206	–
6th	508	289	–
7th	519	319	–
8th	544	370	–
9th	565	375	–
10th	566	391	–

The Australian tourists in 1930. Left to right, back: McCabe, Hurwood, Wall, Hornibrook, A'Beckett, Kippax, Grimmett, Oldfield. Front: Bradman, Ponsford, Richardson, Woodfull, Walker, Jackson, Fairfax.

1932–33: Bodyline causes bitterness and injury

The 1932–33 Test series in Australia was to become the most famous in cricket history, and its 50th anniversary saw books, films and a television series made about it.

The controversy it inspired centred on the England tactics employed by their stern captain, D.R. Jardine, and dubbed by the Australian press as 'bodyline', to subdue the prolific scoring of Bradman.

Ironically, Bradman was unfit for the first Test at Sydney. The bodyline tactics, which consisted of fast, short-pitched bowling to a string of close leg-side catchers, were used, but not exclusively, in Australia's innings. McCabe played what is regarded as the best innings against bodyline – a dashing, hooking 187 not out, including 51 of a last-wicket stand of 55. Australia totalled 360. Centuries from Sutcliffe (194), Hammond and the Nawab of Pataudi, on his Test debut, gave England a lead of 164, and they required only one second-innings run for a ten-wicket victory. The fast bowler Larwood, on whom bodyline was based, took ten wickets.

At Melbourne, on a pitch suited to leg-breaker W.J. O'Reilly, who took ten wickets, Australia levelled the series by a 111-run victory. Bradman, on his return, was bowled first ball by Bowes, but made 103 not out in the second innings.

The bodyline argument came to a head at Adelaide, a Test watched by a record 172,926 spectators, including 50,962 on the fateful second day. After England recovered from 30 for four to 341, Australian captain Woodfull was struck over the heart by Larwood and there were angry crowd scenes. After play Woodfull made a much-publicized remark to the England manager that only one side was playing cricket. After a rest day filled with heated

Douglas Jardine, the controversial England captain on the 1932–33 tour of Australia, whose fast leg-theory tactics earned the name 'bodyline' and sparked off a famous row between the countries.

comments from the Australian press, Jardine continued his tactics and Oldfield's skull was fractured by another ball from Larwood. The deliveries causing the main injuries were not strictly bodyline, but were pitched on the off, and Oldfield sportingly admitted later that he had ducked into his, but opinion now was such that the Australian Board of Control sent a cable to MCC which read:

'Bodyline bowling has assumed such proportions as to menace the best interests of the game, making protection of the body by the batsman the main consideration. This is causing intensely bitter feeling between the players as well as injury. In our opinion it is unsportsmanlike. Unless stopped at once it is likely to upset the friendly relations existing between Australia and England.'

That put the majority Australian view clearly. The MCC view was that leg-theory bowling was quite legal and long-

established, that the Australian batsmen made difficulties for themselves with their style of moving across the wicket, that 'unsportsmanlike' was not a term they could countenance and that if the Australian authorities so wished they would abandon the tour.

Eventually the two Governments were drawn into the dispute, but after much diplomacy and cabling the tour continued, with the England tactics unchanged. England won the Adelaide match by 338 runs.

1932–33   34th Series   Eng 4, Aus 1

1 SYDNEY   England won by 10 wkts
Australia 360 (S J McCabe 187, H Larwood 5–96, W Voce 4–110) and 164 (H Larwood 5–28)
England 524 (H Sutcliffe 194, W R Hammond 112, Nawab of Pataudi 102) and 1–0

2 MELBOURNE   Australia won by 111 runs
Australia 228 (J H W Fingleton 83) and 191 (D G Bradman 103)
England 169 (H Sutcliffe 52, W J O'Reilly 5–63, T W Wall 4–52) and 139 (W J O'Reilly 5–66, H Ironmonger 4–26)

3 ADELAIDE   England won by 338 runs
England 341 (M Leyland 83, R E S Wyatt 78, E Paynter 77, T W Wall 5–72) and 412 (W R Hammond 85, L E G Ames 69, D R Jardine 56, W J O'Reilly 4–79)
Australia 222 (W H Ponsford 85, G O B Allen 4–71) and 193 (W M Woodfull 73, D G Bradman 66, G O B Allen 4–50, H Larwood 4–71)

4 BRISBANE   England won by 6 wkts
Australia 340 (V Y Richardson 83, D G Bradman 76, W M Woodfull 67, H Larwood 4–101) and 175
England 356 (H Sutcliffe 86, E Paynter 83, W J O'Reilly 4–120) and 162–4 (M Leyland 86)

5 SYDNEY   England won by 8 wkts
Australia 435 (L S Darling 85, S J McCabe 73, L P J O'Brien 61, W A S Oldfield 52, H Larwood 4–98) and 182 (D G Bradman 71, W M Woodfull 67, H Verity 5–33)
England 454 (W R Hammond 101, H Larwood 98, H Sutcliffe 56, R E S Wyatt 51, P K Lee 4–111) and 168–2 (W R Hammond 75, R E S Wyatt 61)

1932–33 Averages

Batting	I	No	Runs	HS	Avge	
D.G. Bradman (A)	8	1	396	103*	56.57	
H. Sutcliffe (E)	9	1	440	194	55.00	
W.R. Hammond (E)	9	1	440	112	55.00	
R.E.S. Wyatt (E)	9	2	327	78	46.71	
S.J. McCabe (A)	10	1	385	187*	42.77	
M. Leyland (E)	9	0	306	86	34.00	
W.M. Woodfull (A)	10	1	305	73*	33.88	
V. Richardson (A)	10	0	279	83	27.90	

Bowling	O	M	Runs	W	Avge	BB
H. Larwood (E)	220.1	42	644	33	19.51	5–28
T.W. Wall (A)	160.1	33	409	16	25.56	5–72
W.J. O'Reilly (A)	383.4	144	724	27	26.81	5–63
H. Ironmonger (A)	245.3	96	405	15	27.00	4–26
W. Voce (E)	133.3	23	407	15	27.13	4–110
G.O.B. Allen (E)	170.6	29	593	21	28.23	4–50

Larwood, Harold

Larwood was born on 14 November 1904 at Nuncargate, Nottinghamshire. He first appeared for Notts in 1924 and for England two years later. He was a devastating right-arm fast bowler, whose name will always be linked with the 'bodyline' series of 1932–33. He was the ideal fast bowler to implement the English captain's policy of leg-theory bowling, which was calculated to neutralize Bradman. England won the series 4–1, amid tremendous controversy, but for one reason or another Larwood did not play for England again. In 21 Tests from 1926 he took 78 wickets at 28.35 each. He scored valuable Test runs, averaging 19.40. He emigrated to Australia in 1949.

At Brisbane, where England regained the Ashes with a six-wicket win, there were no serious incidents, the batsman Paynter being the hero with a fine four-hour innings after being summoned from a hospital bed where he was being treated for acute tonsillitis. Sadly the brilliant young batsman Archie Jackson died aged 23 on the day Paynter's six settled the series.

At Sydney, England emphasized their superiority with an eight-wicket win, largely due to Verity's bowling; Larwood, who injured his foot, nevertheless getting 98 runs as night-watchman. His 33 wickets at 19.51 won the series, but he did not play another Test, and was the principal sufferer of the bitterness aroused by bodyline.

1934: Ponsford and Bradman make big partnerships

Many behind-the-scenes meetings had been held as a result of the bodyline tour, and one result was the absence from the England team of the three major bodyline figures: Jardine, the captain, and Larwood and

Larwood bowling to Australian captain Woodfull at Brisbane in 1932–33. Woodfull ducks under a bouncer. Notice the ring of six close in on the leg side, the 'bodyline' field.

Voce, the fast bowlers. MCC opinion was now firmly against its use.

C.F. Walters captained England at Trent Bridge as Wyatt was injured. A.G. Chipperfield lunched at 99 not out in his first Test, but failed to get the vital run. Australia won with ten minutes to spare, after O'Reilly had taken 11 wickets in the match.

Fortune favoured England at Lord's where Wyatt returned. England reached 440, during which innings Oldfield became the first wicket-keeper to achieve 100 Test dismissals. Rain made the wicket on the third day a paradise for Hedley Verity, who caused the Australian first innings to collapse and then dismissed the side a second time, taking 14 wickets in the day – a Test record. England won by an innings.

O'Reilly caused England to collapse from 68 without loss to 72 for three at Old Trafford, with three wickets in four balls, but Hendren (132) and Leyland (153) repaired the damage.

G.O.B. Allen's first over included three wides and four no-balls. McCabe made 137 and the match was destined to be a draw.

After England had been dismissed for 200 at Headingley, Bradman scored his second successive triple-century there. With Ponsford (181) he added 388 for the fourth wicket, to create a new record for Ashes matches. Rain on the last day saved England from probable defeat.

The final Test at the Oval was again the decisive match, played to a finish. Australia batted and Ponsford (266) and Bradman (244) broke all Test partnership records with 451 for the second wicket, which remains a record. Australia made 701 and Woodfull batted again with a lead of 380. England

finally needed 708 to win and were beaten by 562. The spin bowlers Grimmett and O'Reilly took 53 wickets in the series.

1934   35th Series   Aus 2, Eng 1, Drawn 2

1 TRENT BRIDGE   Australia won by 238 runs

Australia 374 (A G Chipperfield 99, S J McCabe 65, W H Ponsford 53, K Farnes 5–102) and 273–8 dec (S J McCabe 88, W A Brown 73, K Farnes 5–77)

England 268 (E H Hendren 79, H Sutcliffe 62, G Geary 53, C V Grimmett 5–81, W J O'Reilly 4–75) and 141 (W J O'Reilly 7–54)

2 LORD'S   England won by an innings and 38 runs

England 440 (L E G Ames 120, M Leyland 109, C F Walters 82, T W Wall 4–108)

Australia 284 (W A Brown 105, H Verity 7–61) and 118 (H Verity 8–43)

3 OLD TRAFFORD   Match Drawn

England 627–9 dec (M Leyland 153, E H Hendren 132, L E G Ames 72, H Sutcliffe 63, G O B Allen 61, H Verity 60, C F Walters 52, W J O'Reilly 7–189) and 123–0 (H Sutcliffe 69, C F Walters 50)

Australia 491 (S J McCabe 137, W M Woodfull 73, W A Brown 72, H Verity 4–78) and 66–1

4 HEADINGLEY   Match Drawn

England 200 (C V Grimmett 4–57) and 229–6

Australia 584 (D G Bradman 304, W H Ponsford 181, W E Bowes 6–142)

5 THE OVAL   Australia won by 562 runs

Australia 701 (W H Ponsford 266, D G Bradman 244, W E Bowes 4–164, G O B Allen 4–170) and 327 (D G Bradman 77, S J McCabe 70, W E Bowes 5–55, E W Clark 5–98)

England 321 (M Leyland 110, C F Walters 64) and 145 (C V Grimmett 5–64)

1934 Averages

Batting	I	No	Runs	HS	Avge	
W.H. Ponsford (A)	7	1	569	266	94.83	
D.G. Bradman (A)	8	0	758	304	94.75	
M. Leyland (E)	8	1	478	153	68.28	
S.J. McCabe (A)	9	1	483	137	60.37	
H. Sutcliffe (E)	7	1	304	69*	50.66	
C.F. Walters (E)	9	1	401	82	50.12	
E.H. Hendren (E)	6	0	298	132	49.66	
L.E.G. Ames (E)	7	1	261	120	43.50	
W.A. Brown (A)	9	0	300	105	33.33	

Bowling	O	M	Runs	W	Avge	BB
H. Verity (E)	271.2	93	576	24	24.00	8–43
W.J. O'Reilly (A)	333.4	128	698	28	24.92	7–54
W.E. Bowes (E)	144.3	27	483	19	25.42	6–142
C.V. Grimmett (A)	396.3	148	668	25	26.72	5–64

1936–37: Thanks to Bradman Australia recover from 2–0 down

G.O.B. Allen, who had declined to bowl bodyline on the previous tour, was captain of the next England party to Australia, which included Voce, who had come to terms with the authorities.

Bradman captained Australia for the first time at Brisbane. McCormick claimed Worthington with the first ball of the first Test and reduced England to 20 for three, but lumbago prevented him playing much further part, and England recovered, thanks to Leyland (126), to 358. Fingleton became the first to score centuries in four successive Test innings. But Australia trailed, and, dismissed on a rain-affected pitch for 58 second time round, were beaten by 322 runs.

At Sydney Hammond made his third double-century against Australia and was 231 not out at the end of a rain-affected second day. Allen then declared at 426 for six, the rain came again, and Australia were shot out for 80. Following on, they did better as the pitch improved, but were beaten by an innings.

A record crowd for any match of 350,534 watched the third Test, in which it was Australia's turn for the luck. They reached 200 for nine, rain again played a part and, with the wicket worsening, Bradman declared. England were reduced to 76 for nine, and also declared. Bradman reversed his batting order, sending in his tail-enders and holding back Fingleton, McCabe and himself. He joined Fingleton at 97 for five, with the wicket easing, and they added a record Test sixth-wicket partnership of 346. Bradman made 270. Leyland's unbeaten century in a total of 323 left England still 365 short.

Australia batted first on a good wicket at Adelaide, and were out for 288, England passing this with only five wickets down, thanks to Barnett's century. But the lead was to be only 42, Bradman scored 212 in the

McCabe, Stanley Joseph

McCabe, born on 16 July 1910 at Grenfell, NSW, played two of the most famous Test innings of all time. After making his debut for New South Wales in 1928–29, he made his Test appearance on the tour of England in 1930. He was a brilliant middle-order right-hand batsman, and a medium-paced bowler. He was very strong against fast bowling and could cut and hook powerfully. This helped him to make 187 not out at Sydney in 1932–33, often described as the best innings against bodyline. At Trent Bridge in 1938 he made 232 out of 411, including 72 out of 77 for the last wicket, an innings singled out by Bradman as the best he'd seen. In 39 Tests McCabe scored 2,748 runs, average 48.21, and took 36 wickets at 42.86 each. He died at Mosman, NSW, on 25 August 1968.

Maurice Tate bowling at Old Trafford in 1935 in his last Test match. He was England's most successful bowler in Australia in the 1920s.

1936–37 36th Series Aus 3, Eng 2

1 BRISBANE **England won by 322 runs**
England 358 (M Leyland 126, C J Barnett 69, W J O'Reilly 5–102) and 256 (G O B Allen 68, F A Ward 6–102)
Australia 234 (J H W Fingleton 100, S J McCabe 51, W Voce 6–41) and 58 (G O B Allen 5–36, W Voce 4–16)

2 SYDNEY **England won by an innings and 22 runs**
England 426–6 dec (W R Hammond 231, C J Barnett 57)
Australia 80 (W Voce 4–10) and 324 (S J McCabe 93, D G Bradman 82, J H W Fingleton 73)

3 MELBOURNE **Australia won by 365 runs**
Australia 200–9 dec (S J McCabe 63) and 564 (D G Bradman 270, J H W Fingleton 136)
England 76–9 dec (M W Sievers 5–21) and 323 (M Leyland 111, R W V Robins 61, W R Hammond 51, L O'B Fleetwood-Smith 5–124)

4 ADELAIDE **Australia won by 148 runs**
Australia 288 (S J McCabe 88, A G Chipperfield 57) and 433 (D G Bradman 212, S J McCabe 55, R G Gregory 50, W R Hammond 5–57)
England 330 (C J Barnett 129, L E G Ames 52, W J O'Reilly 4–51, L O'B Fleetwood-Smith 4–129) and 243 (R E S Wyatt 50, L O'B Fleetwood-Smith 6–110)

5 MELBOURNE **Australia won by an innings and 200 runs**
Australia 604 (D G Bradman 169, C L Badcock 118, S J McCabe 112, R G Gregory 80, K Farnes 6–96)
England 239 (J Hardstaff jun 83, W J O'Reilly 5–51, L J Nash 4–70) and 165 (W R Hammond 56)

second innings and Australia won by 148 runs.

In the Ashes decider at Melbourne, Australia again won the toss, Bradman, McCabe and Badcock scored centuries, and the total of 604 was enough for an innings victory. For the first time a side had won a series from 2–0 down.

1936–37 Averages

Batting	I	No	Runs	HS	Avge	
D.G. Bradman (A)	9	0	810	270	90.00	
W.R. Hammond (E)	9	1	468	231*	58.00	
M. Leyland (E)	9	1	441	126	55.12	
S.J. McCabe (A)	9	0	491	112	54.55	
J.H.W. Fingleton (A)	9	0	398	136	44.22	
C.J. Barnett (E)	9	0	395	129	43.88	
J. Hardstaff, jr (E)	9	0	256	83	28.44	

Bowling	O	M	Runs	W	Avge	BB
W. Voce (E)	162.1	20	560	26	21.53	6–41
W.J. O'Reilly (A)	247.6	89	555	25	22.20	5–51
L.O'B.Fleetwood-Smith (A)	131.4	20	463	19	24.36	6–110
W.R. Hammond (E)	88.4	8	301	12	25.08	5–57
G.O.B. Allen (E)	128.7	12	526	17	30.94	5–36

1938: Records tumble at the Oval

Two strong batting sides met in the first Test at Trent Bridge, with Bradman and Hammond the two captains.

Barnett reached 98 by lunch, completing his century off the first ball afterwards. He and Hutton put on 219 for the first wicket, and this set the pattern: there were two double centuries (Paynter and McCabe) and five other centuries in the match.

Compton, at 20 years 19 days, became England's youngest Test century-maker. McCabe's innings was possibly the best, Bradman regarding it as the best he'd seen. He batted 235 minutes for 232, gave no chance, and scored 72 of 77 added for the last wicket. Australia followed on, but the match was drawn.

Hammond made 240 at Lord's, and W.A. Brown carried his bat through the Australian innings for 206 not out. A Bradman

Woodfull, William Maldon

Woodfull was born at Maldon, Victoria, on 22 August 1897, and first played for Victoria in 1921–22. He was a sound defensive opening right-hand batsman. He made his debut for Australia in 1926, and became captain in 1930. He was captain during the controversial bodyline tour of 1932–33, in which he was a central figure. In 35 Tests he scored 2,300 runs, average 46.00. He died while playing golf at Tweed Heads, NSW, on 11 August 1965.

century in the second innings ensured the draw for Australia.

Not a ball was bowled at Old Trafford, the second instance in history, both at the same ground.

At Headingley, England made 223, and, in bad light and on a difficult pitch, Bradman made a century for the sixth consecutive Test, a record. Australia led by 19, and they required only 105 in the fourth innings. Even so, it needed a firm innings of 33 out of 41 by Hassett to get them home by five wickets. O'Reilly's ten wickets were decisive.

The Oval Test was played to a finish. England won the toss and Hutton batted for 13 hours and 17 minutes, stayed while 770 runs were added and made 364, all Test records. England's total of 903 for seven declared remains a record as does Fleetwood-Smith's concession of 298 runs (he took one wicket). With Bradman and

1938   37th Series   Aus 1, Eng 1, Drawn 2

1 TRENT BRIDGE   Match Drawn
England 658–8 dec (E Paynter 216, C J Barnett 126, D C S Compton 102, L Hutton 100, L O'B Fleetwood-Smith 4–153)
Australia 411 (S J McCabe 232, D G Bradman 51, K Farnes 4–106, D V P Wright 4–153) and 427–6 dec (D G Bradman 144, W A Brown 133)

2 LORD'S   Match Drawn
England 494 (W R Hammond 240, E Paynter 99, L E G Ames 83, W J O'Reilly 4–93, E L McCormick 4–101) and 242–8 dec (D C S Compton 76)
Australia 422 (W A Brown 206, A L Hassett 56, H Verity 4–103) and 204–6 (D G Bradman 102)

3 HEADINGLEY   Australia won by 5 wkts
England 223 (W R Hammond 76, W J O'Reilly 5–66) and 123 (W J O'Reilly 5–56) L O'B Fleetwood-Smith 4–34)
Australia 242 (D G Bradman 103, B A Barnett 57, K Farnes 4–77) and 107–5

4 THE OVAL   England won by an innings and 579 runs
England 903–7 dec (L Hutton 364, M Leyland 187, J Hardstaff jun 169, W R Hammond 59, A Wood 53)
Australia 201 (W A Brown 69, W E Bowes 5–49) and 123 (K Farnes 4–63)
D G Bradman and J H W Fingleton were absent injured in both innings
(The match arranged to be played at Old Trafford was abandoned without a ball being bowled)

1938 Averages

Batting	I	No	Runs	HS	Avge	
L. Hutton (E)	4	0	473	364	118.25	
D.G. Bradman (A)	6	2	434	144*	108.50	
E. Paynter (E)	6	2	407	216*	101.75	
W.A. Brown (A)	8	1	512	206*	73.14	
W.R. Hammond (E)	6	0	403	240	67.16	
S.J. McCabe (A)	8	0	362	232	45.25	

Bowling	O	M	Runs	W	Avge	BB
H. Verity (E)	154.1	53	354	14	25.28	4–103
W.J. O'Reilly (A)	263	78	610	22	27.72	5–66
K. Farnes (E)	179.4	32	581	17	34.17	4–63
D.V.P. Wright (E)	120	20	426	12	35.50	4–153
L.O'B.Fleetwood-Smith (A)	217.5	34	727	14	51.92	4–34

Bradman (right) and Fingleton in 1938. Bradman had just completed 1,000 runs before the end of May, the only batsman to achieve this feat twice.

Fingleton unable to bat because of injury, Australia were beaten by an innings and 579 runs – another record as the biggest victory in Test cricket.

Below: Hutton receiving congratulations after breaking the Test innings record at the Oval in 1938. W.A. Brown is shaking his hand. Hardstaff is the non-striker.

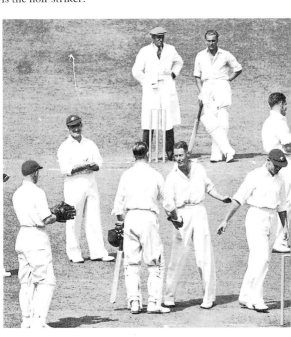

Grimmett, Clarence Victor

Grimmett started his Test career astonishingly late for one who accomplished so much. He was born on Christmas Day, 1891, at Dunedin, New Zealand. He played for Wellington in 1911–12, but after the First World War turned out for Victoria in 1918–19, and switched to South Australia in 1924–25. He was a brilliant leg-break and googly bowler, bowling with a low arm action after a trundle to the wicket. He made his Test debut in 1924–25 aged 33. Short and balding, he did not look dangerous, but he took 11 English wickets in his first Test. Carrying on from there he played in 37 Tests, becoming the first to take 200 Test wickets. He ended with 216, average 24.21. He died on 2 May 1980 in Adelaide.

Oldfield, William Albert Stanley

Oldfield was born on 9 September 1894 at Alexandria, NSW. He began playing for his state in 1919–20, and became the leading wicket-keeper of his time. He made his Test debut in 1920–21 and from 1924–25 was Australia's first-choice keeper for 13 years. It was his being struck and laid out by a delivery from Larwood which climaxed the bodyline argument. In 54 Tests he made 78 catches and 52 stumpings, the aggregate of 130 being a record. He made 1,427 Test runs, average 22.65. He died on 10 August 1976 at Killara, NSW.

Paynter, Edward

Paynter was born at Oswaldtwistle, Lancashire, on 5 November 1901. He made his debut for Lancashire in 1926, but was not a regular until 1931. He was an attacking middle-order left-hand batsman, and although lacking the top joints of two fingers after an early accident he was a brilliant deep fieldsman. He first played for England in 1931, and was not always in favour although he seldom failed in Tests. In 20 matches he scored 1,540 runs, average 59.23, bettered by only four batsmen in the whole history of Tests. In seven Tests against Australia, easily the strongest opposition of the 1930s, his average was a remarkable 84.42. He died in Keighley, Yorkshire, on 5 February 1979.

Verity, Hedley

Verity was born at Headingley, Leeds, on 18 May 1905, and in 1930 made his debut for Yorkshire. He was a slow left-arm bowler, but not of classic mould. He was tall and made the ball turn and lift from little short of medium pace. He became the most successful slow bowler of the 1930s, and achieved the best analysis in first-class cricket, ten for ten for Yorkshire against Notts in 1932. He first appeared in a Test in 1931, and he took 14 wickets in a day against Australia at Lord's in 1934. In 40 Tests he took 144 wickets at 24.37 each. He batted right-hand and once opened in a Test in Australia. His Test average was 20.90. He died of wounds in a prisoner-of-war camp at Casate, Italy, on 31 July 1943.

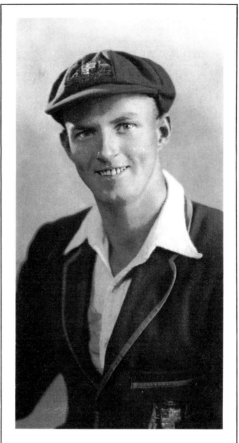

O'Reilly, William Joseph

O'Reilly was born on 20 December 1905 at White Cliffs, NSW, and played for his state from 1927–28. He was a tall leg-break and googly bowler, who bowled quicker than most of that type, with a flurry of whirling arms designed to get maximum life from the pitch. His aggressive style led to the nickname 'Tiger'. He made his Test debut in 1931–32, and in 27 matches took 144 wickets, average 22.59. Some would say he was the best bowler of his era. On retirement he became a distinguished cricket writer.

1946–47: Bradman returns with lucky decision

Bradman and Hammond were rival captains again when Ashes cricket resumed after the Second World War.

An umpiring decision concerning Bradman in the first Test was to have a lasting effect on cricket history. Bradman was not sure if he was fit enough for Test cricket, and might have retired had he been given out after what seemed a legitimate catch in the gully when 28. He went on to 187, adding 276 with Hassett (128) for the third wicket. Australia made 645, and England were forced to bat twice after thunderstorms. Australia's win by an innings and 332 was the largest over England, each side's biggest win having come in successive Tests. Tests in Australia were now limited to 30 hours play, as in England, and Australia's win came in the final session.

England batted first at Sydney, but batted badly and were out for 255. Bradman, coming in at number six, and S.G. Barnes, who opened, both scored 234, and shared a partnership of 405 for the fifth wicket, still a Test record. Evans conceded no byes in Australia's 659 for eight declared, and despite a century by Edrich, England lost by an innings.

There was little in the Melbourne Test until Tallon and Lindwall added 154 in 88 minutes for Australia's eighth wicket in the second innings. England held on for a draw, the first draw in a Test in Australia for 65 years.

The fourth Test at Adelaide was even closer. Australia led by 27 on a high-scoring first innings, and England declared at 340

Below left: The England team at the Oval in 1938.
Below: The Australians in 1938.

for eight in the second, but the match was destined to be another draw. A feature of the match was that Denis Compton and Arthur Morris each scored a century in each innings – the only occasion opposing batsmen have done this in a Test. An oddity was Godfrey Evans batting for 97 minutes in the second innings before scoring.

Yardley took over the England captaincy in the final Test, Hammond having fibrositis. Hutton, 122 not out overnight, took no further part in the match, contracting tonsillitis. Even so England gained a lead of 27, Wright taking seven wickets, but their second innings effort was poor, and Australia won by five wickets.

1946–47 38th Series Aus 3, Eng 0, Drawn 2

1 BRISBANE Australia won by an innings and 332 runs
Australia 645 (D G Bradman 187, A L Hassett 128, C L McCool 95, K R Miller 79, D V P Wright 5–167)
England 141 (K R Miller 7–60) and 172 (E R H Toshack 6–82)

2 SYDNEY Australia won by an innings and 33 runs
England 255 (W J Edrich 71, J T Ikin 60, I W Johnson 6–42) and 371 (W J Edrich 119, D C S Compton 54, C L McCool 5–109)
Australia 659–8 dec (S G Barnes 234, D G Bradman 234)

3 MELBOURNE Match Drawn
Australia 365 (C L McCool 104, D G Bradman 79) and 536 (A R Morris 155, R R Lindwall 100, D Tallon 92)
England 351 (W J Edrich 89, C Washbrook 62, N W D Yardley 61, B Dooland 4–69) and 310–7 (C Washbrook 112, N W D Yardley 53)

4 ADELAIDE Match Drawn
England 460 (D C S Compton 147, L Hutton 94, J Hardstaff jun 67, C Washbrook 65, R R Windwall 4–52) and 340–8 dec (D C S Compton 103, L Hutton 76, E R H Toshack 4–76)
Australia 487 (K R Miller 141, A R Morris 122, A L Hassett 78, I W Johnson 52) and 215–1 (A R Morris 124, D G Bradman 56)

5 SYDNEY Australia won by 5 wkts
England 280 (L Hutton 122, W J Edrich 60, R R Lindwall 7–63) and 186 (D C S Compton 76, C L McCool 5–44)
Australia 253 (S G Barnes 71, A R Morris 57, D V P Wright 7–105) and 214–5 (D G Bradman 63)

1946–47 Averages

Batting	I	No	Runs	HS	Avge
D.G. Bradman (A)	8	1	680	234	97.14
K.R. Miller (A)	7	2	384	141*	76.80
S.G. Barnes (A)	6	0	443	234	73.83
A.R. Morris (A)	8	1	503	155	71.85
C.L. McCool (A)	7	2	272	104*	54.40
L. Hutton (E)	9	1	417	122*	52.12
D.C.S. Compton (E)	10	1	459	147	51.00
A.L. Hassett (A)	7	0	332	128	47.42
W.J. Edrich (E)	10	0	462	119	46.20
C. Washbrook (E)	10	0	363	112	36.30
N.W.D. Yardley (E)	10	2	252	61	31.50

Bowling	O	M	Runs	W	Avge	BB
R.R. Lindwall (A)	122.1	20	367	18	20.38	7–63
K.R. Miller (A)	122.3	15	334	16	20.87	7–60
E.R.H. Toshack (A)	178.4	49	437	17	25.70	6–82
C.L. McCool (A)	182	27	491	18	27.27	5–54
D.V.P. Wright (E)	240.2	23	990	23	43.04	7–105
A.V. Bedser (E)	246.3	37	876	16	54.75	3–97

1948: A great Australian victory at Leeds

The 1948 Australian touring party under Bradman is regarded by common consent as the best of modern times. Based on a fast attack of Lindwall, Miller and Johnston, an experimental rule allowing a new ball every 55 overs considerably helped the tourists.

At Trent Bridge, England were quickly removed for 165 and Australia built up a big lead at 509, Bradman and Hassett scoring centuries. A brilliant innings by Compton, who scored 184, forced Australia to bat again, but they won by eight wickets.

Australia batted first at Lord's and made 350, enough for a lead of 135. With Barnes scoring 141, England were set 596 to win, and failed by 410 runs.

Hutton was dropped for the Old Trafford Test, where Compton played another great innings. After hooking a bouncer onto his forehead, he retired hurt but later resumed to score 145 not out in a total of 363. Pollard pulled a ball into Barnes' midriff, who, after attempting to carry on, spent 10 days in hospital. Australia made only 221, but a day was lost and, after England declared, Morris and Bradman carefully played out time.

The Headingley Test was remarkable for the fourth innings. England won the toss, and passed 400 with only two wickets down, but eventually made only 496. R.N. Harvey made 112 in his first match against England, but England led by 38 and on the last morning declared, setting Australia 404 to win in 344 minutes. Morris and Bradman added 301 in 217 minutes for the second wicket and Australia reached the target to win by seven wickets.

Lindwall breezed through England at the Oval, taking six for 20 in a total of 52. Hutton batted throughout for 30, and was on the field for all but the last 57 minutes. Morris made 196 for Australia, who won by an innings and 149 runs. Bradman, in his last Test, was cheered all the way to the wicket, and bowled by Hollies second ball, needing only four runs for a Test match average of 100.

Hardstaff gets the ball away between Lindwall and McCool at Adelaide in 1946–47.

1 TRENT BRIDGE Australia won by 8 wkts

England 165 (J C Laker 63, W A Johnston 5–36) and 441 (D C S
  Compton 184, L Hutton 74, T G Evans 50, K R Miller 4–125,
  W A Johnston 4–147)
Australia 509 (D G Bradman 138, A L Hassett 137, S G Barnes
  62, J Laker 4–138) and 98–2 (S G Barnes 64)

2 LORD'S Australia won by 409 runs

Australia 350 (A R Morris 105, D Tallon 53, A V Bedser 4–100)
  and 460–7 dec (S G Barnes 141, D G Bradman 89, K R Miller
  74, A R Morris 62)
England 215 (D C S Compton 53, R R Lindwall 5–70) and 186
  (E R H Toshack 5–40)

3 OLD TRAFFORD Match Drawn

England 363 (D C S Compton 145, R R Lindwall 4–99) and
  174–3 dec (C Washbrook 85, W J Edrich 53)
Australia 221 (A R Morris 51, A V Bedser 4–81) and 92–1 (A R
  Morris 54)

4 HEADINGLEY Australia won by 7 wkts

England 496 (C Washbrook 143, W J Edrich 111, L Hutton 81, A
  V Bedser 79) and 365–8 dec (D C S Compton 66, C
  Washbrook 65, L Hutton 57, W J Edrich 54, W A Johnston 4–
  95)
Australia 458 (R N Harvey 112, S J E Loxton 93, R R Lindwall
  77, K R Miller 58) and 404–3 (A R Morris 182, D G Bradman
  173)

5 THE OVAL Australia won by an innings and 149 runs

England 52 (R R Lindwall 6–20) and 188 (L Hutton 64, W A
  Johnston 4–40)
Australia 389 (A R Morris 196, S G Barnes 61, W E Hollies 5–
  131)

1948 Averages

Batting	I	No	Runs	HS	Avge
A.R. Morris (A)	9	1	696	196	87.00
S.G. Barnes (A)	6	2	329	141	82.25
D.G. Bradman (A)	9	2	508	173	72.57
D.C.S. Compton (E)	10	1	562	184	62.44
C. Washbrook (E)	8	1	356	143	50.85
A.L. Hassett (E)	8	1	310	137	44.28
L. Hutton (E)	8	0	342	81	42.75
W.J. Edrich (E)	10	0	319	111	31.90

Bowling	O	M	Runs	W	Avge	BB
R.R. Lindwall (A)	222.5	57	530	27	19.62	6–20
K.R. Miller (A)	138.1	43	301	13	23.15	4–125
W.A. Johnston (A)	309.2	92	630	27	23.33	5–36
A.V. Bedser (E)	274.3	75	688	18	38.22	4–81

Lindwall, Raymond Russell

Lindwall, born on 3 October 1921 at
Mascot, NSW, played for New South
Wales from 1941–42, switching to
Queensland in 1954–55. A right-arm fast
bowler, he was, like Larwood, not tall, but
he had a perfect action and became the
leading fast bowler of the immediate
post-war period. He made his Test debut in
1945–46 and in 61 matches took 228
wickets, average 23.03. He also made two
Test centuries and had an average of
21.15.

Above: The 1948 Australian team at Worcester.
Left to right, back: Johnson, Morris, Toshack,
Miller, Tallon, Lindwall, Harvey. Front: Brown,
Hassett, Bradman, McCool, Barnes.

Top: Dooland dismisses Hammond caught and
bowled for nine in the third Test at Melbourne on
the 1946–47 England tour of Australia.

Bradman, Donald George

Bradman was born on 27 August 1908 at Cootamundra, NSW. He made his debut for NSW in 1927–28, changing to South Australia in 1935–36. He was an outstanding batsman from the start and made his Test debut in 1928–29. He dominated all bowlers from the late 1920s, and his prowess was the reason for England's 'bodyline' tactics in 1932–33. His career averages are about 50 per cent better than those of any other player in history. On his four visits to England he averaged over 84 each time, his 115.66 in 1938 being the highest ever for an English season. In the Test match at Leeds in 1930 he scored 309 on the first day, and his final 334 was at the time a Test record. He played in 52 Tests, captaining Australia in 24. He scored 6,996 runs for an average of 99.94. In his last Test at the Oval in 1948, he was applauded all the way to the wicket, and bowled for a duck, when four runs would have given him an average of 100. He became a leading administrator in Australia and was knighted in 1949.

1950–51: Australia have the luck and win easily

F.R. Brown was third choice captain for the tourists, who included many young and inexperienced players. Hassett was Australia's captain.

England began very unluckily at Brisbane. After a good performance in dismissing Australia for 228, they found a rain-damaged pitch unplayable and declared at 68 for seven. Australia did worse, declaring at 32 for seven. England were all but beaten at close of play on the third day, during

Above: Bradman's reception when he came out to bat at the Oval in 1948 for his last Test innings. He was given three cheers by the England team, but was then dismissed for a duck.

Left: The 1948 Australians at Balmoral, where they were visiting King George VI.

Right: Denis Compton unluckily dismissed at Trent Bridge in 1948, stumbling and falling on his wicket after playing a ball from Miller. He made 184.

which 20 wickets fell while 102 runs were being scored. Hutton, held back to number eight, completed 62 not out of the last 92 runs in a remarkable innings, but could only reduce the deficit to 70.

In a low-scoring match at Melbourne, England, without Compton, led by three runs on first innings and required only 179 to win in the fourth, but tried to make them with extreme caution and fell 29 runs short.

After making 290 at Sydney, England had to bowl on a good pitch with only three bowlers, two having been injured batting. Australia took a lead of 136, and won by an innings when England collapsed to the new 'mystery' spin bowler Jack Iverson, who took six for 27.

There were some remarkable centuries at Adelaide. Morris scored 206 for Australia,

Harvey, Robert Neil

Born on 8 October 1928 at Fitzroy, Victoria, Harvey and his three brothers all played for Victoria. Neil made his debut in 1946–47 and switched to New South Wales in 1958–59. A small man, he was a brilliant middle-order left-hand batsman, noted for his footwork. He was a dynamic fielder, usually at cover point. He made his first appearance for Australia in 1947–48 and played in 79 Tests, at the time an Australian record. His run aggregate was second to Bradman's. He scored 6,419, average 48.41.

Miller, Keith Ross

Born in Sunshine, Victoria, on 28 November 1919, Miller was given the name of the two airmen who made the first flight from England to Australia, Keith Smith and Ross Smith. After playing for Victoria from 1937–38, he became a wartime pilot, and played for the Australian services team in the Victory Tests in England. After the war he switched to New South Wales. He made his Test debut in 1945–46. He was an attacking middle-order right-hand batsman and fast bowler, whose partnership with Lindwall carried all before it. He was an inspirational cricketer, altering his run up and style of bowling as the whim took him, and would play his best when it most mattered. In 55 Tests, he scored 2,958 runs, average 36.97, and took 170 wickets, average 22.97.

who totalled 371. Hutton then demonstrated once more how much the England batting depended on him this tour by carrying his bat for 156 not out from a total of only 272. Hutton's 57 per cent of his side's total was slightly higher than Morris's. J.W. Burke made a century in his first Test and Australia won by 274 runs.

In the final Test Australia were out for 217, and a fine innings by R.T. Simpson of 156 not out, including 64 in a last-wicket stand of 74, gave England a lead of 103. Five wickets for A.V. Bedser for the second time in the match left England needing only 95, of which Hutton scored 60 not out. It was England's first win over Australia since his big innings at the Oval in 1938.

1950–51   40th Series   Aus 4, Eng 1

1 BRISBANE   Australia won by 70 runs
Australia 228 (R N Harvey 74, A V Bedser 4–45) and 32–7 dec (T E Bailey 4–22)
England 68–7 dec (W A Johnston 5–35) and 122 (L Hutton 62, J B Iverson 4–43)

2 MELBOURNE   Australia won by 28 runs
Australia 194 (A L Hassett 52, A V Bedser 4–37, T E Bailey 4–40) and 181 (F R Brown 4–26)
England 197 (F R Brown 62, J B Iverson 4–37) and 150 (W A Johnston 4–26)

3 SYDNEY   Australia won by an innings and 13 runs
England 290 (F R Brown 79, L Hutton 62, K R Miller 4–37) and 123 (J B Iverson 6–27)
Australia 426 (K R Miller 145, I W Johnson 77, A L Hassett 70, A V Bedser 4–107, F R Brown 4–153)

4 ADELAIDE   Australia won by 274 runs
Australia 371 (A R Morris 206, D V P Wright 4–99) and 403–8 dec (J W Burke 101, K R Miller 99, R N Harvey 68)
England 272 (L Hutton 156) and 228 (R T Simpson 61, W A Johnston 4–73)

5 MELBOURNE   England won by 8 wkts
Australia 217 (A L Hassett 92, A R Morris 50, A V Bedser 5–46, F R Brown 5–49) and 197 (G B Hole 63, R N Harvey 52, A V Bedser 5–59)
England 320 (R T Simpson 156, L Hutton 79, K R Miller 4–76) and 95–2 (L Hutton 60)

1950–51 Averages

Batting	I	No	Runs	HS	Avge
L. Hutton (E)	10	4	533	156*	88.83
K.R. Miller (A)	9	1	350	145*	43.75
A.L. Hassett (A)	9	0	366	92	40.66
R.N. Harvey (A)	9	0	362	74	40.22
R.T. Simpson (E)	10	1	349	156*	38.77
A.R. Morris (A)	9	0	321	206	35.66

Bowling	O	M	Runs	W	Avge	BB
T.E. Bailey (E)	75.1	18	198	14	14.14	4–22
J.B. Iverson (A)	138.2	29	320	21	15.23	6–27
A.V. Bedser (E)	195	34	482	30	16.06	5–46
K.R. Miller (A)	106.6	23	301	17	17.70	4–37
W.A. Johnston (A)	153.7	28	422	22	19.18	5–35
F.R. Brown (E)	109	12	389	18	21.61	5–49
R.R. Lindwall (A)	98.3	11	344	15	22.93	3–29

1953: England regain the Ashes after Watson saves them

Hutton had become England's captain by the time Hassett led the Australian tourists to England in 1953.

After Hassett had made 115 at Trent

The England touring party on board ship for Australia in 1950, captain Brown making a farewell speech. On his left is Brian Close, England's youngest Test player.

Bridge, Australia collapsed from 237 for three to 249 all out, Bedser taking seven wickets. England, however, batted poorly and finished 145 behind. Another seven wickets for Bedser shot Australia out for 123, and at the end of the third day England were 42 for one, but rain prevented much more play and the match was drawn.

At Lord's, another century for Hassett saw Australia reach 346, but Hutton (145) and Graveney (78) batted beautifully and England led by 26. With Miller making a century, Australia seemed to have the match won overnight on the fourth day with England, needing 343, already reduced to 20 for three. But Willie Watson played a memorable defensive innings of 109. With Bailey (71) he added 163 in 248 minutes on the last day and saved the game.

Rain ruined the Old Trafford match, with Australia's second-innings 35 for eight (Wardle 4–7) being not too significant.

Australia put England in at Headingley and out again for 167. Australia led by 99, Bedser's sixth wicket taking him past Grimmett's record Test haul of 216. Bailey played another long innings in England's 275: 262 minutes for 38. Australia needed only 177 to win in 115 minutes. They began quickly enough but Bailey again saved the match with legside bowling off a long run – tactics not universally approved but effective.

All was to play for at the Oval, a Test extended to six days. Australia made 275, thanks to a recovery led by Lindwall. England lost nine wickets before passing this total, but managed to gain a valuable lead of 31. Laker and Lock then removed Australia for 162, and England knocked off the runs for the loss of two wickets to regain the Ashes after nearly 19 years. Bedser's 39 wickets was a new Ashes record for England.

Top left: High jinks on board the SS *Stratheden* in 1950. From left: Bailey, Simpson, Parkhouse, Compton, McIntyre, Hutton.

Edrich and Compton (ducking) race for the pavilion after England's Ashes win in 1953.

Top right: Hassett caught by Evans off Bedser for 53 at the Oval in 1953. Edrich is the slip.
Above: Miller, in a cloud of dust, bowls to Bailey at the Oval in 1953. Trueman is the non-striker.

1953 41st Series Eng 1, Aus 0, Drawn 4

1 TRENT BRIDGE Match drawn
Australia 249 (A L Hassett 115, A R Morris 67, K R Miller 55, A V Bedser 7–55 and 123 (A R Morris 67, A V Bedser 7–44)
England 144 (R R Lindwall 5–57) and 120–1 (L Hutton 60)

2 LORD'S Match Drawn
Australia 346 (A L Hassett 104, A K Davidson 76, R N Harvey 59, J H Wardle 4–77, A V Bedser 5–105) and 368 (K R Miller 109, A R Morris 89, R R Lindwall 50, F R Brown 4–82)
England 372 (L Hutton 145, T W Graveney 78, D C S Compton 57, R R Lindwall 5–66) and 282–7 (W Watson 109, T E Bailey 71)

3 OLD TRAFFORD Match Drawn
Australia 318 (R N Harvey 122, G B Hole 66, A V Bedser 5–115) and 35–8 (J H Wardle 4–7)
England 276 (L Hutton 66)

4 HEADINGLEY Match Drawn
England 167 (T W Graveney 55, R R Lindwall 5–54) and 275 (W J Edrich 64, D C S Compton 61, K R Miller 4–63)
Australia 266 (R N Harvey 71, G B Hole 53, A V Bedser 6–95) and 147–4

5 THE OVAL England won by 8 wkts
Australia 275 (R R Lindwall 62, A L Hassett 53, F S Trueman 4–86) and 162 (G A R Lock 5–45, J C Laker 4–75)
England 306 (L Hutton 82, T E Bailey 64, R R Lindwall 4–70) and 132–2 (W J Edrich 55)

1953 Averages

Batting	I	No	Runs	HS	Avge	
L. Hutton (E)	9	1	443	145	55.37	
A.L. Hassett (A)	10	0	365	115	36.50	
R.N. Harvey (A)	10	0	346	122	34.60	
A.R. Morris (A)	10	0	337	89	33.70	
G.B. Hole (A)	10	0	273	66	27.30	

Bowling	O	M	Runs	W	Avge	BB
A.V. Bedser (E)	265.1	58	682	39	17.48	7–44
R.R. Lindwall (A)	240.4	62	490	26	18.84	5–54
J.H. Wardle (E)	155.3	57	344	13	26.46	4–7

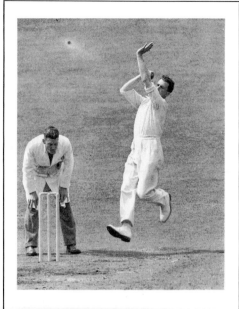

Laker, James Charles

Laker was a Yorkshireman, born on 9 February 1922 in Bradford, but after war service he settled in Surrey and played for them from 1946. He became one of cricket's greatest off-break bowlers, and was one of the principal reasons for Surrey's seven successive Championships in the 1950s. He made his Test debut in 1947–48 on a Tour to West Indies. He did not always have the confidence of the selectors, but in an amazing season in 1956 he twice took all ten Australian wickets in an innings, once for Surrey and once for England. At Old Trafford he set a first-class and Test record with 19 wickets in a match. His 46 wickets in that series is an Ashes record. In 46 Tests he took 193 wickets, average 21.24. He became a television commentator and died on 23 April 1986.

Above: Arthur Morris skies the ball at Trent Bridge in 1953. The ball fell safe and Morris reached 60 in each innings.

Below: Edrich clips the ball to leg at the Oval.

1954–55: Fast bowling by Tyson and Statham wins the rubber

Hutton led England to Australia for the only time in 1954–55, and in the first Test at Brisbane put Australia in, having selected a fast seam attack. Australia survived the early liveliness of the wicket and went on to 601 for eight declared (Morris 153, Harvey 162). Compton had fractured his hand on the fence and England made little show, losing by an innings and 154 runs.

Morris, deputizing for Ian Johnson, put England in at Sydney, and his fast bowlers did better in dismissing England for 154. Australia in return were restricted to 228, which seemed to be enough when England were 55 for three. But May (104) and Cowdrey (54) made a stand of 116, and Australia were eventually set 223. Tyson, who had been knocked unconscious by a Lindwall bouncer when batting, and Statham then bowled with exceptional speed and venom to bowl Australia out for 184, a victory for England by 38. Statham had previously scored 25 in a last-wicket stand of 46. Harvey, undefeated, scored half of Australia's runs. Bedser had been omitted from this Test, to great surprise.

At level pegging, there was great interest in the Melbourne Test. Miller, bowling with great fire, dismissed Hutton, Edrich and Compton for five runs, and England were 41 for four, and reached 191 only because Cowdrey made a splendid 102. However it still needed the last two Australian wickets to add 80 to give Australia a lead of 40. May's 91 helped England to 279, leaving Australia 240 to win. Tyson (7–27) and Statham swept through them again and they made only 111.

In great heat at Adelaide, Australia scored 323 and England plodded to 341 in 541 minutes, the match then looking to be a draw. But Appleyard claimed three quick second-innings wickets and Australia were again all out on their 'unlucky' score of 111. England needed only 94, lost three wickets scoring 18 (to Miller again) but won comfortably by five wickets.

With the Ashes retained, England were unable to start batting until after lunch on the fourth day at Sydney, because of the worst storms seen there in 50 years. They declared at 371 for seven after a Graveney century, forced the follow-on and were four wickets short of another win when play ended.

1954-55 42nd Series   Eng 3, Aus 1, Drawn 1
1 BRISBANE   **Australia won by an innings and 154 runs**
Australia 601–8 dec (R N Harvey 162, A R Morris 153, R R
   Lindwall 64, G B Hole 57)

Top: Denis Compton swings the ball to leg at the Oval in 1953 to win the match and bring back the Ashes to England for the first time since the war.

Ray Lindwall bowling at the Oval in 1953. Trevor Bailey is the non-striking batsman. Bailey played a match-saving innings at Lord's in this series.

England 190 (T E Bailey 88) and 257 (W J Edrich 88)
2 SYDNEY England won by 38 runs
England 154 and 296 (P B H May 104, M C Cowdrey 54)
Australia 228 (F H Tyson 4–45, T E Bailey 4–59) and 184 (R N Harvey 92, F H Tyson 6–85)
3 MELBOURNE England won by 128 runs
England 191 (M C Cowdrey 102, R G Archer 4–33) and 279 (P B H May 91, W A Johnston 5–85)
Australia 231 (J B Statham 5–60) and 111 (F H Tyson 7–27)
4 ADELAIDE England won by 5 wkts
Australia 323 (L V Maddocks 69) and 111
England 341 (L Hutton 80, M C Cowdrey 79, R Benaud 4–120) and 97–5
5 SYDNEY Match Drawn
England 371–7 dec (T W Graveney 111, D C S Compton 84, P B H May 79, T E Bailey 72)
Australia 221 (C C McDonald 72, J H Wardle 5–79) and 118–6

1954–55 Averages

Batting	I	No	Runs	HS	Avge
R.N. Harvey (A)	9	1	354	162	44.25
P.B.H. May (E)	9	0	351	104	39.00
T.E. Bailey (E)	9	1	296	88	37.00
M.C. Cowdrey (E)	9	0	319	102	35.44

Bowling	O	M	Runs	W	Avge	BB
R.G. Archer (A)	97.6	32	215	13	16.53	4–33
F.H. Tyson (E)	151	16	583	28	20.82	7–27
W.A. Johnston (A)	141.4	37	423	19	22.26	5–85
R.R. Lindwall (A)	130.6	28	381	14	27.21	3–27
J.B. Statham (E)	143.3	16	499	18	27.72	5–60

Left: Three happy England pace bowlers in 1954–55 in Australia, Frank Tyson, Peter Loader, who was not in the Test team, and Brian Statham.

Above: Frank Tyson bowling in the fourth Test at Adelaide in 1954–55. Tyson was the main destroyer of the Australian batting during the series.

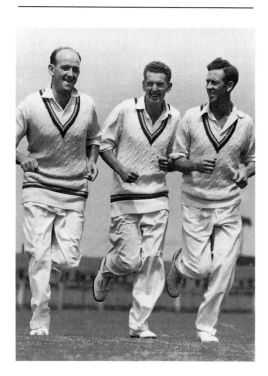

1956: Laker breaks the bowling records at Old Trafford

Peter May was captain of England when Ian Johnson's tourists arrived in 1956.

Peter Richardson made his debut in the first Test at Trent Bridge and made 81 and 73. The second day was washed out, and although England declared twice they could not achieve a result.

At Lord's Australia made 285, after McDonald and Burke had started with 130 for the first wicket. England were then put out for 171, despite Australia's new bowler, W.P.A. Crawford, breaking down in his fifth over. Miller took five for 72. Australia recovered from 112 for six when Benaud made a dashing 97. A total of 257 left England needing 372, and Australia won easily by 185 runs. Miller took ten wickets in the match for the only time in his career, and Gil Langley established a Test record with nine dismissals behind the stumps.

At Headingley England recalled a selector, Washbrook, whose last Test had been five years earlier. Washbrook joined May after Archer had reduced England to 17 for three on the first morning. The two added 157, with May scoring a century and Washbrook being lbw for 98. With the wicket taking spin, Laker and Lock ran through Australia twice, taking 11 and 7 wickets respectively. Only Harvey provided much resistance as England levelled the series with victory by an innings and 42 runs.

The Old Trafford Test will never be forgotten because of the astonishing bowling of Jim Laker. The Rev David Sheppard was recalled and made 113. Richardson and Cowdrey also scored well and England reached 459. On a pitch becoming dusty, Laker then went through the Australian first innings, taking nine for 37, finishing it off with a spell of seven for eight in 22 balls. At the close of the second day he had captured Harvey's wicket for his second duck of the day. A storm then allowed less than two hours play on the third and fourth days. On the fifth Laker completed his amazing analysis: 10 for 53, 19 for 90 in the match. McDonald resisted for 337 minutes over five sessions for 89 and held out until after tea on the fifth day, but England won by an innings and 170 with only an hour to spare.

England recalled Compton for the Oval Test and completed a hat-trick of inspired selections. Compton, minus a knee-cap after an operation, made 94, rescuing England from 66 for three to 222 for four in company with May. England got a lead, declared, but could not force a result. Laker took seven wickets, establishing an Ashes record of 46 for the series, second only in all Tests to Barnes' 49 in South Africa in 1913–14.

1956 43rd Series Eng 2, Aus 1, Drawn 2
1 TRENT BRIDGE Match Drawn
England 217–8 dec (P E Richardson 81, P B H May 73, K R Miller 4–69) and 188–3 dec (M C Cowdrey 81, P E Richardson 73)
Australia 148 (R N Harvey 64, J C Laker 4–58) and 120–3 (J W Burke 58)
2 LORD'S Australia won by 185 runs
Australia 285 (C C McDonald 78, J W Burke 65) and 257 (R Benaud 97, F S Trueman 5–90, T E Bailey 4–64)
England 171 (P B H May 63, K R Miller 5–72) and 186 (P B H May 53, K R Miller 5–80, R G Archer 4–71)
3 HEADINGLEY England won by an innings and 42 runs
England 325 (P B H May 101, C Washbrook 98)
Australia 143 (J C Laker 5–58, G A R Lock 4–41) and 140 (R N Harvey 69, J C Laker 6–55)
4 OLD TRAFFORD England won by an innings and 170 runs
England 459 (D S Sheppard 113, P E Richardson 104, M C Cowdrey 80, I W Johnson 4–151)
Australia 84 (J C Laker 9–37) and 205 (C C McDonald 89, J C Laker 10–53)
5 THE OVAL Match Drawn
England 247 (D C S Compton 94, P B H May 83, R G Archer 5–53, K R Miller 4–91) and 182–3 dec (D S Sheppard 62)
Australia 202 (K R Miller 61, J C Laker 4–80) and 27–5

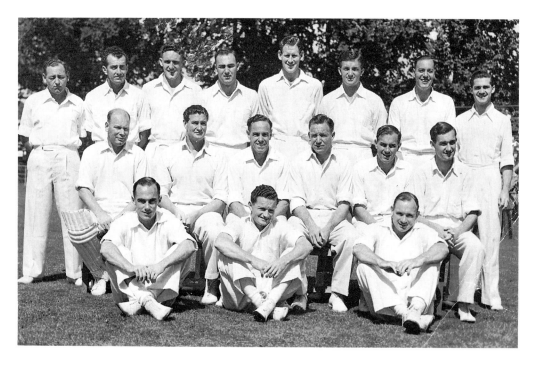

1956 Averages

Batting

	I	No	Runs	HS	Avge
P.B.H. May (E)	7	2	453	101	90.60
P.E. Richardson (E)	8	0	364	104	45.50
J.W. Burke (A)	10	1	271	65	30.11

Bowling

	O	M	Runs	W	Avge	BB
J.C. Laker (E)	283.5	127	442	46	9.60	10.53
K.R. Miller (A)	205.1	44	467	21	22.23	5–72
G.A.R. Lock (E)	237.2	115	337	15	22.46	4–41
R.G. Archer (A)	207.4	67	451	18	25.05	5–53

The 1956 Australians about to leave for England. Left to right, standing: Wilson, Mackay, Davidson, Burge, Crawford, Benaud, Archer, Harvey. Sitting: Langley, Miller, Johnson, Lindwall, McDonald, Burke. Front: Craig, Maddocks, Rutherford.

1958–59: England well-beaten amid complaints of chucking

England took what was regarded as a strong side to Australia in 1958–59, but met an Australian side in which Benaud and Davidson realized their potential as all-rounders and Norman O'Neill made his debut as a Test batsman. But the story of the series was one of bitterness over the Australian bowling actions. Four bowlers – Meckiff, Slater, Rorke and Burke – were considered to throw, and in addition the giant Rorke had a drag which took him well past the bowling crease before he released the ball.

For the first time Australians saw a Test live on television, but ironically Brisbane provided some of the slowest scoring ever. England were out for 134 and Australia for 186 before Bailey made 68 second innings runs in over 7½ overs. Australia needed only 147 to win, and on the last day opener Jack Burke took over four hours making 28 of them. Australia won by eight wickets.

At Melbourne, Davidson took three wickets in his second over: England were seven for three. They totalled 259 thanks to a century from May, Davidson finishing with six for 64. Statham then took seven for 57 for England, but Harvey made a brilliant 167 and Australia led by 49. Meckiff played his biggest role of the series by taking six for 38 as England collapsed for only 87. Australia won again by eight wickets.

Benaud was the destructive bowler at Sydney. England were dismissed for 219

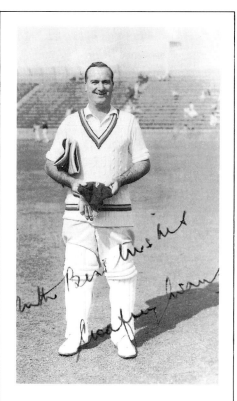

Evans, Thomas Godfrey

Born on 18 August 1920 at Finchley, Middlesex, Evans made his debut for Kent in 1939 and took over as Kent and England wicket-keeper from L.E.G. Ames immediately after the war. A brilliant, acrobatic keeper, he was also a hard-hitting lower-order batsman. In Tests he stood up to A.V. Bedser, forming an effective partnership with the medium-paced bowler. In his 91 Tests he caught 173 batsmen and stumped 46, the aggregate of 219 being a record at the time. He also scored 2,439 runs, average 20.49.

and Australia led by 138. A third-wicket stand of 182 between May (92) and Cowdrey (100 not out) saved England.

May put Australia in at Adelaide, which was generally regarded as a mistake. Australia had 276 on the board before the second wicket fell and totalled 476, thanks mainly to McDonald (170), who was almost bowled by the first ball of the match from Statham. During this innings there were a number of umpiring mistakes.

Lindwall was recalled by Australia and Rorke made his debut. Benaud bowled best, however, as England were put out for 240 and asked to follow on. They did little better second time, making 270, and Australia scored the 35 needed without loss to recapture the Ashes.

Benaud put England in at Melbourne in the last Test, and helped dismiss them for 205. McDonald then made his second successive century (133) and Australia built a lead of 146. England failed again second time round and Australia made the 69 needed for the loss of one wicket. Lindwall passed Grimmett's Australian record of 216 Test wickets.

1958–59 44th Series Aus 4, Eng 0, Drawn 1

1 BRISBANE Australia won by 8 wkts
England 134 and 198 (T E Bailey 68, R Benaud 4–66)
Australia 186 (P J Loader 4–56) and 147–2 (N C O'Neill 71)

2 MELBOURNE Australia won by 8 wkts
England 259 (P B H May 113, A K Davidson 6–64) and 87 (I Meckiff 6–38)
Australia 308 (R N Harvey 167, J B Statham 7–57) and 42–2

3 SYDNEY Match Drawn
England 219 (R Benaud 5–83) and 287–7 dec (M C Cowdrey 100, P B H May 92, R Benaud 4–94)
Australia 357 (N C O'Neill 77, A K Davidson 71, K D Mackay 57, L E Favell 54, J C Laker 5–107, G A R Lock 4–130) and 54–2

4 ADELAIDE Australia won by 10 wkts
Australia 476 (C C McDonald 170, J W Burke 66, N C O'Neill 56, F S Trueman 4–90) and 36–0
England 240 (M C Cowdrey 84, R Benaud 5–91) and 270 (P B H May 59, T W Graveney 53, R Benaud 4–82)

5 MELBOURNE Australia won by 9 wkts
England 205 (P E Richardson 68, R Benaud 4–43) and 214 (T W Graveney 54)
Australia 351 (C C McDonald 133, A T W Grout 74, R Benaud 64, F S Trueman 4–92) and 69–1 (C C McDonald 51)

1958–59 Averages

Batting

	I	No	Runs	HS	Avge
C.C. McDonald (A)	9	1	520	170	65.00
N.C. O'Neill (A)	7	2	282	77	56.40
R.N. Harvey (A)	9	3	291	167	48.50
M.C. Cowdrey (E)	10	1	391	100*	43.44
P.B.H. May (E)	10	0	405	113	40.50
T.W. Graveney (E)	10	1	280	54	31.11

Bowling

	O	M	Runs	W	Avge	BB
I. Meckiff (A)	112.2	24	292	17	17.17	6–38
R. Benaud (A)	233.2	65	584	31	18.83	5–83
A.K. Davidson (A)	183.5	45	456	24	19.00	6–64
J.C. Laker (E)	127.6	24	318	15	21.20	5–107
J.B. Statham (E)	104	12	286	12	23.83	7–57

1961: Australia's great win at Old Trafford

By 1961 Australia had eliminated the chuckers. The main bowler in the first Test at Edgbaston was, surprisingly, all-rounder Ken Mackay, who broke the back of England's batting with three wickets in four balls, making the score 122 for six. England made 195. Bill Lawry made 57 in his first

Test innings and, with Harvey's 114 the best of other good scores, Australia were able to declare at 516 for nine. Dexter's brilliant innings of 180 on the last day, with support from Subba Row's 112, ensured the draw.

Cowdrey set a Test record by winning his ninth successive toss at Lord's, but good bowling by Davidson removed England for 206. Lawry made 130 on a lively pitch (the Lord's ridge was discovered) with the tail-enders helping him retrieve a poor start, and Australia to reached 340. Graham McKenzie, making his debut, took five wickets in England's second-innings 202, and Australia were left with only 69 to get. They lost five wickets to Trueman and Statham, but made the runs. Harvey captained Australia for the only time, because of Benaud's injury.

Benaud and May were back as captains at Headingley and after 12 successful English tosses, May lost. Australia, however, made only 237, thanks mainly to Trueman. England led with only four men out, but collapsed, and the lead was only 62. Australia then collapsed even more dramatically, with Trueman enjoying a spell of five for nothing as they subsided from 99 for two to 120 all out. England won by eight wickets.

The Old Trafford Test, although it did not start until 2.40 on the first day, proved to be one of the most exciting for years. Australia were rapidly dismissed for 190, despite Lawry's gritty 74, Statham taking five wickets. England passed this with only three wickets down, and reached 358 for six, but Bobby Simpson then took the last four wickets, including Barrington, for two runs and England's lead was kept to 177. Australia, in turn, knocked these off with only two men out, Lawry making a century, but wickets fell and nine were out for 334, a lead of only 157. On the last morning McKenzie joined Davidson, who suddenly hit Allen, who had taken four wickets, for 20 in an over. The two added 98 for the last wicket before McKenzie was bowled, leaving Davidson 77 not out. England needed 256 to win at 67 an hour.

When Pullar was out, Dexter played what Benaud described as the finest innings he

The 1961 Australians in England. Left to right, back: Booth, Lawry, Misson, Gaunt, McKenzie. Middle row: A. James (physiotherapist), J. Cameron (scorer), Jarman, Quick, R. Steele (treasurer), Kline, O'Neill, Burge, Simpson. Front: Grout, Davidson, Benaud, S.G. Webb (manager), Harvey, McDonald, Mackay.

had seen in a Test match. But after he had scored 76 in 84 minutes he was caught behind off Benaud. The score was 150 for two, but Benaud, bowling round the wicket, then bowled May round his legs for a duck, and went on to a spell of five for 12 in 25 balls. Suddenly, after England had looked sure to win, the pendulum had tipped Australia's way. With 20 minutes remaining Davidson bowled Statham, and Australia had won by 54 runs to keep the Ashes.

Benaud, Richard

Benaud, known throughout his cricket career as 'Richie', was born on 6 November 1930 at Penrith, NSW. Beginning as a right-hand batsman for New South Wales in 1948–49, he developed great skill as a leg-break and googly bowler and with his catching and captaincy he was an excellent Test all-rounder. He made his Test debut in 1951–52 and captained Australia 28 times from 1958–59. He was captain in the first tied Test against West Indies in 1960–61. In 63 Tests he scored 2,201 runs, average 24.45, and took 248 wickets, average 27.03. He was the first to score 2,000 runs and take 200 wickets. He is now a respected cricket writer and TV commentator.

At the Oval, England made 256, but any hopes they had of squaring the rubber disappeared with a chanceless innings by Peter Burge of 181. With O'Neill (117) and Booth (71) he helped add 308 runs for the fourth and fifth wickets. Australia made 494. There was rain on the third and fourth days, and England had made 370 for eight (Subba Row 137) by the close. It was May's last Test match.

1961   45th Series   Aus 2, Eng 1, Drawn 2

1 EDGBASTON   Match Drawn
England 195 (R Subba Row 59, K D Mackay 4–57) and 401–4 (E R Dexter 180, R Subba Row 112;
Australia 516 (R N Harvey 114, N C O'Neill 82, R B Simpson 76, K D Mackay 64, W M Lawry 57)

2 LORD'S   Australia won by 5 wkts
England 206 (A K Davidson 5–42) and 202 (K F Barrington 66, G D McKenzie 5–37)
Australia 340 (W M Lawry 130, K D Mackay 54, F S Trueman 4–118) and 71–5

3 HEADINGLEY   England won by 8 wkts
Australia 237 (R N Harvey 73, C C McDonald 54, F S Truman 5–58) and 120 (R N Harvey 53, F S Trueman 6–30)
England 299 (M C Cowdrey 93, G Pullar 53, A K Davidson 5–63) and 62–2

4 OLD TRAFFORD   Australia won by 54 runs
Australia 190 (W M Lawry 74, J B Statham 5–53) and 432 (W M Lawry 102, A K Davidson 77, N C O'Neill 67, R B Simpson 51, D A Allen 4–58)
England 367 (P B H May 95, K F Barrington 78, G Pullar 63, R B Simpson 4–23) and 201 (E R Dexter 76, R Benaud 6–70)

5 THE OVAL   Match Drawn
England 256 (P B H May 71, K F Barrington 53, A K Davidson 4–83) and 370–8 (R Subba Row 137, K F Barrington 83, K D Mackay 5–121)
Australia 494 (P J P Burge 181, N C O'Neill 117, B C Booth 71, D A Allen 4–133)

1961 Averages

Batting	I	No	Runs	HS	Avge	
W.M. Lawry (A)	8	0	420	130	52.50	
P.J.P. Burge (A)	8	1	332	181	47.42	
R. Subba Row (E)	10	0	468	137	46.80	
K.F. Barrington (E)	9	1	364	83	45.50	
R.N. Harvey (A)	8	0	338	114	42.25	
E.R. Dexter (E)	9	0	378	180	42.00	
N.C. O'Neill (A)	8	0	324	117	40.50	
P.B.H. May (E)	8	1	272	95	38.85	
G. Pullar (E)	10	1	287	63	31.88	

Bowling	O	M	Runs	W	Avge	BB
A.K. Davidson (A)	280.2	86	572	23	24.86	5–42
F.S. Trueman (E)	164.4	21	529	20	26.45	6–30
D.A. Allen (E)	134	53	354	13	27.23	4–58
J.B. Statham (E)	201.4	41	501	17	29.47	5–53
R. Benaud (A)	214.3	76	488	15	32.53	6–70
K.D. Mackay (A)	273	87	525	16	32.81	5–121

Peter Burge sweeps in the fifth Test at the Oval in 1961. Murray is the wicket-keeper. Burge scored 181 to end a successful series.

Subba Row, batting with a runner, sweeps a boundary at the Oval.

A turning point in 1961. Dexter is caught by Grout off Benaud for a brilliant 76 at Old Trafford.

1962–63: A disappointing finale to a drawn series

Ted Dexter captained England in Australia in 1962–63. The first Test at Brisbane was a high-scoring match with 14 innings passing 50, although only Brian Booth went on to a century. After an Australian second-innings declaration, England needed 378 in a day to win – long before the end the match was clearly destined to be a draw.

At Melbourne each team used seven bowlers. A third-wicket stand of 175 by Dexter (93) and Cowdrey (113) enabled England to pass Australia's 316 by 15. Booth's second century of the series left England needing 234. Sheppard, who had made a duck and dropped some vital catches, now scored 113 as Australia dropped catches. Sheppard was run out going for the winning run, but England won by seven wickets. Trueman took eight wickets.

England were dismissed for 279 at Sydney, with Bobby Simpson taking five wickets. That Australia led by only 40 was due to Titmus, who took seven for 79 after Simpson and Harvey had added 160 for Australia's second wicket. Davidson struck early with three quick wickets in England's second innings and they never recovered, being out for 104. Davidson had nine wickets in the match. Australia won comfortably by eight wickets to level the series.

At Adelaide, both sides seemed frightened of defeat. Harvey and O'Neill made centuries for Australia, Harvey's 154 being the last of his 21 Test centuries. England batted steadily to reach 331, 62 behind. Davidson broke down in his fourth over. In Australia's second-innings 293, Statham passed Bedser's Test record of 236 wickets. Needing 356 at 89 an hour, England easily drew, with Barrington scoring an unbeaten century.

With everything to play for at Sydney, the fifth Test was a disappointment. With Barrington's second century, England spent the first day reaching 195 for five. The final total of 321 was passed by Australia's 349, Burge making a century. England then declared with eight wickets down, setting Australia a reasonable target of 241 in 240 minutes, but Lawry batted out time amid much barracking.

This was the last Test for Harvey, whose 79 Tests were an Australian record, and Davidson.

1962–63 46th Series Eng 1, Aus 1, Drawn 3

1 BRISBANE Match Drawn
Australia 404 (B C Booth 112, K D Mackay 86, R B Simpson 50) and 362–4 dec (W M Lawry 98, R B Simpson 71, R N Harvey 57, N C O'Neill 56)
England 389 (P H Parfitt 80, K F Barrington 78, E R Dexter 70, R Benaud 6–115) and 278–6 (E R Dexter 99, G Pullar 56, D S Sheppard 53)

2 MELBOURNE England won by 7 wkts
Australia 316 (W M Lawry 52, F J Titmus 4–43) and 248 (B C Booth 103, W M Lawry 57, F S Trueman 5–62)
England 331 (M C Cowdrey 113, E R Dexter 93, A K Davidson 6–75) and 237–3 (D S Sheppard 113, M C Cowdrey 58, E R Dexter 52)

3 SYDNEY Australia won by 8 wkts
England 279 (M C Cowdrey 85, G Pullar 53, R B Simpson 5–57, A K Davidson 4–54) and 104 (A K Davidson 5–25)
Australia 319 (R B Simpson 91, B K Shepherd 71, R N Harvey 64, F J Titmus 7–79) and 67–2

4 ADELAIDE Match Drawn
Australia 393 (R N Harvey 154, N C O'Neill 100) and 293 (B C Booth 77, R B Simpson 71, F S Trueman 4–60)
England 331 (K F Barrington 63, E R Dexter 61, F J Titmus 59, G D McKenzie 5–89) and 223–4 (K F Barrington 132)

5 SYDNEY Match Drawn
England 321 (K F Barrington 101) and 268–8 dec (K F Barrington 94, D S Sheppard 68, M C Cowdrey 53)
Australia 349 (P J P Burge 103, N C O'Neill 73, R Benaud 57, F J Titmus 5–103) and 152–4 (P J P Burge 52)

1962–1963 Averages

Batting	I	No	Runs	HS	Avge
K.F. Barrington (E)	10	2	582	132*	72.75
B.C. Booth (A)	10	2	404	112	50.50
E.R. Dexter (E)	10	0	481	99	48.10
R.B. Simpson (A)	10	1	401	91	44.55
M.C. Cowdrey (E)	10	1	394	113	43.77
R.N. Harvey (A)	10	0	395	154	39.50
W.M. Lawry (A)	10	1	310	98	34.44
N.C. O'Neill (A)	9	0	310	100	34.44
D.S. Sheppard (E)	10	0	330	113	33.00

Bowling	O	M	Runs	W	Avge	BB
A.K. Davidson (A)	176.2	30	480	24	20.00	6–75
F.S. Trueman (E)	158.3	9	521	20	26.05	5–62
F.J. Titmus (E)	236.3	54	616	21	29.33	7–79
G.D. McKenzie (A)	205.3	25	619	20	30.95	5–89
R. Benaud (A)	228	56	688	17	40.47	6–115
J.B. Statham (E)	165.2	16	580	13	44.61	3–66

Norman O'Neill was one of the most exciting Australian batsmen throughout the 1960s.

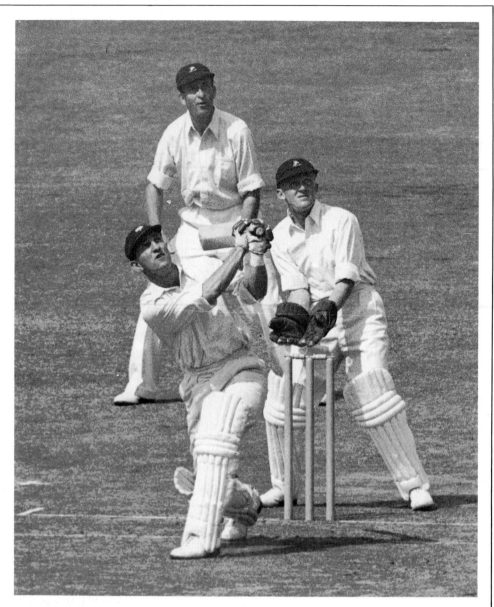

Hutton, Leonard

Hutton was born in Pudsey, Yorkshire, on 23 June 1916. A stylish right-hand opening batsman, he made his Yorkshire debut in 1934, and his Test debut three years later. He made a worldwide impact on cricket at the Oval in 1938, when, just 22, he broke the Test innings record with 364 against Australia. An accident during the war left him with a shortened left arm, but he overcame this handicap and played as brilliantly as ever. He had all the strokes but for England was often forced to play in a restrained manner. In 1952 he became the first professional to be selected to captain England. In 79 Tests he scored 6,971 runs, average 56.67. He was knighted in 1956.

1964: Rain the winner as Australia retain Ashes

Bobby Simpson led the 1964 tourists to England, when the series was spoilt by the weather.

At Trent Bridge, where Geoff Boycott made his Test debut, England declared at 216 for eight after rain had interrupted the play. Australia were dismissed for only 164, and England declared their second innings at 193 for nine, but rain, which had allowed only one full day, had the last word.

Rain prevented play until the third day at Lord's. Australia were put in by Dexter and again dismissed cheaply, for 176, Trueman taking five wickets, and with John Edrich making a century England took a lead of 70. But rain again ended the match soon after lunch on the last day.

A result was achieved at Headingley. England made 268, Neil Hawke and McKenzie getting the wickets. The match turned with Australia struggling against the off-spin of Titmus at 187 for seven. Dexter took the new ball, and Peter Burge played a magnificent innings of 160, hoisting Australia to 389. England were restricted to 229 and Australia scored the 109 needed to win by seven wickets.

Australia won the toss on a perfect Old Trafford wicket, and Lawry and Simpson began with a stand of 201. Simpson went on to 311. He batted 762 minutes, the third longest in first-class cricket. Australia declared at 656 for eight. England replied with 611, Barrington (256) and Dexter (174) putting on 246 for the third wicket. There was time for two overs in the second innings.

At the Oval, England made 182, Hawke

taking six for 47. Hawke achieved more fame in this match, however, by becoming Trueman's 300th Test victim, the first time this figure had been reached. Australia reached 379, and England 381 for four, with Boycott making his first Test century, before rain wiped out the last day of a frustrating series.

1964 47th series Aus 1, Eng 0, Drawn 4

1 TRENT BRIDGE Match Drawn

England 216–8 and 193–9 dec (E R Dexter 68, G D McKenzie 5–53)

Australia 168 (R B Simpson 50) and 40–2

2 LORD'S Match Drawn

Australia 176 (T R Veivers 54, F S Trueman 5–48) and 168–4 (P J P Burge 59)

England 246 (J H Edrich 120, G E Corling 4–60)

3 HEADINGLEY Australia won by 7 wkts

England 268 (J M Parks 68, E R Dexter 66, N J N Hawke 5–75, G D McKenzie 4–74) and 229 (K F Barrington 85)

Australia 389 (P J P Burge 160, W M Lawry 78, F J Titmus 4–69) and 111–3 (I R Redpath 58)

4 OLD TRAFFORD Match Drawn

Australia 656–8 dec (R B Simpson 311, W M Lawry 106, B C Booth 98) and 4–0

England 611 (K F Barrington 256, E R Dexter 174, J M Parks 60, G Boycott 58, G D McKenzie 7–153)

5 THE OVAL Match Drawn

England 182 (N J N Hawke 6–47) and 381–4 (G Boycott 113, M C Cowdroy 93, F J Titmus 56, K F Barrington 54)

Australia 379 (W M Lawry 94, B C Booth 74, T R Veivers 67, F S Trueman 4–87)

1964 Averages

Batting	I	No	Runs	HS	Avge	
R.B. Simpson (A)	8	2	458	311	76.33	
K.F. Barrington (E)	8	1	531	256	75.85	
G. Boycott (E)	6	0	291	113	48.50	
E.R. Dexter (E)	8	0	384	174	48.00	
P.J.P. Burge (A)	8	1	322	160	46.00	
W.M. Lawry (A)	9	1	317	106	39.62	

Bowling	O	M	Runs	W	Avge	BB
G.D. McKenzie (A)	256	61	654	29	22.55	7–153
F.S. Trueman (E)	133.3	25	399	17	23.47	5–48
N.J.N. Hawke (A)	242.1	80	496	18	27.55	6–47
G.E. Corling (A)	193.1	50	447	12	37.25	4–60

1965–66: Nothing between the sides in another drawn series

M.J.K. Smith was England's captain on the 1965–66 tour. In the first and third Tests his opposite number was Brian Booth, standing in for an injured or ill Bobby Simpson.

Booth won the toss at Brisbane, where Doug Walters made his debut with 155. Lawry batted 419 minutes for 166 after rain had washed out 1½ days, and although England followed on the match was clearly going to be drawn.

There were big scores at Melbourne, where Australia's 358 was overshadowed by England's 558, John Edrich and Cowdrey making centuries. In Australia's second innings Parks missed a stumping of Burge with Australia 204 for four, and Burge and Walters took the score to 374, both topping the hundred to ensure the draw.

England made a great start at Sydney, Boycott (84) and Barber (185) putting on 234 for the first wicket in 242 minutes. Barber's score is the highest by an Englishman on the first day of a Test in Australia. With Edrich making his second successive century, England made 488, despite Hawke's seven for 105. David Brown then took five wickets to help force Australia to follow on at 221, and with the wicket taking spin David Allen and Titmus took four wickets each as Australia were dismissed again for 174, leaving England winners by an innings and 93.

McKenzie removed Barber and Edrich with only 25 on the board at Adelaide, and England could make only 241, McKenzie finishing with six for 48. Australia passed this without loss, Simpson (225) and Lawry (119) putting on 244, an Australian first wicket record in Ashes matches. Australia scored 516, Jeff Jones taking six for 118. Barrington made 102, his tenth score over 50 in ten innings at Adelaide, but at 266 England were beaten by an innings and 9.

In the decider at Melbourne, Barrington made another century, taking only 122 balls, but the momentum was not maintained. England declared at 485 for nine, but Australia made 543 for eight declared, with Bob Cowper scoring the only triple century made by an Australian at home. It took 727 minutes, the longest first-class innings in Australia. Lawry too made a century, but for the second consecutive Ashes series, the deciding Test at Melbourne ended in a disappointing stalemate.

Wally Grout ended his Test career with 187 dismissals, at the time an Australian wicket-keeping record.

A record for Fred Trueman. Cowdrey at first slip grabs a snick from Neil Hawke and Trueman becomes the first player to take 300 wickets in Test matches. Peter Parfitt is the other slip and Jim Parks the wicket-keeper.

1965–66 48th Series Eng 1, Aus 1, Drawn 3

1 BRISBANE Match Drawn

Australia 443–6 dec (W M Lawry 166, K D Walters 155, T R Veivers 46)

England 280 (F J Titmus 60, K F Barrington 53, J M Parks 52, P I Philpott 5–90) and 186–3 (G Boycott 63)

2 MELBOURNE Match Drawn

Australia 358 (R M Cowper 99, W M Lawry 88, R B Simpson 59, B R Knight 4–84) and 426 (P J P Burge 120, K D Walters 115, W M Lawry 78, R B Simpson 67)

England 558 (J H Edrich 109, M C Cowdrey 104, J M Parks 71, K F Barrington 63, F J Titmus 56, G Boycott 51, G D McKenzie 5–134) and 5–0

3 SYDNEY England won by an innings and 93 runs

England 488 (R W Barber 185, J H Edrich 103, G Boycott 84, D A Allen 50, N J N Hawke 7–105)

Australia 221 (R M Cowper 60, G Thomas 51, D J Brown 5–63) and 174 (F J Titmus 4–40, D A Allen 4–47)

4 ADELAIDE Australia won by an innings and 9 runs

England 241 (K F Barrington 60, G D McKenzie 6–48) and 266 (K F Barrington 102, F J Titmus 53, N J N Hawke 5–54)

Australia 516 (R B Simpson 225, W M Lawry 119, G Thomas 52, I J Jones 6–118)

5 MELBOURNE Match Drawn

England 485–9 dec (K F Barrington 115, J M Parks 89, J H Edrich 85, M C Cowdrey 79, K D Walters 4–53) and 69–3

Australia 543–8 dec (R M Cowper 307, W M Lawry 108, K D Walters 60)

1965–66 Averages

Batting	I	No	Runs	HS	Avge	
R.B. Simpson (A)	4	0	355	225	88.75	
W.M. Lawry (A)	7	0	592	166	84.57	
R.M. Cowper (A)	6	0	493	307	82.16	
K.D. Walters (A)	7	1	410	155	68.33	
K.F. Barrington (E)	8	1	464	115	66.28	
F.J. Titmus (E)	6	2	258	60	64.50	
M.C. Cowdrey (E)	6	1	267	104	53.40	
J.M. Parks (E)	6	0	290	89	48.38	
J.H. Edrich (E)	8	0	375	109	46.87	
G. Boycott (E)	9	2	300	84	42.85	
R.W. Barber (E)	9	1	328	185	41.00	

Bowling	O	M	Runs	W	Avge	BB
N.J.N. Hawke (A)	142.7	29	419	16	26.18	7–105
G.D. McKenzie (A)	133.4	20	467	16	29.18	6–48
I.J. Jones (E)	129	15	533	15	35.53	6–118

1968: Mopping up at the Oval saves the rubber

Bill Lawry and Colin Cowdrey were the captains in the 1968 series in England. At Old Trafford Australia made 357, and England unaccountably collapsed after Edrich and Boycott had put on 86 for the first wicket. The score became 97 for five, and eventually 165 all out. Pocock (6–79) bowled well to dismiss Australia for 220 second time, but England's 253 meant defeat by 159 runs.

Strangely Pocock and D'Oliveira, England's top scorer at Old Trafford, were both omitted at Lord's where England batted solidly down the order to declare at 351 for seven. Australia were then shot out for 78, with Brown taking five for 42, but rain had interrupted throughout and Australia, following on, saved the match at 127 for four.

The first day's play was lost to rain at Edgbaston, where Cowdrey celebrated his 100th Test (a record) with a century, and became the second player after Hammond to score 7,000 Test runs. Other good scores took England to 409, and Australia were dismissed for 222. England declared at 143 for three, leaving Australia to score 530 in just over a day, but rain washed out play at 12.30 with the score 68 for one.

Cowdrey and Lawry were injured at Edgbaston, and at Headingley Graveney and Jarman captained their countries for the only time. Keith Fletcher and John Inverarity were among the debutants. Australia made 315, and England 302 (Connolly 5–72), thanks partly to Underwood scoring 45 not out at number eleven. Illingworth took six for 87 in Australia's 312, setting England 326 in 295 minutes, but they made only 230 for four.

At the Oval, D'Oliveira was recalled when Prideaux was injured, and made 158. With Edrich making 164, England scored 494. Lawry replied with 135, but at 324 Australia

trailed by 170. They bowled well in the second innings on a wearing wicket to dismiss England for 181, leaving themselves 352 to win. At lunch on the final day they appeared well beaten at 85 for five, but in the interval a freak storm left much of the ground

covered in water. The sun came out, and spectators helped the ground staff to mop up to such effect that play resumed at 4.45, with 75 minutes remaining. Thirty-nine minutes were safely negotiated before D'Oliveira bowled Jarman. Underwood then came on

Barrington, Kenneth Frank

Barrington was born on 24 November 1930 at Reading, and made his debut for Surrey in 1953. He was initially a brilliant attacking batsman but made a false start in Tests in 1955. He was dropped after two matches, and restyled his game, eliminating risk and becoming an on-side player. Regaining his Test place four years later, he became the most reliable batsman in the team. In 82 Tests he scored 6,806 runs, average 58.67. He also took 29 wickets with his leg-break mixture. He retired in 1968 after a mild heart attack, but he died of a second heart attack while assistant manager of the touring party in West Indies, at Bridgetown on 14 March 1981.

Left: The incredible scene as Inverarity is out lbw to Underwood and England win the final Test at the Oval with five minutes to spare. All the England players are in the picture.

and took the last four wickets, the last being Inverarity, who batted throughout the innings for 56 out of 124. England levelled the series with five minutes to spare, Underwood recording seven for 50.

1968 49th Series Aus 1, Eng 1, Drawn 3
1 OLD TRAFFORD   **Australia won by 159 runs**
Australia 357 (A P Sheahan 88, W M Lawry 81, K D Walters 81, I M Chappell 73, J A Snow 4–97) and 220 (K D Walters 86, P I Pocock 6–79)
England 165 (R M Cowper 4–48) and 253 (B L D'Oliveira 87)
2 LORD'S   **Match Drawn**
England 351–7 dec (C Milburn 83, K F Barrington 75)
Australia 78 (D J Brown 5–42) and 127–4 (I R Redpath 53)
3 EDGBASTON   **Match Drawn**
England 409 (M C Cowdrey 104, T W Graveney 96, J H Edrich 88, E W Freeman 4–78) and 142–3 dec (J H Edrich 64)
Australia 222 (I M Chappell 71, R M Cowper 57) and 68–1
4 HEADINGLEY   **Match Drawn**
Australia 315 (I R Redpath 92, I M Chappell 65, D L Underwood 4–41) and 312 (I M Chappell 81, K D Walters 56, R Illingworth 6–87)
England 302 (R M Prideaux 64, J H Edrich 62, A N Connolly 5–72) and 230–4 (J H Edrich 65)
5 THE OVAL   **England won by 226 runs**
England 494 (J H Edrich 164, B L D'Oliveira 158, T W Graveney 63) and 81 (A N Connolly 4–65)
Australia 324 (W M Lawry 135, I R Redpath 67) and 125 (R J Inverarity 56, D L Underwood 7–50)

1968 Averages

Batting	I	No	Runs	HS	Avge	
B.L. D'Oliveira (E)	4	1	263	158	87.66	
J.H. Edrich (E)	9	0	554	164	61.55	
W.M. Lawry (A)	7	1	270	135	45.00	
I.M. Chappell (A)	10	2	348	81	43.50	
T.W. Graveney (E)	9	1	337	96	41.12	
K.D. Walters (A)	9	0	343	86	38.11	
I.R. Redpath (A)	10	0	310	92	31.00	
Bowling	**O**	**M**	**Runs**	**W**	**Avge**	**BB**
D.L. Underwood (E)	209.5	103	302	20	15.10	7–50
R. Illingworth (E)	183.2	82	291	13	22.39	6–87
A.N. Connolly (A)	267.1	75	591	23	25.69	5–72
J.A. Snow (E)	203	44	508	17	29.88	4–97
D.J. Brown (E)	144	34	401	12	33.41	5–42
J.W. Gleeson (A)	193.5	65	417	12	34.75	3–44
G.D. McKenzie (A)	264	77	595	13	45.76	3–33

1970–71: Snow helps England regain Ashes after 16 years

Illingworth was preferred to Cowdrey as England captain in Australia in 1970–71. Lawry continued to lead Australia. Rodney Marsh was the most notable debutant at Brisbane, where Keith Stackpole hit 207 after Boycott had clearly indicated he thought he had run him out at 18. With Walters making 112, the score reached 418 for three, but an astonishing collapse saw the side out for 433, Snow taking six for 114. England, with all the batsmen contributing, made 464, Cowdrey establishing a new Test record aggregate by passing Hammond's 7,249. Australia were then dismissed for 214, but there was not time to force a win.

The second Test was the first played at the WACA ground at Perth. Greg Chappell made his debut, but had to wait to bat as Lawry put England in. Boycott (70) and Brian Luckhurst (131 in his second Test) put on 171 for the first wicket, and England totalled 397. Redpath made 171, and Greg

Trueman, Frederick Sewards

Born on 6 February 1931 at Stainton, Yorkshire, Trueman first appeared for the county in 1949. He was a strong, aggressive right-arm fast bowler, with a classical action and a belligerent fiery nature. His debut for England in 1952 was sensational, for he took three quick wickets in the second innings. With Bedser getting one, India were nought for four. A tendency to air his views might have cost him a few Test appearances, but he made 67, and was the first player to take 300 Test wickets. He ended with 307, average 21.57. He became a radio commentator.

Chappell, on his debut, 108 (batting number seven) and Australia reached 440. Edrich then made a century and an England declaration at 287 for six left Australia to make 245 in 145 minutes. Lawry did not accept the challenge, taking over an hour for six and the match was drawn.

The third Test at Melbourne was abandoned on the third day without a ball being bowled. A one-day game played on what would have been the final day established the current enthusiasm for one-day internationals.

At Sydney Bob Willis made his Test debut after being flown out to Australia when Alan Ward was injured. England made 332 and led by 96 when Australia were dismissed for 236. Boycott made 142 not out as England reached 319 for five before declaring, setting Australia 416 to win. Lawry was the only batsman to withstand Snow, who took seven for 40, as Australia were beaten by 299 runs. Lawry carried his bat for 60 not out. McKenzie, hit by a ball from Snow, retired hurt in his last Test match.

A fifth Test at Melbourne was an additional Test arranged to replace the washed-out third Test. It was an unsatisfactory match. Amid many missed catches, particularly by Cowdrey, Ian Chappell made a century, at which the crowd invaded the pitch and retired with a stump and two players' caps. Lawry declared at 493 for nine. England made 392, with Luckhurst, despite a broken finger, and D'Oliveira scoring centuries. Lawry declared but there was no chance of a result, and the crowd demonstrated against the pointlessness of the last day.

The sixth Test at Adelaide saw the first appearance of Dennis Lillee. He took five for 84 when England batted, but Edrich made 130 and England 470. Australia could manage only 235, but Illingworth did not enforce the follow-on. Instead he declared at 233 for four. Boycott made a century and he and Edrich opened each innings with a century stand. The pitch was easing and with Stackpole and Ian Chappell making centuries, Australia easily saved the match.

Lawry's Test career ended when he was dropped for the seventh Test at Sydney, which Australia had to win, and Ian Chappell preferred as captain. Chappell put England in, and achieved success by dismissing them for 184. When Australia batted, at 195 for seven, a ball from Snow hit Jenner on the head, Jenner being taken to hospital. Snow was warned about bouncers, and the crowd threw a few beer cans. When Snow went to field near the fence, a drunken spectator grabbed his shirt, and more cans were thrown. Illingworth led the team off the field, but returned when the umpires threatened to award the match to Australia. Australia led by 80, but determined batting by England accrued 302 runs, and Australia were set 223 to win. Snow bowled Eastwood without a run on the board, but injured his hand on the fence attempting to catch Stackpole, and retired. Nevertheless steady bowling by the other bowlers (six England bowlers took a wicket) saw Australia dismissed for 160, and England regained the Ashes by 2–0.

1970–71 50th Series Eng 2, Aus 0, Drawn 4
1 BRISBANE   **Match Drawn**
Australia 433 (K R Stackpole 207, K D Walters 112, I M Chappell 59, J A Snow 6–114) and 214 (W M Lawry 84, K Shuttleworth 5–47)
England 464 (J H Edrich 79, B W Luckhurst 74, A P E Knott 73, B L D'Oliveira 57) and 39–1
2 PERTH   **Match Drawn**
England 397 (B W Luckhurst 131, G Boycott 70, G D McKenzie 4–66) and 287–6 dec (J H Edrich 115, G Boycott 50)
Australia 440 (I R Redpath 171, G S Chappell 108, I M Chappell 50, J A Snow 4–143) and 100–3
3 SYDNEY   **England won by 299 runs**
England 332 (G Boycott 77, J H Edrich 55, A A Mallett 4–40, J W Gleeson 4–83) and 319–5 dec (G Boycott 142, B L D'Oliveira 56, R Illingworth 53)
Australia 236 (I R Redpath 64, K D Walters 55, D L Underwood 4–66) and 116 (W M Lawry 60, J A Snow 7–40)
4 MELBOURNE   **Match Drawn**
Australia 493–9 dec (I M Chappell 111, R W Marsh 92, W M Lawry 56, I R Redpath 72, K D Walters 55) and 169–4 dec
England 392 (B W Luckhurst 109, B L D'Oliveira 117) and 161–0
(G Boycott 76, J H Edrich 74)
5 ADELAIDE   **Match Drawn**

England 470 (J H Edrich 130, K W R Fletcher 80, G Boycott 58, J H Hampshire 55, D K Lillee 5–84) and 233–4 dec (G Boycott 119)

Australia 235 (K R Stackpole 87, P Lever 4–49) and 328–3 (K R Stackpole 136, I M Chappell 104)

6 SYDNEY **England won by 62 runs**

England 184 and 302 (B W Luckhurst 59, J H Edrich 57)

Australia 264 (G S Chappell 65, I R Redpath 59) and 160 (K R Stackpole 67)

After the match at Perth, the next Test should have been played at Melbourne, but bad weather prevented a ball being bowled and the match was re-arranged

1970–71 Averages					
Batting	I	No	Runs	HS	Avge
G. Boycott (E)	10	3	657	142*	93.85
J.H. Edrich (E)	11	2	648	130	72.00
B.W. Luckhurst (E)	9	1	455	131	56.87
K.R. Stackpole (A)	12	0	627	207	52.25
I.R. Redpath (A)	12	2	497	171	49.70
W.M. Lawry (A)	10	2	324	84	40.50
I.M. Chappell (A)	12	0	452	111	37.66
K.D. Walters (A)	12	2	373	112	37.30
R. Illingworth (E)	10	1	333	53	37.00
B.L. D'Oliveira (E)	10	0	369	117	36.90
Bowling	O	M	Runs	W	Avge	BB
J.A. Snow (E)	225.5	47	708	31	22.83	7–40
R.G.D. Willis (E)	88	16	329	12	27.41	3–58
D.L. Underwood (E)	194.6	50	520	16	32.50	4–66
P. Lever (E)	143.5	25	439	13	33.76	4–49
J.W. Gleeson (A)	221	57	605	14	43.21	4–83
A.L. Thomson (A)	189.7	33	654	12	54.50	3–79

1972: Problems over the pitch at Headingley

Illingworth and Ian Chappell remained captains for the 1972 series, when Tony Greig made his debut in the first Test at Old Trafford, and was England's top scorer in each innings. England made 249 in the first, and good bowling by Snow and Arnold removed Australia for 142. Lillee took six for 66 in the second innings, England making 234, but a target of 342 was too much for Australia. Snow took four wickets for the second time and although Marsh hit a defiant 91 England won by 89 runs.

The Lord's Test provided one of the most amazing performances of modern cricket. Bob Massie, making his debut, so bamboozled England with his swing that he took eight for 84 as England crashed to 272. Australia made 308 thanks mainly to Greg Chappell's 131, whereupon Massie again went through England with eight for 53. Australia required only 81 to win by eight wickets. Massie's 16 wickets is easily the most by a bowler in his first Test, and only two players have achieved more in the whole of Test cricket.

Snow took five wickets again in Australia's first innings at Trent Bridge, but, helped by dropped catches, Stackpole made 114 and Australia 315. Lillee and Massie dismissed England for 189, allowing Chappell to declare at 324 for four, with Ross Edwards 170 not out. England easily saved the game at 290 for four.

The Headingley pitch for the fourth Test caused great controversy. It took spin from the first day, when Australia were dismissed for 146, Underwood getting four wickets. Underwood had been recalled for this match, which caused many Australians to become suspicious. England did a little better against Mallett and Inverarity, reaching 263 mainly

through Illingworth and Snow adding 104 for the eighth wicket. It was a decisive stand, as Underwood's six for 46 meant Australia made only 136, leaving England only 20 to get for a three-day victory. The explanation for the grassless and uneven wicket was freak weather conditions (storm and sunshine) which caused an outbreak of a fungus called *Fusarium oxysporum*. As John Snow pointed out to disgruntled Australians, by batting first they should have won.

It meant England retained the Ashes but Australia fought well to level the rubber at the Oval. England were all out for 284, thanks to five wickets for Lillee, three of them in four balls. Then 201 runs were added for Australia's third wicket by Ian Chappell (118) and Greg Chappell (113), the first instance of brothers scoring centuries in the same Test innings. Australia made 399. Lillee took another five wickets in the second innings, but England batted well to get 356. Australia were set to get 242, and when Illingworth, Snow and D'Oliveira were unfit to bowl, they made them for the loss of five wickets. Lillee's 31 wickets and Marsh's 23 behind the stumps were Australian records for a tour of England.

Greg Chappell caught by Peter Parfitt at Trent Bridge in 1972. John Snow is the bowler. Chappell was second in the batting averages in a drawn series.

1972 51st Series Eng 2, Aus 2, Drawn 1

1 OLD TRAFFORD **England won by 89 runs**

England 249 (A W Greig 57) and 234 (A W Greig 62, D K Lillee 6–66)

Australia 142 (K R Stackpole 53, J A Snow 4–41, G G Arnold 4–62) and 252 (R W Marsh 91, K R Stackpole 67, A W Greig 4–53, J A Snow 4–87)

2 LORD'S **Australia won by 8 wkts**

England 272 (A W Greig 54, R A L Massie 8–84) and 116 (R A L Massie 8–53)

Australia 308 (G S Chappell 131, I M Chappell 56, R W Marsh 50, J A Snow 5–57) and 81–2 (K R Stackpole 57)

3 TRENT BRIDGE **Match Drawn**

Australia 315 (K R Stackpole 114, D J Colley 54, J A Snow 5–92) and 324–4 dec (R Edwards 170, G S Chappell 72, I M Chappell 50)

England 189 (D K Lillee 4–35, R A L Massie 4–43) and 290–4 (B W Luckhurst 96, B L d'Oliveira 50)

4 HEADINGLEY **England won by 9 wkts**

Australia 146 (K R Stackpole 52, D L Underwood 4–37) and 136 (D L Underwood 6–45)

England 263 (R Illingworth 57, A A Mallett 5–114) and 21–1

5 THE OVAL **Australia won by 5 wkts**

England 284 (A P E Knott 92, P H Parfitt 51, D K Lillee 5–58) and 356 (B Wood 90, A P E Knott 63, D K Lillee 5–123)

Australia 399 (I M Chappell 118, G S Chappell 113, R Edwards 79, D L Underwood 4–90) and 242–5 (K R Stackpole 79)

1972 Averages					
Batting	I	No	Runs	HS	Avge
K.R. Stackpole (A)	10	1	485	114	53.88
G.S. Chappell (A)	10	1	437	131	48.55
R. Edwards (A)	7	1	291	170*	48.50
A.W. Greig (E)	9	1	288	62	36.00
I.M. Chappell (A)	10	0	334	118	33.40
Bowling	O	M	Runs	W	Avge	BB
D.L. Underwood (E)	125	49	266	16	16.62	6–45
D.K. Lillee (E)	249.5	83	548	31	17.67	6–66
R.A.L. Massie (A)	199.1	58	409	23	17.78	8–53
G.G. Arnold (E)	110.5	25	279	13	21.46	4–62
J.A. Snow (E)	205.5	46	555	24	23.12	5–57

Bob Massie made the most sensational debut in modern Test history at Lord's in 1972, taking 16 wickets in his first Test, a record.

1974–75: Lillee and Thomson come together to defeat England

Mike Denness had taken Illingworth's place as captain when England toured Australia in 1974–75. Boycott, whom some thought might have succeeded Illingworth, withdrew from the party for personal reasons.

At Brisbane, the pitch was prepared by the Lord Mayor, who did not like the way the curator was preparing it and, as he was also a member of the cricket ground trust, dismissed him. Australia had first use of it and made 309. Despite Greig's 110, England finished 44 behind. Chappell's declaration at 288 for five set England a task of scoring 333 in 400 minutes, but Jeff Thomson, whom they were meeting for the first time, took six for 46 (nine in the match) and their score of 166 meant defeat by the same amount. Amiss batted in the second innings with a broken thumb and Edrich with a broken hand, and Cowdrey was flown out to reinforce the batting.

At Perth, Titmus reappeared for the first time since losing four toes in an accident in the West Indies in 1968. Chappell put England in, and rapidly out again for 208. Ross Edwards and Walters made centuries for Australia, Walters between tea and the close on the second day. Australia led by 272 and needed only 21 in the fourth innings to win by nine wickets.

England were put in again at Melbourne, and made 242. Five wickets for Willis helped England to dismiss Australia for 241. They then made 244, with Amiss scoring 90, and a very close match was finally drawn with Australia eight runs short of victory with two wickets left.

Denness dropped himself for the fourth Test at Sydney, where Australia won the toss again, but this time batted. Australia made 405, and led by 110 on first innings, then declared at 289 for four with Redpath

and Greg Chappell each getting centuries and adding 220 for the second wicket. England made 228, Australia winning with just over 10 overs left. Edrich captained England but was forced to go to hospital when hit in the ribs by Lillee when facing his first ball in the second innings. He suffered his second fracture of the series, but returned to be 33 not out at the end of the innings.

At Adelaide, Denness returned as captain and put Australia in on a damp pitch after the first day was lost to rain. Underwood reduced Australia to 84 for five, but the tail wagged and 304 was too many against Lillee and Thomson. England were out for 172, and Australia declared at 272 for five, Underwood having taken 11 of the 15 Australian wickets to fall. Thomson could not bowl in the second innings, having injured his shoulder playing tennis on the rest day, but England still fell 164 short of the target of 405.

Peter Lever replaced the injured Willis for the sixth Test at Melbourne and took six for 38 as Australia were rushed out for 152. Lillee bruised his foot after six overs and retired. Without Lillee or Thomson bowling England prospered, Denness (188) and Fletcher (146), two disappointments of the tour, adding 192 for the fourth wicket. England reached 529, with Max Walker

Jeff Thomson was the outstanding bowler in the 1974–75 series. This catch at Melbourne shows one wicket-keeper dismissing another: Knott caught Marsh bowled Thomson for four.

taking eight for 143, his best Test figures. Despite Greg Chappell's century, Australia were beaten by an innings and four runs.

1974–75 52nd Series   Aus 4, Eng 1, Drawn 1

1 BRISBANE   Australia won by 166 runs

Australia 309 (I M Chappell 90, G S Chappell 58, R G D Willis 4–56) and 288–5 dec (G S Chappell 71, K D Walters 62, R Edwards 53)

England 265 (A W Greig 110, M H N Walker 4–73) and 166 (J R Thomson 6–46)

2 PERTH   Australia won by 9 wkts

England 208 (A P E Knott 51) and 293 (F J Titmus 61, J R Thomson 5–93)

Australia 481 (R Edwards 115, K D Walters 103, G S Chappell 62) and 23–1

3 MELBOURNE   Match Drawn

England 242 (A P E Knott 52, J R Thomson 4–72) and 244 (D L Amiss 90, A W Greig 60, A A Mallett 4–60, J R Thomson 4–72)

Australia 241 (I R Redpath 55, R G D Willis 5–61) and 238–8 (G S Chappell 61, A W Greig 4–56)

4 SYDNEY   Australia won by 171 runs

Australia 405 (G S Chappell 84, R B McCosker 80, I M Chappell 53, G G Arnold 5–86, A W Greig 4–104) and 289–4 dec (G S Chappell 144, I R Redpath 105)

England 295 (A P E Knott 82, J H Edrich 50, J R Thomson 4–74) and 228 (A W Greig 54, A A Mallett 4–21)

5 ADELAIDE   Australia won by 163 runs

Australia 304 (T J Jenner 74, K D Walters 55, D L Underwood 7–113) and 273–5 dec (K D Walters 71, R W Marsh 55, I R Redpath 52, D L Underwood 4–102)

England 172 (M H Denness 51, D K Lillee 4–49) and 241 (A P E Knott 106, K W R Fletcher 63, D K Lillee 4–69)

6 MELBOURNE   England won by an innings and 4 runs

Australia 152 (I M Chappell 65, P Lever 6–38) and 373 (G S Chappell 102, I R Redpath 83, R B McCosker 76, I M Chappell 50, A W Greig 4–88)

England 529 (M H Denness 188, K W R Fletcher 146, A W Greig 89, J H Edrich 70, M H N Walker 8–143)

1974–75 Averages

Batting	I	No	Runs	HS	Avge
G.S. Chappell (A)	11	0	608	144	55.27
J.H. Edrich (E)	7	1	260	70	43.33
I.R. Redpath (A)	12	1	472	105	42.90
K.D. Walters (A)	11	2	383	103	42.55
A.W. Greig (E)	11	0	446	110	40.54
A.P.E. Knott (E)	11	1	364	106*	36.40
K.W.R. Fletcher (E)	9	0	324	146	36.00
M.H. Denness (E)	9	0	318	188	35.33
I.M. Chappell (A)	12	1	387	90	35.18
R.W. Marsh (A)	11	2	313	55	34.77
R. Edwards (A)	9	1	261	115	32.62

Bowling	O	M	Runs	W	Avge	BB
J.R. Thomson (A)	175.1	34	592	33	17.93	6–46
A.A. Mallett (A)	140.6	47	339	17	19.94	4–21
D.K. Lillee (A)	182.6	36	596	25	23.84	4–49
M.H.N. Walker (A)	218.7	46	684	23	29.73	8–143

Right: Tony Greig driving at Sydney in the fourth Test, where he was top scorer in England's second innings. Greig was defiant in a losing side.

Far right: Rodney Marsh, whose total dismissals in Tests is a record for a wicket-keeper. Marsh's career was almost exactly contemporary with Lillee's, and each achieved a record number of Test victims.

Left: In 1974–75 the Australian fast bowlers, Dennis Lillee (left) and Jeff Thomson, routed the English tourists and became known collectively as 'Lillian Thomson'. Between them they took 58 wickets.

Left: The Australian team at Sydney in 1974–75. Left to right, back: Walters, Thomson, Lillee, Walker, Mallett, McCosker, Jenner. Front: Marsh, Redpath, Ian Chappell, Edwards, Greg Chappell. Australia won by 171 runs, and took the series by four matches to one.

Knott, Alan Philip Eric

Born in Belvedere, Kent, on 9 April 1946, Knott made his debut for the county in 1964. He became the third in a line of Kent wicket-keepers (Ames, Evans, Knott) who kept for England for most of 50 years. A fitness fanatic, he frequently performed his callisthenics at the wicket. Small and agile, he batted in the same darting and quick-footed manner as he kept wicket. He made his Test debut in 1967, and in 95 Tests he caught 250 and stumped 19 batsmen, at the time a record. He also scored 4,389 runs, average 32.75, making him a genuine all-rounder. His Test career was cut short by a combination of World Series Cricket, a 'rebel' South African tour and a final distaste for touring every winter.

69

1975: Australia win a short series

England played a four-match series with Australia after the first Prudential World Cup in 1975. At Edgbaston, Denness put Australia in, who went on to make 359. After one over of England's reply, a thunderstorm wrecked the wicket and England were shot out for 101 by Lillee and Walker. Following on they made 173, Thomson this time getting five wickets, and lost by an innings and 85. Graham Gooch, in his first Test, bagged a pair. Denness was much criticized for his decision to field, and was dropped for the second Test.

Greig assumed the captaincy at Lord's and prudently batted. He also scored 96, helping England recover from a bad start to 315. David Steele made 50 in his first Test. Australia made 268, recovering from 133 for eight thanks to 99 from Ross Edwards and a career first-class best score from Lillee of 73 not out. Edrich made 175, enabling England to declare at 436 for seven, but Australia easily batted out time for a draw.

The prospect of an exciting finish at Headingley was ruined by vandals. England made 288 and rushed through Australia, who could manage only 135, with Phil Edmonds, in his first Test, taking five for 28. In the second knock England made 291 (Steele top-scored in each innings) and set Australia to get 445 to win. At the end of the fourth day they were making a good attempt at 220 for three, with McCosker 95 not out. Overnight, however, vandals protesting the innocence of a man serving a prison sentence, damaged the pitch with knives and oil, ending the play. Rain for most of the afternoon might well have meant a draw in any case.

In the fourth and last Test at the Oval, Australia made 532 for nine declared, with McCosker (127) and Ian Chappell (192) making centuries. England could manage only 191 and followed on. They recovered well, however, saving the match with 538 in the second innings, Bob Woolmer, in only his second Test, making 149 in 499 minutes. This was the longest first-class match played in England, covering six days with just over three hours for stoppages.

1975   53rd Series   Aus 1, Eng 0, Drawn 3

1 EDGBASTON   Australia won by an innings and 85 runs
Australia 359 (R W Marsh 61, R B McCosker 59, R Edwards 56, I M Chappell 52)
England 101 (D K Lillee 5–15, M H N Walker 5–48) and 173 (K W R Fletcher 51, J R Thomson 5–38)

2 LORD'S   Match Drawn
England 315 (A W Greig 96, A P E Knott 69, D S Steele 50, D K Lillee 4–84) and 436–7 dec (J H Edrich 175, B Wood 52)
Australia 268 (R Edwards 99, J A Snow 4–66) and 329–3 (I M Chappell 86, R B McCosker 79, G S Chappell 73, R Edwards 52)

3 HEADINGLEY   Match Drawn
England 288 (D S Steele 73, J H Edrich 62, A W Greig 51, G J Gilmour 6–85) and 291 (D S Steele 92)
Australia 135 (P H Edmonds 5–28) and 220–3 (R B McCosker 95, I M Chappell 62)

4 THE OVAL   Match Drawn
Australia 532–9 dec (I M Chappell 192, R B McCosker 127, K D Walters 65) and 40–2
England 191 (J R Thomson 4–50, M H N Walker 4–63) and 538 (R A Woolmer 149, J H Edrich 96, G R J Roope 77, D S Steele 66, A P E Knott 64, K D Walters 4–34, D K Lillee 4–91)

1975 Averages

Batting	I	No	Runs	HS	Avge
R.B. McCosker (A)	7	2	414	127	82.80
I.M. Chappell (A)	6	0	429	192	71.50
D.S. Steele (E)	6	0	365	92	60.83
R.A. Woolmer (E)	4	0	218	149	54.50
J.H. Edrich (E)	8	0	428	175	53.50
R. Edwards·(A)	6	1	253	99	50.60
A.P.E. Knott (E)	8	1	261	69	37.28
A.W. Greig (E)	8	0	284	96	35.50

Bowling	O	M	Runs	W	Avge	BB
D.K. Lillee (A)	207	72	460	21	21.90	5–15
J.R. Thomson (A)	175.1	56	457	16	28.56	5–38
J.A. Snow (E)	135.5	31	355	11	32.27	4–66
M.H.N. Walker (A)	204.1	59	486	14	34.71	5–48

Below left: Ian Chappell, captain of the 1975 Australians to England, driving at the Oval, and *below right* Max Walker bowling to John Edrich at Lord's. Walker and Edrich were the consistent players who did not always attract the headlines, but were vital to their sides.

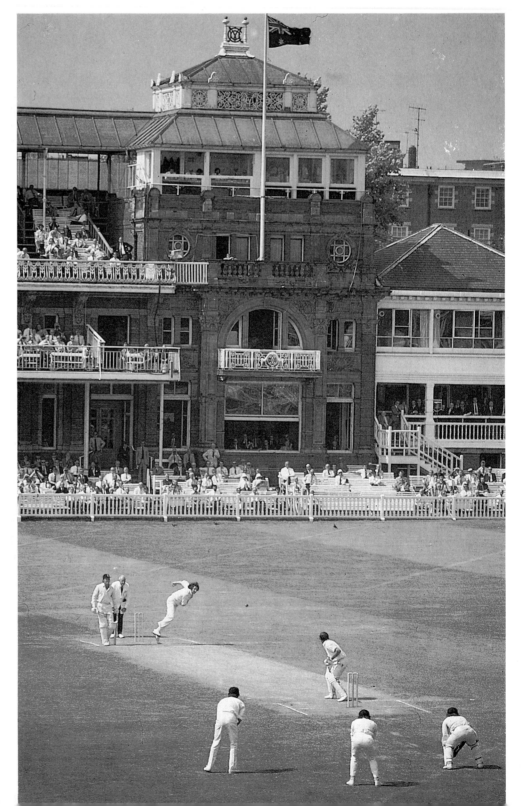

1976–77: The Centenary Test provides exciting match

On their way home from a tour of India and Sri Lanka, England called in at Melbourne to play a match there to celebrate the first Test at Melbourne 100 years earlier.

All past Ashes cricketers were invited to what was an outstanding cricket and social occasion.

Greig and Greg Chappell were captains, and England put Australia in, performing well to dismiss them for 138. However Australia, particularly Lillee (6–26) and Walker (4–54), did even better and England were shot out for 95. Sanity returned to the batting in the second innings, and Marsh became the first Australian wicket-keeper to score a century against England. Australia declared at 419 for nine, setting England to get 463 to win. Lillee took five wickets again, but for 139, and England made a great attempt, getting to 346 for four at one stage. Derek Randall batted brilliantly for 174, but the tail-enders could not quite sustain the effort, and the innings closed at 417. Australia's winning margin, 45 runs, was by coincidence the same as that in the first Test 100 years before.

The two teams for the Centenary Test Match at Melbourne on 12–17 March 1977. *Left to right, back*: D.L. Amiss, D.W. Hookes, R.A. Woolmer, G.J. Gilmour, J.K. Lever, K.J. O'Keeffe, R.G.D. Willis, G.J. Cosier, C.M. Old, S.J. Rixon, G.D. Barlow, R.J. Bright, I.C. Davis, D.W. Randall. *Front*: K.W.R. Fletcher, M.H.N. Walker, A.P.E. Knott, R.W. Marsh, A.W. Greig, G.S. Chappell, J.M. Brearley, K.D. Walters, D.L. Underwood, D.K. Lillee. Another player, R.B. McCosker, was absent with a broken jaw.

Below: The Centenary Test at Melbourne in 1977 was a splendid occasion attended by many old Test cricketers. Derek Randall was the man of the match for his second-innings 174, and is shown staring belligerently at the most successful bowler, Dennis Lillee.

1976–77 54th Series (Centenary Test) Aus 1, Eng 0
MELBOURNE **Australia won by 45 runs**
Australia 138 and 419–9 dec (R W Marsh 110, I C Davis 68, K
 D Walters 66, D W Hookes 56, C M Old 4–104)
England 95 (D K Lillee 6–26, M H N Walker 4–54) and 417 (D W
 Randall 174, D L Amiss 64, D K Lillee 5–139)

1977: Botham arrives and Boycott returns in triumph

The 1977 tour to England came after the revelation that Kerry Packer had : gned up many of the world's leading cricketers for World Series Cricket. Greig lost the England captaincy (but not his place), through his part in the operation, Brearley taking over. Lillee did not tour.

The first Test at Lord's was staged as a Jubilee Test, celebrating 25 years of Queen Elizabeth's reign. England batted and made only 216. Willis then bowled well, taking seven for 78, but Australia took a first-innings lead of 80. In the second innings Woolmer made 120, but England lost four wickets at 286, and totalled only 305. The England bowlers were on top in the final innings, but because nearly a day had been lost to rain, Australia held out for a draw at 114 for six.

At Old Trafford, all six England bowlers got at least one wicket, but Australia made a respectable 297. Woolmer's 137, made in partnerships with Randall and Greig, led to England getting 437 and leading by 140. Greg Chappell made an elegant 112 in Australia's second knock, but he was one of Underwood's victims in his six for 66, and he had little support, scoring over half Australia's 218. England needed only 79 and won by nine wickets.

At Trent Bridge Ian Botham made his debut and took five for 74 as Australia were dismissed for 243. Boycott returned to Test cricket after missing 30 matches and in an eventful innings ran out Randall, made 20 in his first three hours and was dropped in the slips by McCosker. England were 82 for five when Knott joined him. The two added 215, Boycott making 107 and Knott 135, the highest by a wicket-keeper in Ashes matches. England made 364. McCosker made a century in 309, but England needed only 189 to win, and won by seven wickets. Boycott (80 not out) became the second batsman (after M.L. Jaisimha) to bat on all five days of a Test.

At Headingley Boycott was centre stage again, becoming the first batsman to score his hundredth century in a Test match. He went on to 191 in a total of 436. Australia fell to some excellent swing bowling by Hendrick (4–41) and Botham (5–21). All out 103, they followed on and were dismissed again for 248, Randall performing a somersault after catching Marsh to retain the Ashes. Boycott who batted throughout England's innings, was on the field for the whole of the match.

Australia put England in at the Oval and out again for 214, by courtesy of M.F. Malone (5–63 in his first Test) and Thomson. After a shaky start Australia made 385; but nearly 12 hours, including the whole of the first day, had been lost to rain, and a draw was obvious from early in the game.

Greig, Malone and Walker ended their Test careers, largely because of WSC. Boycott averaged 147.33, a record for Ashes matches.

1977 Averages

Batting	I	No	Runs	HS	Avge	
G. Boycott (E)	5	2	442	191	147.33	
R.A. Woolmer (E)	8	1	394	137	56.28	
G.S. Chappell (A)	9	0	371	112	41.22	
A.P.E. Knott (E)	7	0	255	135	36.42	
D.W. Hookes (A)	9	0	283	85	31.44	
R.B. McCosker (A)	9	0	255	107	28.33	

Bowling	O	M	Runs	W	Avge	BB
R.G.D. Willis (E)	166.4	36	534	27	19.77	7–78
M. Hendrick (E)	128.4	33	290	14	20.71	4–41
J.R. Thomson (A)	200.5	44	583	23	25.34	4–41
D.L. Underwood (E)	169.1	61	362	13	27.84	6–66
L.S. Pascoe (A)	137.4	35	363	13	27.92	4–80
M.H.N. Walker (A)	273.2	88	551	14	39.35	3–40

Left: A shot that was a landmark in Test history. Geoff Boycott drives Greg Chappell for four runs and becomes the first player to score his 100th century in a Test match.

1978–79: England much too good for a Packer-depleted Australia

The 1978–79 series in Australia was played in opposition to the World Series Cricket matches. Those players who had signed for Kerry Packer's rival to Test cricket were not considered. Australia suffered most. While England lost four of her best players, Australia had to find almost a whole new team.

Brearley, although not considered worthy of a Test place as a batsman, retained the England captaincy, while Graeme Yallop led Australia.

In the first Test, England's fast bowlers reduced Australia to 26 for six, which became 116 all out. England took a first-innings lead of 170, despite Rodney Hogg taking six for 74 in his first Test. Hughes and Yallop both made centuries, but Randall ensured England's seven-wicket victory.

At Perth, Yallop put England in, but after three quick wickets had fallen Gower made a century and England reached 309. Good bowling by Willis then helped put out Australia for 190. England set Australia to score 328 and won easily by 166 runs. Hogg took five wickets in each innings. There was criticism of some umpiring decisions, and on the last day umpire Tom Brookes announced his retirement.

The Melbourne pitch had numerous bare patches, and Australia were lucky enough to win the toss and bat. Allan Border made his debut and a determined century by Graeme Wood was the foundation of a score of 258. Fourteen wickets tumbled on a second day in which only 122 runs were scored. England were out for 143, and after Australia's 167 needed 283 to win. They made just 179, Wood's being the only innings over 50. Hogg again took five wickets in each innings to have 26 in his first three Tests.

England were dismissed for 152 at Sydney in temperatures so hot that Australia's wicket-keeper John Maclean retired with heat exhaustion. When Australia scored 294 they looked likely to level the series; Randall, batting very slowly in the tremendous heat, scored 150, allowing England to set a reasonable target of 203. Australia then collapsed before the off-spin of Emburey and Miller for 111, and were defeated by 93. Border was not out in each innings.

Put in at Adelaide, England were 27 for five, but thanks to Botham reached 169. Botham was also prominent in dismissing Australia for five fewer. They weren't helped by an accident to Darling, who was struck on the heart by a ball from Willis in the first over, and was given the kiss of life by Emburey and umpire O'Connell before being stretchered off. He resumed later. Bob Taylor made 97, his highest Test score, in the second innings, and Australia, needing 366, lost by 205.

At Sydney, Yallop, coming in at 19 for two, scored 121 of the last 179 runs. His share of the whole Australian innings of 198 was 61.11 per cent. England made 308, and with Miller and Emburey again getting to work on a

1978–79   56th Series   Eng 5, Aus 1

1 BRISBANE   England won by 7 wkts
Australia 116 (R G D Willis 4–44) and 339 (K J Hughes 129, G N Yallop 102)
England 286 (D W Randall, 75, R M Hogg 6–74, A G Hurst 4–93) and 170–3 (D W Randall 74)

2 PERTH   England won by 166 runs
England 309 (D I Gower 102, G Boycott 77, R M Hogg 5–65) and 208 (R M Hogg 5–57)
Australia 190 (P M Toohey 81, R G D Willis 5–44) and 161 (G M Wood 64, J K Lever 4–28)

3 MELBOURNE   Australia won by 103 runs
Australia 258 (G M Wood 100) and 167
England 143 (R M Hogg 5–30) and 179 (R M Hogg 5–36)

4 SYDNEY   England won by 93 runs
England 152 (I T Botham 59, A G Hurst 5–28) and 346 (D W Randall 150, J M Brearley 53, J D Higgs 5–148, R M Hogg 4–67)
Australia 294 (W M Darling 91, A R Border 60) and 111 (J E Emburey 4–46)

5 ADELAIDE   England won by 205 runs
England 169 (I T Botham 74, R M Hogg 4–26) and 360 (R W Taylor 97, G Miller 64, A G Hurst 4–97)
Australia 164 (I T Botham 4–42) and 160

6 SYDNEY   England won by 9 wkts
Australia 198 (G N Yallop 121, I T Botham 4–57) and 143 (B Yardley 61, G Miller 5–44, J E Emburey 4–52)
England 308 (G A Gooch 74, D I Gower 65, J D Higgs 4–69) and 35–1

1978–79 Averages

Batting	I	No	Runs	HS	Avge
D.I. Gower (E)	11	1	420	102	42.00
D.W. Randall (E)	12	2	385	150	38.50
G.N. Yallop (A)	12	0	391	121	32.58
I.T. Botham (E)	10	0	291	74	29.10
K.J. Hughes (A)	12	0	345	129	28.75
G.M. Wood (A)	12	0	344	100	28.66
G. Boycott (E)	12	0	263	77	21.91

Bowling	O	M	Runs	W	Avge	BB
R.M. Hogg (A)	217.4	60	527	41	12.85	6–74
G. Miller (E)	177.1	54	346	23	15.04	5–44
M. Hendrick (E)	145	30	299	19	15.73	3–19
J.E. Emburey (E)	144.4	49	306	16	19.12	4–46
R.G.D. Willis (E)	140.3	23	461	20	23.05	5–44
A.G. Hurst (A)	204.2	44	577	25	23.08	5–28
J.D. Higgs (A)	196.6	47	468	19	24.63	5–148
I.I. Botham (E)	158.4	25	567	23	24.65	4–42

Above: England easily won the 1978–79 series played without the WSC players. Gooch catches Maclean off Miller in the second Test at Perth.

Below: Ray Illingworth was a successful English captain in the 1970s, whose main achievement was the winning of the Ashes in 1970–71.

wearing wicket, England were set only 44 to get, and won the series by 5–1. Hogg, however, with 41 wickets, set a new series record for Australia against England.

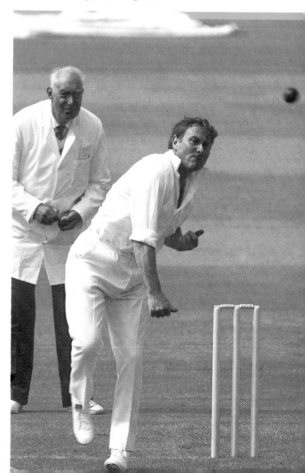

1979–80: Post-Packer Australians take their revenge for the previous season

When the rift between 'establishment' cricket and WSC was healed, part of the deal involved the cancellation of the Indian tour to Australia in 1979–80, with both England and West Indies touring and playing three-match series against the home side. England claimed the Ashes were not at stake, but Australia reckoned they were.

All the WSC cricketers returned to the Australian side, captained by Greg Chappell, but England took only Underwood of the Packer players.

Brearley put Australia in at Perth, but early success was cancelled by 99 from Kim Hughes, Australia getting 244 (Botham 6–78). Lillee began to bat with a bat made of aluminium, and held up play with a ten-minute tantrum when asked to change it for a wooden one. A century by Border helped Australia to 337 in the second innings, when the score-card entry everybody had been waiting for appeared: Lillee c Willey b Dilley. Botham took 11 wickets in the match. Boycott batted throughout England's second innings, but was left on 99 not out when the innings closed at 215. Dymock took six for 34.

The pitch at Sydney was left exposed to a pre-match storm, and when Chappell won the toss the match was virtually settled on the shortened first day, when England were 90 for seven. Australia also had difficulty on the second day, but established a lead of 22. Gower, batting at number seven, made 98 not out as the pitch began to ease, but Greg Chappell made an identical score as Australia won an unsatisfactory match by six wickets.

England began well at Melbourne, collapsed, and then rallied to reach 306. Gooch was run out attempting a silly run when 99, and Lillee (6–60) passed 200 Test wickets. Solid batting by Australia, highlighted by Greg Chappell's century, took them to 477,

Above: Australian jubilation as Miller is caught by Maclean off Hurst in the fourth Test at Sydney in 1978–79.

and England were still well behind at 92 for six in the second innings. Botham then made a magnificent 119 not out, but Australia still had a target of only 103 and made a clean sweep of the three matches.

1980: The second Centenary Test Match

The 1980 match at Lord's was to celebrate the centenary of the first Test in England, in 1880 at the Oval. Botham led England.

The match was marred by rain, and will be remembered for its off-the-pitch incidents more than the play. Chappell batted, and centuries by Wood and Hughes allowed a declaration at 385 for five. But play had been lost on the first two days, and when the umpires returned from a pitch inspection on Saturday afternoon they and Botham were jostled by MCC members when entering the pavilion. There was little hope of a result, despite a second Australian declaration which set England 370 in 350 minutes. Boycott made a not-out century as a sad match fizzled out into a draw.

1980 58th Series (Centenary Test)   Drawn 1
LORD'S   **Match Drawn**
Australia 385–5 dec (K J Hughes 117, G M Wood 112, A R
    Border 56) and 189–4 dec (K J Hughes 84, G S Chappell 59)
England 205 (G Boycott 62, L S Pascoe 5–59, D K Lillee 4–43)
    and 244–3 (G Boycott 128, M W Gatting 51)

1981: Botham's magnificent season as he and England recover

The 1981 series was one of the most exciting of modern times, rivalling 1902 in its twists, and in dramatic finishes.

Ian Botham and Kim Hughes led their countries in the first Test at Trent Bridge,

1979–80 57th Series   Aus 3, Eng 0
1 PERTH   **Australia won by 138 runs**
Australia 244 (K J Hughes 99, I T Botham 6–78) and 337 (A R
    Border 115, J M Wiener 58, I T Botham 5–98)
England 228 (J M Brearley 64, D K Lillee 4–73) and 215 (G
    Boycott 99, G Dymock 6–34)
2 SYDNEY   **Australia won by 6 wkts**
England 123 (D K Lillee 4–40, G Dymock 4–42) and 237 (D I
    Gower 98)
Australia 145 (I T Botham 4–29) and 219–4 (G S Chappell 98)
3 MELBOURNE   **Australia won by 8 wkts**
England 306 (G A Gooch 99, J M Brearley 60, D K Lillee 6–60)
    and 273 (I T Botham 119, G A Gooch 51, D K Lillee 5–78, L
    S Pascoe 4–80)
Australia 477 (G S Chappell 114, I M Chappell 75, B M Laird 74,
    A R Border 63, J K Lever 4–111) and 103–2

1979–80 Averages

Batting	I	No	Runs	HS	Avge	
G.S. Chappell (A)	6	2	317	114	79.25	
Bowling	O	M	Runs	W	Avge	BB
G. Dymock (A)	130.3	40	260	17	15.29	6–34
D.K. Lillee (A)	155.1	41	388	23	16.86	6–34
I.T. Botham (E)	173.1	62	371	19	19.52	6–78
L.S. Pascoe (A)	93.5	17	241	10	24.10	4–80
D.L. Underwood (E)	160.2	48	405	13	31.15	3–71

Underwood, Derek Leslie

Underwood was born on 8 June 1945 at Bromley, Kent, and first appeared for Kent in 1963. He was a left-arm slow or slow-medium bowler, devastating on damaged pitches. He first played for England in 1966 and played in 86 Tests, taking 297 wickets, average 25.83. Had he not joined WSC and then the 'rebel' tour to South Africa, which virtually ended his Test career, he would probably have become the leading wicket-taker in Tests.

Kim Hughes in the Centenary match at Lord's in 1980, when between the showers he made 117 and 84.

the first Test match in England in which cricket was played on Sunday – there was no rest day in the middle. Terry Alderman and Trevor Chappell made debuts for Australia – Chappell being the brother of Ian and Greg, the first instance of three brothers all playing for Australia.

England were put in in conditions favouring swing bowling, and Alderman (4–68), supported by Lillee and Hogg, dismissed them for 185. Australia however fared no better against England's seamers and were removed for 179. At the end of three days interrupted by rain and bad light, England were 94 for six. Sunday was at last a sunny day, and Australia, needing 132 to win, made them for a four-wicket victory. Alderman took nine wickets.

There were more interruptions at Lord's, and more scenes of crowd dissatisfaction when the sun shone brightly after play had been abandoned on the second day. England were put in again but the match was destined for a draw when they compiled a slow 311, Lawson taking seven for 81. Play was well into the fourth day when Australia were dismissed for 345 (of which 32 were no-balls). An England declaration was no more than a formality. Botham made a pair and resigned as England captain while the selectors were considering his sacking. Brearley was appointed captain for the rest of the series.

The third Test at Headingley was one of the most extraordinary in the series, and was a great personal triumph for Ian Botham. Australia batted first and a century by Dyson was the basis of a good score of 401 for nine declared. Botham took six for 95, and when England batted was the only

player to reach 50, the side being all out for 174. The follow-on was enforced and Gooch was out for the second time in one day. Botham came in at 105 for five, which soon became 135 for seven. At this stage, with 92 still required to avoid the innings defeat, England were quoted in the betting tent at 500–1, odds which Lillee and Marsh actually took for a small amount. With Dilley (56) in support, Botham's batting on the Monday evening was magical – he reached his century in 87 balls, having scored 62 of the last 64 in boundaries. The pair added 117 for the eighth wicket, when Old (29) provided further support in a stand of 67 for the ninth. Willis helped add a last-wicket 37, leaving Botham not out 149 and England 129 ahead. Botham scored 106 in the final session on Monday.

The last wicket fell very early on the last day – it still seemed a formality for Australia. But Willis began to take wickets with regularity after Botham had got the first, and in a remarkable spell the score slid from 56 for one to 75 for eight. A mini-stand of 35 between Bright and Lillee threatened the story-book ending but both fell to Willis and England won by 18 runs. Willis took eight for 43 on the last day. It was only the second time in Test cricket that a side had won after following on, and this was a much more incredible fight-back. Two Australians, however, had something to celebrate: Alderman again had nine wickets in the match, and Marsh passed Knott's wicket-keeping record of 263 dismissals in Tests.

In the fourth Test, England were dismissed for 189, Alderman getting five wickets. Australia took a lead of 69 (with the help of 44 extras) and having put England out again for 219 needed only 151 to win. Forty-six were needed with five wickets left when Botham came into the attack. Botham claimed them all for 11 runs and England won by 29. No batsman reached 50 – the first such occurrence for 46 years.

At Old Trafford, England reached 231, of which 92 came from the last two wickets. Australia, however, could do no better than 130. England then batted so slowly that in the Saturday pre-lunch session only 29 runs were scored in the 28 overs bowled. Tavare, the principal reason, eventually scored 78 in 423 minutes, including the slowest-ever first-class 50 in England. Botham, coming in at 104 for five, despite first playing himself in, then reached 100 in 86 balls, batting with controlled power and brilliance. Some thought it his best innings. When Lillee and Alderman took the new ball he scored 66 in eight overs. Knott and Emburey consolidated, and England reached 404.

Yallop and Border, who batted with a broken finger, each made centuries, Yallop stylishly and Border grittily and Australia reached 402, but lost by 103. Botham, for the third match running, was chosen Man of the Match. Whitney played the first of his

The two England captains of 1981, Ian Botham, left, and Mike Brearley. The series was a triumph for both.

two Tests, having been summoned from Gloucestershire when about to play only his seventh first-class match (Hogg and Lawson were injured).

At the Oval, Australia led on the first innings after centuries by Border and Boycott and Dirk Wellham made a century in his first Test in the second innings. England saved the game with three wickets to spare. Botham took 10 wickets in the match and Lillee 11, but Alderman's five made him the leading bowler of the series. His 42 wickets remain second to Grimmett's 44 against South Africa among Australians.

Boycott lbw to Lillee in 1981.

1981 59th Series Eng 3, Aus 1, Drawn 2

1 TRENT BRIDGE **Australia won by 4 wkts**
England 185 (M W Gatting 52, T M Alderman 4–68) and 125 (D K Lillee 5–46, T M Alderman 5–62)
Australia 179 (A R Border 63) and 132–6 (G R Dilley 4–24)

2 LORD'S **Match Drawn**
England 311 (P Willey 82, M W Gatting 59, G F Lawson 7–81) and 265–8 dec (D I Gower 89, G Boycott 60)
Australia 345 (A R Border 64) and 90–4 (G M Wood 62)

3 HEADINGLEY **England won by 18 runs**
Australia 401–9 dec (J Dyson 102, K J Hughes 89, G N Yallop 58, I T Botham 6–95) and 111 (R G D Willis 8–43)
England 174 (I T Botham 50, D K Lillee 4–49) and 356 (I T Botham 149, G R Dilley 56, T M Alderman 6–135)

4 EDGBASTON **England won by 29 runs**
England 189 (T M Alderman 5–42) and 219 (R J Bright 5–68)
Australia 258 (J E Emburey 4–43) and 121 (I T Botham 5–11)

5 OLD TRAFFORD **England won by 103 runs**
England 231 (C J Tavare 69, P J W Allott 52, D K Lillee 4–55, T M Alderman 4–88) and 404 (I T Botham 118, C J Tavare 78, A P E Knott 59, J E Emburey 57, T M Alderman 5–109)
Australia 130 (M F Kent 52, R G D Willis 4–63) and 402 (A R Border 123, G N Yallop 114)

6 THE OVAL **Match Drawn**
Australia 352 (A R Border 106, G M Wood 66, M F Kent 54, I T Botham 6–125, R G D Willis 4–91) and 344–9 dec (D M Wellham 103, A R Border 84, R W Marsh 52, M Hendrick 4–82, I T Botham 4–128)
England 314 (G Boycott 137, M W Gatting 53, D K Lillee 7–89) and 261–7 (A P E Knott 70, M W Gatting 56, J M Brearley 51, D K Lillee 4–70)

1981 Averages

Batting	I	No	Runs	HS	Avge	
A.R. Border (A)	12	3	533	123*	59.22	
I.T. Botham (E)	12	1	399	149*	36.27	
G. Boycott (E)	12	0	392	137	32.66	
M.W. Gatting (E)	12	0	370	59	30.83	
G.M. Wood (A)	12	1	310	66	28.18	
G.N. Yallop (A)	12	0	316	114	26.33	
D.I. Gower (E)	10	0	250	89	25.00	
K.J. Hughes (A)	12	0	300	89	25.00	

Bowling	O	M	Runs	W	Avge	BB
G.R. Dilley (E)	98	24	275	14	19.64	4–24
I.T. Botham (E)	272.3	81	700	34	20.58	6–95
T.M. Alderman (A)	325	76	893	42	21.26	6–135
D.K. Lillee (A)	311.4	81	870	39	22.30	7–89
R.G.D. Willis (E)	252.4	56	666	29	22.96	8–43
G.F. Lawson (A)	106.1	30	285	12	23.75	7–81
R.J. Bright (A)	191.4	82	390	12	32.50	5–68
J.E. Emburey (E)	193.5	58	399	12	33.25	4–43

Border, Allan Robert
Born on 27 July, 1955 at Cremorne, New South Wales, Border became an all-rounder whose bowling declined as his stubborn left-handed batting developed. He switched from NSW to become captain of Queensland. His Test career began in 1978–79, and he took over the captaincy in 1984–85, often playing his best in a beaten side. He became the first batsman to score 150 in each innings of a Test against Pakistan at Lahore in 1979–80. After many failures, he led Australia in a triumphant tour of England in 1989, winning back the Ashes 4–0. By the end of that season he had played in 108 Tests, scoring 8,273 runs, average 53.37. His Test aggregate is second only to that of India's Gavaskar.

Botham and Taylor after the sensational English victory at Headingley in 1981, 'Botham's Match'.

1982–83: Captains put in opposition and Australia regain Ashes

A 'rebel' tour of South Africa, which was estranged from cricket because of its racial policies, by an English side of Test match strength, and the subsequent three-year ban on those players, weakened the England party to Australia in 1982–83.

At Perth, however, England batted solidly to reach 411 after being put in by Chappell. When the 400 was reached, some drunken supporters of England ran on to the field, and a skirmish developed. Alderman tackled one but so damaged a shoulder that he missed the rest of the season. Greg Chappell scored a century to give Australia a small lead, but Randall replied with another on an easy wicket and the match was drawn.

England were put in again at Brisbane, and were dismissed for 216 by Lawson, who took six for 47. South African-born Kepler Wessels, making his debut as one of five Queensland players in the side, was dropped at 15, and then went on to 162, giving Australia a lead of 122. The England captain Willis took five wickets. England batted better in the second innings, although the total of 309 owed much to an Australian record of 52 extras. Lawson and a restored Thomson shared the wickets equally, Lawson totalling 11 for the match, while Marsh equalled Langley's record of nine catches in a match. Australia won by seven wickets.

Willis made the mistake of putting Australia in at Adelaide. His opposing captain Chappell scored a century in a total of 438. England collapsed from 181 for three to 216 all out, and followed on. This time they reached 247 for three, but collapsed again to 304. Only Gower and Botham batted well in each innings. Lawson took nine wickets in the match, and Australia won comfortably.

England needed to win the last two Tests to square the series. At Melbourne they were put in again. This Test was remarkable in that all four innings were within ten runs of each other. Once again the last seven wickets crashed, 217 for three becoming 284 all out. Australia achieved a lead of three. After England made 294, with the lower order at last contributing well, excellent bowling by Norman Cowans reduced Australia to 218 for nine. Needing 74 more to win, Border and Thomson made half of them by the close on the fourth day, and 18,000 watched free as they attempted the last 37 on the last day. When three short of the England total, Thomson snicked Botham to Tavare at second slip. He could only knock the ball over his head, but Miller came behind him from first slip to catch the ball low down. During the match Marsh claimed his 27th victim of the series, beating the record of J.H.B. Waite of South Africa, which he had equalled seven years earlier.

For the first time in the series, the captain winning the toss batted at Sydney. Australia had a big slice of luck in the first over when Dyson was shown by TV replays to be run

out by a very long way. He was allowed to stay (for over five hours), and made 79 out of 314. England, pressing, made 237, but a century from Hughes made a win impossible. Night-watchman Hemmings made 95 on the last day, but the match was drawn, Australia regaining the Ashes. Marsh's record of 28 dismissals remains a series record.

1982–83   60th Series   Aus 2, Eng 1, Drawn 2
1 PERTH   Match Drawn
England 411 (C J Tavare 89, D W Randall 78, D I Gower 72, B Yardley 5–107) and 358 (D W Randall 115, A J Lamb 56, G F Lawson 5–108)
Australia 424–9 dec (G S Chappell 117, K J Hughes 62, D W Hookes 56, J Dyson 52, G F Lawson 50, G Miller 4–70) and 73–2
2 BRISBANE   Australia won by 7 wkts
England 219 (A J Lamb 72, G F Lawson 6–47) and 309 (G Fowler 83, G Miller 60, J R Thomson 5–73, G F Lawson 5–87)
Australia 341 (K C Wessels 162, G S Chappell 53, B Yardley 53, R G D Willis 5–66) and 190–3 (D W Hookes 66)
3 ADELAIDE   Australia won by 8 wkts
Australia 438 (G S Chappell 115, K J Hughes 88, I T Botham 4–112) and 83–2
England 216 (A J Lamb 82, D I Gower 60, G F Lawson 4–56) and 304 (D I Gower 114, I T Botham 58, G F Lawson 5–66)
4 MELBOURNE   England won by 3 runs
England 284 (C J Tavare 89, A J Lamb 83, R M Hogg 4–69, B Yardley 4–89) and 294 (G Fowler 65, G F Lawson 5–107)
Australia 287 (K J Hughes 66, D W Hookes 53, R W Marsh 53) and 288 (D W Hookes 68, A R Border 62, N G Cowans 6–77)
5 SYDNEY   Match Drawn
Australia 314 (A R Border 89, J Dyson 79, I T Botham 4–75) and 382 (K J Hughes 137, A R Border 83, K C Wessels 53)
England 237 (D I Gower 70, D W Randall 70, J R Thomson 5–50) and 314–7 (E E Hemmings 95, B Yardley 4–139)

1982–83 Averages

Batting	I	No	Runs	HS	Avge
K.J. Hughes (A)	8	1	469	137	67.00
D.W. Hookes (A)	8	1	344	68	49.14
G.S. Chappell (A)	10	2	389	117	48.62
K.C. Wessels (A)	8	0	386	162	48.25
D.W. Randall (E)	8	0	365	115	45.62
A.R. Border (A)	9	2	317	89	45.28
D.I. Gower (E)	10	0	441	114	44.10
A.J. Lamb (E)	10	0	414	83	41.40
J. Dyson (A)	10	2	283	79	35.37
I.T. Botham (E)	10	0	270	58	27.00

Bowling	O	M	Runs	W	Avge	BB
J.R. Thomson (A)	128.4	22	411	22	18.68	5–50
G.F. Lawson (A)	230.4	51	687	34	20.20	6–47
R.G.D. Willis (E)	166.3	28	486	18	27.00	5–66
G. Miller (E)	171	50	397	13	30.53	4–70
B. Yardley (A)	292.2	91	793	22	36.04	5–107
I.T. Botham (E)	213.5	35	729	18	40.50	4–75

Graham Gooch, who returned to the England colours in 1985 and made 196 at the Oval.

Gooch is caught by Phillips at Edgbaston in 1985 and Jeff Thomson claims his 200th Test wicket.

1985: A day at Edgbaston turns the series England's way

Allan Border was captain of Australia when the 1985 tourists arrived in England. His counterpart was David Gower. The South African 'rebels' were now eligible again.

At Headingley, Andy Hilditch made 119 for Australia, who passed 200 with only two men out but then collapsed to 331. Opener Tim Robinson then made 175, and with good support helped the England total to 533. With rain and bad light playing a part, there was a rush to get Australia out again in time to win. England finally needed 123 in 200 minutes and won by five wickets.

Border put England in at Lord's – and out again for 290 (McDermott 6–70). He then scored an impressive 196, adding 216 for the fifth wicket with Ritchie (94). Australia reached 451, and dismissing England for 261 (Holland 5–68), needed only 127 to win. Five wickets were down for 65, including a run-out by Gower of Wessels from silly point off a defensive stroke. Australia held together, however, to win by four wickets.

At Trent Bridge Gower made 166 on a good pitch, adding 187 with Gatting for the third wicket, which fell at 358. England's 456 was passed by Australia who made 539, with Wood making 172 and Greg Ritchie 146, the pair adding 161 for the sixth wicket. Breaks for rain ensured the match was a high-scoring draw.

Rain also affected the Old Trafford Test, where Gower successfully put Australia in – they made only 257. Gatting made his first Test century in England (160), and with most of the batsmen scoring well, England declared at 482 for nine. Craig McDermott was the only bowler to get a wicket – he took eight for 148 and there was a run-out. On the last day England needed six Australian wickets, but play started late, Border was missed in the first over (he went on to 146 not out) and the match was drawn.

There was plenty of rain at Edgbaston, where Australia, put in, had scored 335 for eight, apparently safe from defeat. But Saturday's exciting play determined the series. The last two wickets were taken in the first over, Richard Ellison finishing with six for 77. By close of play England were ahead at 355 for one. Robinson (148) and Gower (215) played brilliantly, eventually adding 331 for the second wicket. Gatting scored a century, and England declared at 595 for five. The only bright spot for Australia was the 200th Test wicket for the recalled Jeff Thomson. Rain seemed the only hope for Australia after they finished the fourth day at 35 for five (Ellison having claimed four for one), and indeed play did not start till 2.30, when Wayne Phillips and Ritchie batted till tea. The break-through was controversial. Phillips, on 59, slashed Edmonds square, and Lamb at silly point, jumped to avoid injury. The ball hit his foot in mid-air and was caught by Gower. The incident occurred so fast that umpire Shepherd and most of the players were unsure of what happened, but square-leg umpire Constant confirmed that Phillips was out. England won with 14 overs to spare. It was the first Ashes Test to be won with the loss of no more than five wickets.

Australia needed to win at the Oval to save the series and the Ashes, but on a fast pitch this seemed unlikely after the first day, when England were 376 for three. This state of affairs arose from a stand of 351 for the second wicket between Gooch (196) and Gower (157). The innings subsided somewhat to 464, but Australia could manage only 241, and then, following on, they batted feebly (apart from Border) before Ellison, who took five for 46, and were out for 129. England thus regained the Ashes 3–1.

1985 61st Series Eng 3, Aus 1, Drawn 2

1 HEADINGLEY England won by 5 wkts
Australia 331 (A M J Hilditch 119) and 324 (W B Phillips 91, A M J Hilditch 80, K C Wessels 64, J E Emburey 5–82, I T Botham 4–107)
England 533 (R T Robinson 175, I T Botham 60, P R Downton 54, M W Gatting 53, C J McDermott 4–134) and 123–5

2 LORD's Australia won by 4 wkts
England 290 (D I Gower 86, C J McDermott 6–70) and 261 (I T Botham 85, M W Gatting 75, R G Holland 5–68)
Australia 425 (A R Border 196, G M Ritchie 94, I T Botham 5–109) and 127–6

3 TRENT BRIDGE Match Drawn
England 456 (D I Gower 166, G A Gooch 76, M W Gatting 74, G F Lawson 5–103) and 196–2 (R T Robinson 77)
Australia 539 (G M Wood 172, G M Ritchie 146)

4 OLD TRAFFORD Match Drawn
Australia 257 (D C Boon 61, P H Edmonds 4–40, I T Botham 4–79) and 340–5 (A R Border 146, K C Wessels 50, J E Emburey 4–99)
England 482–9 dec (M W Gatting 160, G A Gooch 74, A J Lamb 67, C J McDermott 8–141)

5 EDGBASTON England won by an innings and 118 runs
Australia 335 (K C Wessels 83, G F Lawson 53, R M Ellison 6–77) and 142 (W B Phillips 59, R M Ellison 4–27)
England 595–5 dec (D I Gower 215, R T Robinson 148, M W Gatting 100)

6 THE OVAL England won by an innings and 94 runs
England 464 (G A Gooch 196, D I Gower 157, G F Lawson 4–101)
Australia 241 (G M Ritchie 64) and 129 (A R Border 58, R M Ellison 5–46)

1985 Averages

Batting	I	No	Runs	HS	Avge
M.W. Gatting (E)	9	3	527	160	87.83
D.I. Gower (E)	9	0	732	215	81.33
A.R. Border (A)	11	2	597	196	66.33
R.T. Robinson (E)	9	1	490	175	61.25
G.A. Gooch (E)	9	0	487	196	54.11
G.M. Ritchie (A)	11	1	422	146	42.20
A.M.J. Hilditch (A)	11	0	424	119	38.54
A.J. Lamb (E)	8	1	256	67	36.57
W.B. Phillips (A)	11	1	350	91	35.00
K.C. Wessels (A)	11	0	368	83	33.45
G.M. Wood (A)	9	0	260	172	28.88

Bowling	O	M	Runs	W	Avge	BB
R.M. Ellison (E)	75.5	20	185	17	10.88	6–77
I.T. Botham (E)	251.4	36	855	31	27.58	5–109
J.E. Emburey (E)	248.4	75	544	19	28.63	5–82
C.J. McDermott (A)	234.2	21	901	30	30.03	8–141
P.H. Edmonds (E)	225.5	59	549	15	36.60	4–40
G.F. Lawson (A)	246	38	830	22	37.72	5–103

The 1985 Australian party in England. Left to right, back: G.R. Mackay (physiotherapist), R.B. Phillips, Ritchie, Gilbert, McDermott, O'Donnell, Bennett, Holland, Matthews, Wellham, M.P. Ringham (scorer). Front: Wood, Wessels, Thomson, Border, R.F. Merriman (manager), G. Dymock (assistant manager), Hilditch, Lawson, W.B. Phillips, Boon.

Boycott, Geoffrey
Born on 21 October 1940 at Fitzwilliam, Yorkshire, Boycott made his debut for Yorkshire in 1962. He was a very sound and correct opening batsman. He wore spectacles when making his first appearance for England in 1964. Later he changed to contact lenses. He played in 108 Test matches, scoring 8,114 runs, average 47.72. His aggregate was a record until passed by Gavaskar. The highlight of his career was the scoring of his 100th century in a Test match at Headingley in 1977.

1986–87: England keep Ashes with all-round performance

Gatting was Border's opposing captain when England visited Australia in 1986–87. England's form had been wretched in the games before the first Test, in which Border put them in, but the early batsmen applied themselves well, and then Botham came in to play a commanding innings of 138. He hit 22 in an over from Merv Hughes, equalling the 22 he and Tavare (3) had taken from Lillee in 1981. Dilley took five for 68 to help dismiss Australia for 248 and just enforce the follow-on. Geoff Marsh batted the whole of the fourth day for Australia, but nobody stayed with him long enough. Emburey took five for 80 in nearly 43 overs and England needed just 75, winning by eight wickets. DeFreitas, making his debut, was given out, caught, but reinstated after non-striker Botham had intervened and the umpires had conferred.

At Perth, England chose to bat and never looked back after Broad (162) and Athey (96) had put on 223 for the first wicket. Gower added 136 and Jack Richards 133 in his second Test, England declaring at 592 for eight. Border, with 125, led a rearguard action which this time just avoided the follow-on. England declared at 199 for eight, but the Australians found plenty of determination to bat out time.

All the Australian batsmen, led by David Boon (103), got runs at Adelaide, allowing Border to declare at 514 for five. Board and Gatting also scored centuries, however, and England's 455 doomed the match to another draw. Border declared on reaching his hundred on a rain-affected last day, but it was a formality.

At Melbourne, Gatting put Australia in on a true pitch and hustled them out for 141, excellent bowling by Botham and Gladstone Small allowing them to share the wickets. Broad then scored his third century in consecutive Ashes Tests, Hobbs and Hammond having previously achieved this feat. Few Australian batsmen offered much resistance in the second innings, and 194 all out meant an innings defeat in three days and England retaining the Ashes.

In the last Test at Sydney, Dean Jones made a splendid 184 not out for Australia, more than half the team's total of 343. Small again took five wickets. England began badly but recovered somewhat to 275. Peter Taylor, an off-spinner making his Test debut, took six of the last seven wickets for 78. He had played only six first-class matches, and his selection was so surprising that Australian commentators only half-jokingly suggested his selection was a case of mistaken identity.

At 145 for seven, Australia faced defeat again, but Taylor scored 42, helping Waugh set a target of 320 to win. Emburey took seven for 78. When the final 20 overs began, England needed 90 with five wickets left, but when Gatting was out for 96 it became a question of saving the game. Peter Sleep, however, took his fifth wicket with the last ball of the penultimate over to end Australia's record sequence of 15 Tests without a win.

1986–87 62nd Series Eng 2, Aus 1, Drawn 2

1 BRISBANE England won by 7 wkts
England 456 (I T Botham 138, C W J Athey 76, M W Gatting 61, D I Gower 51) and 77–3
Australia 248 (G R Marsh 56, G R J Matthews 56, G R Dilley 5–68) and 282 (G R Marsh 110, J E Emburey 5–80)

2 PERTH Match Drawn
England 592–8 dec (B C Broad 162, D I Gower 136, C J Richards 133, C W J Athey 96, B A Reid 4–115) and 199–8 dec (M W Gatting 70, S R Waugh 5–69)
Australia 401 (A R Border 125, S R Waugh 71, G R Dilley 4–79) and 197–4 (D M Jones 69)

3 ADELAIDE Match Drawn
Australia 514–5 dec (D C Boon 103, D M Jones 93, S R Waugh 79, G R Matthews 73, A R Border 70) and 201–3 dec (A R Border 100)
England 455 (B C Broad 116, M W Gatting 100, C W J Athey 55, B A Reid 4–64, P R Sleep 4–132) and 39–2

4 MELBOURNE England won by an innings and 14 runs
Australia 141 (D M Jones 59, I T Botham 5–41, G C Small 5–48) and 194 (G R Marsh 60)
England 349 (B C Broad 112, B A Reid 4–78, C J McDermott 4–83)

5 SYDNEY Australia won by 55 runs
Australia 343 (D M Jones 184, G C Small 5–75) and 251 (S R Waugh 73, J E Emburey 7–78)
England 275 (D I Gower 72, J E Emburey 69, P L Taylor 6–78) and 264 (M W Gatting 96, P R Sleep 5–72)

1986–87 Averages

Batting	I	No	Runs	HS	Avge
B.C. Broad (E)	9	2	487	162	69.57
D.I. Gower (E)	8	1	404	136	57.71
D.M. Jones (A)	10	1	511	184*	56.78
A.R. Border (A)	10	1	473	125	52.56
S.R. Waugh (A)	8	1	310	79	44.29
M.W. Gatting (E)	9	0	393	100	43.67
G.R. Marsh (A)	10	0	429	110	42.90
C.J. Richardson (E)	7	0	264	133	37.71
C.W.J. Athey (E)	9	0	303	96	33.67

Bowling	O	M	Runs	W	Avge	BB
G.C. Small (E)	78.4	23	180	12	15.00	5–48
B.A. Reid (A)	198.4	44	527	20	26.35	4–64
G.R. Dilley (E)	176.1	38	511	16	31.94	5–68
P.H. Edmonds (E)	261.4	78	538	15	35.87	3–45
J.E. Emburey (E)	315.5	86	663	18	36.83	7–78

Botham, Ian Terence

Botham was born on 24 November 1955 at Heswall, Cheshire, and made his debut for Somerset, to where his family moved, in 1974. His Test debut came in 1977. He became a very hard-hitting right-hand middle-order batsman, a fast-medium swing bowler and an outstanding close fielder. Among his all-round achievements, he became the first to score a century and take ten wickets in a Test match, against India in 1979–80. He became the first player to pass 3,000 runs and 300 wickets in Tests. He captained England in 12 Tests, but was unfortunate to meet the strong West Indian side in nine of those, and lost the job. His most famous match followed immediately, when an innings of 149 not out at Headingley against Australia in 1981 won the match from an almost impossible position. In 97 Tests to the end of 1989 he had scored 5,119 runs, average 34.35, and taken 376 wickets, average 28.27. His aggregate wickets was a world record until passed by New Zealand's Hadlee. Always in the news with brushes with authority and with charity walks, he left Somerset for Worcestershire amid much publicity in 1987. He was cricket's biggest box-office attraction of the 1980s.

Above: Emburey bowls McDermott at Melbourne in 1986–87 and England retain the Ashes with an innings victory and with one match to come. Emburey's 18 wickets were the most by an England bowler in the series.

Far Left: David Boon batting at Adelaide in 1986–87 where he scored a century and saved his Test place which was in danger after two disappointing Tests.

Left: The Adelaide ground during the Australia v England third Test in 1986–87. Adelaide is one of the most beautiful and peaceful of Australian grounds, although some of the most tense cricket has been played there.

1987–88: Bicentennial Test drawn

In 1988 Australia celebrated her Bicentenary, and among the celebrations was a Bicentennial Test between the old enemies, played at Sydney on 29, 30 and 31 January and 1 and 2 February 1988. England were touring New Zealand, and played the Test and a one-day international in Australia. The England side for the Test consisted of Gatting (captain), Broad, Moxon, Robinson, Athey, Capel, Emburey, French, Foster, Hemmings and Dilley. Australia were represented by Border (captain), Boon, Marsh, Jones, Veletta, Waugh, Sleep, Dyer, Taylor, Dodemaide and McDermott.

A parade of 'Living Legends' preceded the match, led by Sir Donald Bradman in a veteran Rolls-Royce.

England won the toss and took first innings on a perfect day for batting, Broad and Moxon giving them a solid start, although not without giving three straightforward but unaccepted chances before lunch, taken at 71. They proceeded to 93, when Moxon was out, and England continued to bat unadventurously to 221 for two by the close, Gatting taking 67

Right: Gatting and Border, the rival captains in the Bicentennial Test. *Below:* Dilley takes his sweater as England celebrate a wicket.

minutes to end on 3 not out. All the English batsmen except the not-out Hemmings were to make double figures, but only one passed 50 – Broad, who made 139 and then disgraced himself by knocking out his off stump when finally dismissed. He was promptly fined £500 (A$1,000) and apologized. England's 425 was always too much for the Aussies, who subsided to 214, Jones being top scorer with 56.

By now play was into the fourth day, most of the session after tea on the third being lost, but England had excellent prospects of a win provided they could capture a wicket or two. However, Boon and Marsh opened with an undefeated 101 before the light became bad and the players retired an hour and a half early, considerably improving Australia's prospects of saving the game.

These got steadily better as the last day progressed. Boon and Marsh took their stand to 162 before Marsh was out, and the fielding, poor throughout the match, got no better as England lost interest. Jones scored 24, and Boon (184 not out) and Border (48 not out) saw out time. It was a grand occasion, but not a particularly distinguished match.

1987–88   63rd Series (Bicentennial Test)   Aus 0, Eng 0, Drawn 1

1 SYDNEY   **Drawn**
England 425 (B C Broad 139, P L Taylor 4–84)
Australia 214 (D M Jones 56) and 328–2 (D C Boon 184, G R Marsh 56)

Above: David Boon gets the ball away to leg in the Bicentennial Test. He was top scorer with 184 not out in Australia's second innings.

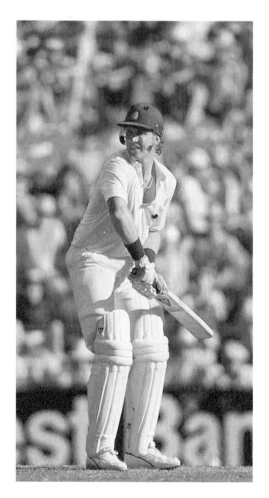

Below left: Dean Jones receives his medal for taking part. *Below right:* Chris Broad, who made 139, but petulantly broke his wicket when dismissed.

1989: Australia trounce England and regain Ashes

Australian and English cricket had both been in the doldrums for several seasons before the 1989 tour, yet both sides had shown signs of revival and the series was looked forward to with great interest.

Allan Border was named captain of the touring party. The main disappointment for the Australians was that Bruce Reid, their leading fast bowler, was ruled out after major surgery to his back, which had troubled him since his successful tour of Pakistan the previous season.

The main controversy in the 17 named for the trip concerned the fast bowling and centred on the omission of the New South Wales left-armer Mike Whitney, who led the wicket-takers in the Australian season with 58 wickets, including nine West Indian wickets in the Test match at Adelaide. He was the first Australian bowler since the Second World War to have headed the wicket table and not to have been picked for the Ashes Tour (except for the unavailable Lillee in 1977).

The quickish bowlers selected were Terry Alderman and Geoff Lawson, both in their thirties, and Carl Rackemann, these three being expected to be the main Test strike force. Hughes was expected to lend support, while the surprise selection was Greg Campbell, of Tasmania. The first-choice spinner was Tim May, an off-breaker, while more spin was provided by leg-spinner Trevor Hohns. This was another slightly surprising selection in that at 35 Hohns was the oldest in the party on his first overseas tour.

The Australian batting looked promisingly solid. The likely opening pair for the Test matches was Geoff Marsh and left-hander Mark Taylor, the leading run-maker in the Australian season, while David Boon, who had opened the innings for a few seasons with Marsh, would bat at number three. Border would follow, with Dean Jones and all-rounder Steve Waugh completing a strong line-up. The back-up batsmen were the 6ft 8in Tom Moody and Mike Veletta, both of West Australia. Ian Healy was first-choice wicket-keeper, while Tim Zoehrer, first choice until a couple of seasons earlier, was his understudy.

Only Border, Lawson and Boon had been on the 1985 tour, but Alderman had been an outstanding success in 1981, and would have toured in 1985 but for injury. The full party was: A.R. Border (Queensland), the captain, G.R. Marsh (West Australia), the vice-captain, T.M. Alderman (West Australia), D.C. Boon (Tasmania), G.D. Campbell (Tasmania), I.A. Healy (Queensland), T.V. Hohns (Queensland), M.G. Hughes (Victoria), D.M. Jones (Victoria), G.F. Lawson (New South Wales), T.B.A. May (South Australia), T.M. Moody (West Australia), C.G. Rackemann (Queensland), M.A.

Above: Century-maker Mark Taylor ducks below a Foster bouncer in the first Test. *Below:* Dean Jones hooks on his way to 79. *Right:* Merv Hughes during his surprise 71.

Taylor (New South Wales), M.R.J. Veletta (West Australia), S.R. Waugh (New South Wales) and T.J. Zoehrer (West Australia). The manager was L.M. Sawle and the coach was former captain R.B. Simpson.

England, meanwhile, appointed a new chairman of selectors in succession to Peter May. He was Ted Dexter, another former Test captain, who would be joined by the team manager, Mickey Stewart, and *ex officio* members Alan Smith and Ossie Wheatley, to form a new 'England committee' for the purposes of selecting the Test teams. The old selectors lost their positions. Dexter's post carried a salary – he was the first chairman of selectors to be paid. He immediately appointed David Gower as captain of the Test team for the whole summer. Gower had been the successful captain in 1985, but had lost the post to Mike Gatting in the middle of the losing series against India in 1986. In 1988

England had used four captains during the series against West Indies: Gatting, Emburey, Chris Cowdrey and Gooch. The partnership of the cavalier Dexter and the stylish Gower promised a series of flair and adventure from England's point of view.

The Texaco Trophy one-day series served to increase the appetite for the Tests, as in brilliant sunshine not a minute was lost to the weather. England won the first match comfortably by 95 runs, the second was tied, and Australia won the third by six wickets. Australia's win at Lord's was accomplished by making a record second-innings score between the countries of 279 for four, and was enlivened by a shapely pre-tea interval streaker. Nevertheless England were the official Trophy winners on the grounds of having lost fewer wickets in the tied match.

In the first Test at Headingley, Australia were without Rackemann, who had fallen at Hove and required an operation to his knee – he was not to play in the series –

and thus gave a Test debut to Greg Campbell, playing him with Hughes, Lawson and Alderman and no front-line spinner. England, too, did not play a spinner.

In light of the absence of spinners, Gower's decision to put the Australians in when winning the toss was surprising. Border let it be known that he would still have batted had he won the toss. Perhaps Gower's decision was based on the cloudy skies and the knowledge that the Headingley pitch had a reputation for being at its most difficult on the first morning – but this pitch was a new one and groundsman Keith Boyce had promised that it would play true, which it did.

England were without Botham, whose long-awaited return to the Test fold was put back by a triple fracture of the cheekbone caused when he top-edged a

Robin Smith doubles up as he is hit by a bouncer. He made 66 in England's first innings.

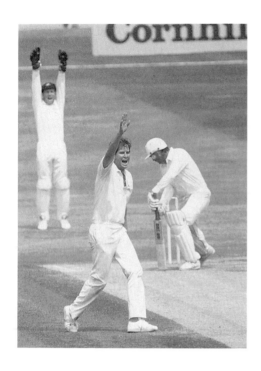

Left: Terry Alderman and Ian Healy appeal for lbw against Gooch, who had to go.

score 80 in 118 balls before becoming an unlucky lbw victim of Alderman.

Lamb had partnered Barnett in a stand of 114, and he and Gower looked safe till Gower was hit painfully on the arm by Hughes and was then well caught by keeper Healy from a glance off Lawson in the next over for 26. Lamb passed the 100 mark for the first time in a Test against Australia, and with another former South African, Robin Smith, saw England to 280 for four by the end of Saturday, with the match apparently well on the way to a draw.

Lamb and Smith attacked on the

Below: Australian dressing-room jubilation.
Bottom: Mike Gatting out for a duck in the second Test at Lord's.

Monday morning until Lamb was caught off bat and pad for 125, of which 96 had come in fours. The percentage of his runs to come in boundaries (76.80 per cent) was a record for an Ashes century, beating the 76.51 per cent of Botham's famous innings on the same ground in 1981. After that, only Newport (36) helped Smith (66) to offer much more resistance, but England's total of 430 had easily saved the follow-on.

Australia went in again with a determination to score quickly enough to make a declaration sufficiently challenging to make a match of it, and by the close on Monday had rattled up 158 for three, Taylor following his 136 with 60, only K.C. Wessels and A.A. Jackson having scored more than his 196 in a first Test against England. Border (60 not out) and Jones (40 not out) cracked 72 more in ten

ball onto his face, as well as Gatting, who had injured a thumb, and Dilley, also injured.

Marsh and Taylor remained together for the shortened session till lunch, but Marsh was lbw to DeFreitas on the first ball afterwards – he made 16 of 44. Boon lasted less than half an hour for 9, but skipper Border (66) helped Taylor take the score to 174. Taylor, in his first Ashes Test, was still there at close of play on 96, with the score 207 for three.

On an overcast second day, Taylor quickly became the 16th Australian to score a century in his maiden Test, and he went on to a solid 136. Dean Jones (79) and Steve Waugh then put the English attack to the sword, scoring 138 runs at slightly better than a run-a-minute. After Healy had gone, Waugh and Hughes then put on 139 by the close, which was taken at 580 for six, 373 runs having come in the day: 120 before lunch, 114 in the afternoon, and 139 in the evening. Gower's decision not to bat had already proved to be wrong, and the tone was set for the series.

Border batted on on the third day before finally declaring at 601 for seven, the highest Ashes score recorded at Leeds. Steve Waugh had taken his score to 177 not out, which was both his first Test century and his highest first-class innings. The only England player to gain any satisfaction from this huge total was Jack Russell, keeping wicket in his second Test. He allowed no byes, this being the highest total made in a Test in England without a bye.

England's first target was the 402 needed to save the follow-on, and they started moderately with Gooch (13) lbw to Alderman, and Broad (37) deceived by Hughes' exaggerated slow donkey-drop, both out by 81. But Kim Barnett, in his first Ashes match, batted brilliantly to

overs on Tuesday morning, and England were set a theoretical 402 in a minimum 83 overs to win – it would be more a question of attempting to bat out the time.

Broad soon went, but Gooch was firm and Barnett batted as he had in the first innings, 34 coming in only 51 minutes. However when he left, Lamb was out as in the first innings, caught from bat and pad by Boon off Alderman, and Gower, like Barnett, also scored a quick 34 in 51 minutes. He, too, was out as in the first innings, glancing Lawson and being caught by the wicket-keeper.

All this feverish activity was not what was wanted, and once the stolid Gooch had

Right: Merv Hughes is introduced to Her Majesty the Queen at Lord's. *Below:* Robin Smith makes his way past Dickie Bird at Lord's and Gower practises as Australia grab another wicket.

Above: Steve Waugh puts short leg's life at risk as he turns the match with 152 not out in the first innings. *Left:* Allan Border drives John Emburey back over his head.

gone, lbw to a big swinger from Hughes, the remaining batsmen subsided rapidly. England were 191 all out, and Australia had 27 overs to spare. Terry Alderman, the Man of the Match, claimed five wickets in each innings, registering ten in a Test for the first time.

The Australians made only one change for the second Test at Lord's, bringing in leg-spinner Hohns for Campbell. England were forced to make a batting change as Lamb was injured, so Gatting returned, but the wholesale ditching of the bowlers from Headingley suggested bad selection in the first place. Only Foster kept his place as DeFreitas, Newport and Pringle were dropped for Dilley, Jarvis and off-spinner Emburey. Angus Fraser of Middlesex was in the 12 selected, but omitted on the morning.

Gower won the toss (his ninth in succession against Border) and this time batted. He had no option after Leeds, but in fact there would have been more justification at Lord's for fielding, and he must have pondered on his luck when he went to the wicket at 58 for three.

The men out were Broad (18), Barnett (14) and Gatting, who faced only one ball and was caught close in by Boon off Hughes. Gooch, in his solid introspective style, remained, and he and Gower survived to lunch, at 80 for three, although Gower was very lucky early on when he hooked to Jones on the long leg boundary and Jones spilled the catch.

Gooch finally went for a good 60, but Gower and Smith batted with freedom until Gower chopped Lawson onto his stumps. His 57 came from only 62 balls and Smith was just as fluent, but there seemed no need for the hurry unless it was a laudable attempt to seize the initiative. It came to grief when Emburey lasted two balls and then Smith went, but Russell (64 not out) gave England hope by batting sensibly for nearly three hours, during which Foster and Dilley supported him well. However England's 286 was not enough, and Australia began their innings with one over on the first day.

Next morning, Marsh was soon caught behind off Dilley, but Taylor (62), continuing where he left off at Headingley, and Boon (94) put on 144 and Australia once again assumed the initiative. England's new attack, however, was more persistent than the old, and in a very competitive session after tea took four wickets, so that with Australia at 276 for

Right: A big appeal by Healy against Graham Dilley, who took part in a stubborn last-wicket stand. *Below right:* David Boon drives square in his first innings 94.

Gower, David Ifon

Gower was born on April Fool's Day, 1 April, 1957, and some of his experiences as England captain in the 1980s, when his side was soundly beaten by most of the Test-playing countries, must have led him to believe that his birth-date was ominous. However, he is one of the most stylish and elegant batsmen of his day, and when in form his left-handed cover-driving is the equal of any batsman's. Born in Tunbridge Wells, Kent, he spent his early years in Tanganyika before making his debut for Leicestershire in 1975 when only 18. He made his Test debut in 1978, and was captain on and off from 1982 to 1987, and again in 1989. To the end of 1989 he had played in 106 Tests, scoring 7,383 runs, average 43.42. His highest score is 215 against Australia, and his Ashes aggregate is fourth behind Bradman, Hobbs and Boycott.

six overnight the match looked well poised.

The Saturday of the Lord's Test, so often a day of significance, proved to be so again, as Australia completely dominated England and turned a close position into one of great ascendancy. Waugh batted beautifully for the second successive Test and found support from Hughes (30), Hohns (21) and, most surprisingly, from Lawson (74), with whom he added 130 for the ninth wicket. Even Alderman survived for 39 balls, by which time Australia had made 528, their second highest total on his ground, and Waugh was left on 152 not out. He had now made 329 without being dismissed, and England, having hoped to face a deficit of 30 or 40 when play began, were 242 in arrears, having conceded 263 for the last four wickets.

It was a dejected side which went out to bat again, and Alderman, after his batting 'success' followed up by getting Gooch lbw with the third ball of the innings. Nought for one became 18 for two when Barnett was out, and 28 for three when Broad followed. Gatting and Gower steadied the ship, but at the close of a momentous day for Australia England were still 184 behind at 58 for three. More than 300 runs had been scored in the day. Gower, who came in for severe criticism over the handling of his bowlers, left the post-play press conference abruptly, claiming he had to

Opposite: The Aussie captain Border, the centre of attention in the nets. *Above:* Jack Russell ducks a bouncer during his innings of 42. *Right:* a rare Test wicket for Steve Waugh as Kim Barnett is caught behind. *Below:* Ian Botham in his usual place in the slips on his Test return. Barnett and Tavaré are his neighbours.

Opposite: Dean Jones drives handsomely during his dashing innings of 57 at Edgbaston in the third Test. *Above:* Mark Taylor cuts through the slips. *Above right:* Ian Botham hits Alderman to leg while compiling his patient 46. *Below:* Geoff Lawson clean bowled by Test debutant Angus Fraser. *Right:* Steve Waugh, an outstanding batting success, enthusiastically congratulated by team-mates on one of his two wickets.

catch a cab for a show. This was an understandable reaction from a skipper after such a day, but one for which he was obliged to apologise.

Gower batted at his elegant best on Monday and made 106, taking his Test aggregate into the top ten, and to sixth in England–Australia clashes. He soon lost Gatting, who shouldered arms in his mistaken manner to be given lbw, but Smith stayed with him to add 139 for fifth wicket. Smith made 96 in his hard-hitting style before being bowled by Alderman just short of a deserved first Test century. The tail took the score to 322 for nine at the close, and Emburey and Dilley raised the total to 359 on the last morning, but there was no sign of the rainstorm needed to prevent Australia winning, although 67 for four would have had the 1981 team quaking. Waugh came in and hoisted his aggregate to 350 without being out as Australia reached the 118 required to win by six wickets. Waugh was Man of the Match, but Alderman, with nine wickets, was proving the main difference between the sides. His 19 wickets to date were nine more than the hauls of Hughes and Foster.

Australia naturally fielded the same side for the third Test at Edgbaston, but England, having made changes, were forced into more by injuries and bereavement. First of all, Botham returned to the side, as did Lamb, both recovered from injury. Broad and Jarvis were dropped from the Lord's 12, implying that Fraser would play. However, Lamb and Smith then dropped out with injuries and Tim Curtis and Chris Tavaré were picked to replace them. The day before the match Gatting returned home when his mother-in-law died, and at the last minute Foster retired with a blistered finger. Jarvis was recalled to replace him. The comings and goings meant only four changes from the Lord's team in the end.

Border at last won the toss and decided to bat. In a storm-threatening atmosphere Marsh and Taylor again got Australia off to a good start and batted through to lunch. Botham returned to the England attack for the first time in 22 months, and his first ball rapped Taylor's pads and there was a loud appeal – but, strange to relate, the umpire said 'not out'. After lunch, however, Emburey and Botham removed the openers, and then Emburey bowled Border for 8 (he had just passed his 8,000th Test run): 105 for three.

Jones then came in and helped Boon (38) to take the score to 210 when Boon was unluckily run out, Jarvis deflecting Jones' straight drive onto the stumps with Boon backing up. At 232 for four a terrific storm finished play for the day and for

Robin Smith acknowledging the applause of the spectators on reaching his first Test hundred in the fourth Test at Old Trafford, after reaching 96 at Edgbaston.

most of the next. Waugh, 17 not out, had now scored 367 without being dismissed, thus passing Hutton's 364 in the 1938 Oval Test.

Next day, Waugh was at last out for 43 (average 393), becoming Fraser's first Test victim, and Australia ended the day at 294 for six, Jones having reached 101.

Saturday consisted of 31 overs only. Jones advanced to 141, and Australia to 391 for seven. An oddity was the powerful throw from Emburey at third man which continued to the long-on boundary, giving Australia seven leg-byes. It was a fine day on Monday, the fourth day, and Border relentlessly batted on. He was already safe from defeat, but he had suffered so much as Australia's captain that perhaps it was understandable that now he was in the driving seat he should be ruthless. Jones was eventually out for 157, and Australia

Left: Gooch out for 11, and the congratulations are for Geoff Lawson. *Below:* Men under pressure at Old Trafford: Gower, Stewart and Dexter, with Alan Knott on the left.

were all out for 424. Fraser's four for 63 in 35 overs was an excellent start.

England were soon in deep trouble on a pitch which now started to play tricks. Gooch (8) was lbw to one that didn't rise, Gower (8) followed suit, Tavaré scored only 2, Curtis' two-hour stay ended with another lbw for 41 and an injured Barnett was out for 10 – 75 for five.

Botham (46) and Russell (42) then added 96, each batting for over 2½ hours, but they left together at 171, with 54 still needed to avoid the follow-on. England were still 40 short when the last day began, and Fraser was stupidly run out in the first over: 185 for eight. Emburey (26) was out with ten still needed, but the last wicket pair, Dilley (11 not out in nearly 1½ hours) and Jarvis, who chanced his arm and hit 22, saved the indignity, and possibly the match. Australia made a sedate 158 for two in the time left, and the match was drawn. Dean Jones was Man of the Match.

The Australians naturally were not prepared to make any changes for the fourth Test at Old Trafford: at two up with three to play they were most of the way to regaining the Ashes. England made four changes. Smith and Foster returned after injury, and Tim Robinson and left-arm spinner Nick Cook came back into the side for the first time in the season. The players omitted were Barnett, Tavaré, Dilley, who was again injured, and Jarvis.

Right: Jack Russell, England's Man of the Series, just dodges a bouncer during his 128 not out at Old Trafford. *Below:* England's bowling success, Angus Fraser, a Test new boy.

Ashes victory! *Top left:* Border finds the celebrations boisterous. *Left:* Geoff Marsh joins his beer-soaked skipper. *Above:* Popular Merv Hughes gets his share of the amber liquid. *Right:* Chairman of selectors Ted Dexter and David Gower are naturally more subdued at the outcome. *Below:* The moment of truth (or joy!) — the Australians leap into the air as David Boon sweeps the Ashes-winning boundary.

Opposite: Geoff Marsh and Mark Taylor walk out at Trent Bridge to continue a partnership which went on to a new Ashes record opening stand.

England won the toss and batted on a grey day – the sunshine of the first two Tests having temporarily disappeared. They were soon in trouble, Lawson bowling Gooch and then getting Robinson lbw for a duck which lasted 15 minutes. Curtis and Smith saw the innings to lunch at 48 for two, England at one time taking more than an hour for two runs. Curtis (11) was out to Lawson soon after lunch, whereupon Smith and Gower played the best cricket of the innings. They added 75 before the elegant Gower completely misjudged a hook against Hohns and was lbw. Hohns then bowled Botham for a duck, Botham clearly trying to hit the spinner for six and missing. Two more wickets tumbled and England were 158 for seven before the second worthwhile stand of the innings took place. Smith and Foster (39) added 74 before Lawson got

Right: Geoff Marsh returns to the pavilion at the end of his knock of 138; the stand had reached 329, six more than Hobbs and Rhodes made at Melbourne in 1911–12. *Below:* Gower leans on Smith (as he did metaphorically all through the series) as England await the next man in.

Above: Not exactly Keats, but a decorative band of Aussies aren't worried about that.
Right: Taylor and Marsh, the record-breakers, with some of the well-earned 'gold award'.
Below: A determined looking Merv Hughes after bowling Smith in the second innings.
Bottom: No need for the umpire to raise a finger as the Aussies dance a jig. Moxon is caught off Alderman: 1 for one wicket.

Above: Geoff Lawson bowling in the fifth Test. His 29 wickets in the series were a valuable contribution to the victory effort. *Below:* Mark Taylor takes a break during his 554-minute innings.

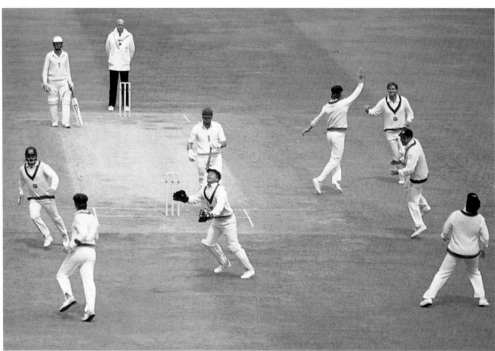

both Foster and Fraser, leaving Smith to be last out for 143, his first Test century. England were all out for 260, with Lawson taking six for 72.

England's total was soon put into perspective as Marsh and Taylor produced their usual sound opening. The two made the first century opening stand of the series, taking the score to 135 before Botham claimed Marsh who was caught behind for 47. Taylor, who had been outscoring Marsh, left seven overs later when he was stumped off Emburey for 85. When Fraser bowled Boon for 12, England were fighting back at 154 for three, but Border and Jones played attacking cricket and took the score to 219 by the close.

Australia coasted into the lead on Saturday, the third day, and were 14 ahead when Botham bowled Jones for 69. The man who replaced him was the prolific Waugh, who proceeded to bat with freedom while Border, still single-mindedly pursuing the Ashes, decided to play an anchor role. It was a surprise when Border (80) eventually groped outside the off stump and was caught behind the wicket. He had hoisted his aggregate of Test runs to 8,081, overtaking Sobers and now standing third to Gavaskar and Boycott in the all-time list. On his dismissal, Border could reflect that Australia were over 100 ahead, but Healy was out first ball, Foster being on a hat-trick which Waugh foiled. Australia were finally out for 447, Waugh being out for a second time in the series. He made 92, but his average dropped to 242.50!

England began their second innings early on the fourth morning 187 behind, with the prospect of needing to bat for at least a day and a half to save the Ashes. They began in a totally dispirited manner, and soon after lunch were 59 for six, with all six main batsmen out. There then came a brave flourish from Russell and Emburey, who stayed together until heavy rain ended play for the day at tea time when England were 123 for six.

Next morning, one possible reason for England's lack of spirit became known. Sixteen English cricketers had signed for a rebel tour to South Africa, and nine of them were players who had taken part in the current series. They were putting their Test careers on ice for four or five years – some like Emburey and Foster probably ending their Test careers altogether. Foster and Gatting were likely to be the two most missed in the immediate future.

As if released from tension now that the secret was out, Russell and Emburey continued to resist stoutly on the last day and, with rain always likely to return, the Australians grew more and more frustrated and anxious. The innings defeat was avoided at 187 and 200 was passed – but only just. Emburey was finally bowled by

Allan Border with some of the material rewards for winning — an envelope containing a cheque.

Alderman for 64, the seventh-wicket stand of 142 failing by one to equal England's record against Australia, set at Sydney in 1911–12. Russell continued bravely on, and with the three tail-enders staying with him for another hour and a half he finally made 128 not out for his first century in first-class cricket. It was his fifth Test, and significantly his previous highest score (94) also came in a Test.

Australia needed only 78 to win and symbolically the sun began to shine brightly again as they made their way calmly to the target. Taylor and Marsh were not to make them, for Marsh was out at 62 and it was Boon who made the hit which won back the Ashes. It was the first time Australia had regained the Ashes in England since Woodfull's team had done so after the 'bodyline' tour in 1934. It was Australia's 100th victory over England in the 267th match – England had won 88.

Left: Ever-present wicket-keeper Jack Russell takes a high return in the sixth Test at the Oval.
Below: Chin Chin. Gooch and Gower give it all a bit of thought.

England needed to make changes for the fifth Test at Trent Bridge after the announcement of the names of the players for the rebel South African tour. Two new Test players were selected in the 12 named: batsman Mike Atherton and fast bowler Devon Malcolm. Three previous Test players made reappearances: Martyn Moxon, Gladstone Small and veteran Eddie Hemmings. Two days before the Test, Gladstone Small withdrew injured and Greg Thomas was chosen in his place. On the morning of the match Thomas was the one to be omitted.

Australia were again unchanged – although anybody looking at the close of play score on the first day would know only that the openers were the same, because Mark Taylor and Geoff Marsh so dominated proceedings that they batted all day. Without interruptions for wickets, England bowled 102 overs and, as the day progressed, so the batting records began to go. A few edges early on and some lusty lbw appeals were all that disturbed the batsmen as they went serenely on, first passing Australia's previous highest

Gladstone Small, not a noted batsman, in his only Test innings of the series scored 59 at number 9 and saved the follow-on.

opening stand in England (201), then the highest in Australia (244) – both held by Bobby Simpson (the current tour coach) and Bill Lawry. At the close the pair had put on 301 without being parted.

Next day came the biggest prize of all – the record opening stand in Ashes history, which was previously 323 between Jack Hobbs and Wilfred Rhodes, scored in Melbourne in 1911–12. The stand ended soon afterwards, at 329, with Marsh caught by Botham off Cook for 138. Taylor went on to pass 200 by square-cutting Hemmings for four, and eventually reached 219 before being stumped off Cook. Australia ended the day at 560 for five, which was a disappointing total after the first day's run spree, but Border was showing his desire to grind every run and advantage out of his side's supremacy. He himself was batting at the close, and he continued into the third day before declaring at 602 for six.

The Australian total was seen in perspective after Alderman's first over: Moxon caught at slip off the fourth ball and Atherton lbw two balls later, both for ducks. One run for two wickets became 37 for four, and it took Robin Smith again to lead any resistance there was. His 101 at least kept England at the crease for the rest of the day. But only just – the last wicket fell on the Monday morning and England were asked to follow on.

With Botham hurt – he had resisted for nearly an hour on Saturday with a badly dislocated finger – the batting order was revised. Gower opened and Moxon dropped down to give the middle order substance, but the story was the same. Atherton averted a first-Test pair, and made top score of 47, and Hemmings made a popular 35, but England were bowled out for 167. Botham did not bother to make the futile gesture of coming in to bat. The match ended a day early, and a thunderstorm flooded the ground as if to emphasise the depth of England's fall.

The despairing England selectors named 13 players for the sixth and last test at The Oval. Botham was out injured but, despite tabloid newspaper speculation, the skipper, Gower, had not resigned. The other established member of the side, Gooch, returned after having requested a rest for the fifth Test while he sought to recover his form. Gower and wicket-keeper Russell, perhaps England's outstanding success of the series, were thus the only two original selections for the first Test to have retained this status throughout the series. Apart from Russell, only Smith, Lamb and Fraser had advanced their reputations.

Two newcomers brought in were the Essex batsmen John Stephenson and

Above left: Terry Alderman during his 5-wicket haul. *Above right:* A wicket for Trevor Hohns as Derek Pringle is out. *Left:* England's debutant bowler Alan Igglesden fails to stop an off-drive of his own bowling. *Below:* England's other new player, John Stephenson. *Opposite:* Allan Border with the Ashes.

Left: The well-known contributor to this book (he also does a little umpiring), Dickie Bird, in action. *Below:* Steve Waugh, who scored 393 runs before being dismissed, an Ashes record. *Right:* Michael Atherton, Test debutant in 1989.

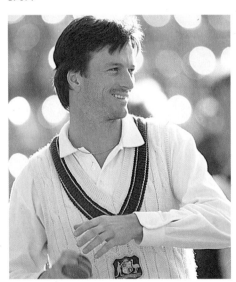

Nasser Hussain, both Durham University graduates. They replaced Curtis and Moxon. Small, recovered from injury, was again selected, and Capel replaced Botham.

The days before the Test produced their usual mishaps, however. Malcolm pulled a muscle and was replaced by Philip DeFreitas, who had been one of those who signed for the rebel South African tour, but who, together with the other black player in the party, Roland Butcher, had withdrawn after second thoughts. Having expressed his desire to play, DeFreitas himself withdrew through injury next day, as did Fraser. The likeliest replacement, Greg Thomas, ruled himself out by announcing that he had filled the vacancy in the South African rebel party. Called into the Test party were Kent's 6ft 6in Alan Igglesden, and Derek Pringle, one of the most picked and discarded of Test cricketers. Both played, and it was Hussain and Hemmings, the youngest and oldest of the party, who were the two discarded on the morning. The England selectors must have envied their Australian counterparts. Australia were again unchanged, having made only one change in the whole series.

Border won the toss and batted on a good pitch. At 149 for three in mid-afternoon honours were fairly even, but then Dean Jones joined Border and played another of the memorable innings with which the series had been studded. By the close he had made 114 not out from only 141 balls, Border was 66 and the total was 325 for three. England had tried seven bowlers.

The bowlers did better next day, when the glorious sunshine gave way to thick cloud cover, and Australia were out for a 'mere' 468, but in the new conditions this looked very good, especially when Gooch was lbw to Alderman for 0 – his fifth lbw in eight innings. At 1 for one the rains came.

Rain curtailed the Saturday play, and in the intervals England lost wickets steadily: 124 for six was not a score to enjoy over the weekend.

Monday was a better day for England, however, as the follow-on was averted, first by Gower batting at his silkiest for 79 and then by a ninth-wicket stand of 73 from Small (58) and Cook (31). Australia were 87 for one at the close, still hoping for a record-breaking five Test victories in England.

They did their best on the last day, too. Taylor (48) took his aggregate for the series to 839 – only Bradman and Hammond have scored more in a Test series – and a lunch-time declaration at 219 for four left England a purely notional 403 to win in a minimum 67 overs. Even now Border was being ultra-cautious.

He might have regretted this caution as wickets fell regularly: 67 for four became 138 for five after a little stand, but only Smith showed the necessary determination and technique to bat to the end. He was 77 not out and there were still 21 overs left when bad light eventually ended the series with England 143 for five.

It had been a resounding series victory for Australia – one of the most one-sided ever played.

1989 64th Series Aus 4, Eng 0, Drawn 2

1 HEADINGLEY Australia won by 210 runs
Australia 601–7 dec (S R Waugh 177, M A Taylor 136, D M Jones 79, M G Hughes 71, A R Border 66) and 230–3 dec (M A Taylor 60, A R Border 60)
England 430 (A J Lamb 125, K J Barnett 80, R A Smith 66, T M Alderman 5–107) and 191 (G A Gooch 68, T M Alderman 5–44)

2 LORD'S Australia won by 6 wkts
England 286 (R C Russell 64, G A Gooch 60, D I Gower 57, M G Hughes 4–71) and 359 (D I Gower 106, R A Smith 96, T M Alderman 6–128)
Australia 528 (S R Waugh 152, D C Boon 94, G F Lawson 74, M A Taylor 62, J E Emburey 4–88) and 119–4 (D C Boon 58)

3 EDGBASTON Match Drawn
Australia 424 (D M Jones 157, A R C Fraser 4–63) and 158–2 (M A Taylor 51)
England 242

4 OLD TRAFFORD Australia won by 9 wkts
England 260 (R A Smith 143, G F Lawson 6–72) and 264 (R C Russell 128, J E Emburey 64, T M Alderman 5–66)
Australia 447 (S R Waugh 92, M A Taylor 85, A R Border 80, D M Jones 69) and 81–1

5 TRENT BRIDGE Australia won by an innings and 180 runs
Australia 602–6 dec (M A Taylor 219, G R Marsh 138, D C Boon 73, A R Border 65)
England 255 (R A Smith 101, T M Alderman 5–69) and 167

6 THE OVAL Match Drawn
Australia 468 (D M Jones 122, A R Border 76, M A Taylor 71, D R Pringle 4–70) and 219–4 dec (A R Border 51, D M Jones 50)
England 285 (D I Gower 79, G C Small 59, T M Alderman 5–66) and 143–5 (R A Smith 77)

1989 Averages

Batting	I	No	Runs	HS	Avge
S.R. Waugh (A)	8	4	506	177*	126.50
M.A. Taylor (A)	11	1	839	219	83.90
A.R. Border (A)	9	3	442	80	73.66
D.M. Jones (A)	9	1	566	157	70.75
R.A. Smith (E)	10	1	553	143	61.44
D.C. Boon (A)	11	3	442	94	55.25
R.C. Russell (E)	11	3	314	128*	39.25
D.I. Gower (E)	11	0	383	106	34.81
G.R. Marsh (A)	11	0	347	138	31.54

Bowling	O	M	Runs	W	Avge	BB
T.M. Alderman (A)	269.2	68	712	41	17.36	6–128
G.F. Lawson (A)	277.1	68	791	29	27.27	6–72
M.G. Hughes (A)	189.2	41	615	19	32.36	4–71
N.A. Foster (E)	167	42	421	12	35.08	3–39

Below: Spectacular dismissal. Smith bowled by Lawson at the Oval.

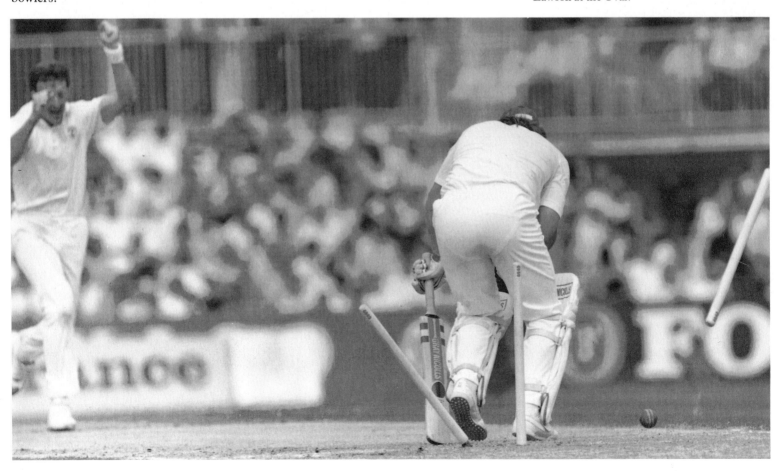

Dickie Bird warns Merv Hughes for bowling too many short-pitched balls at the Oval. Big Merv doesn't look too impressed.

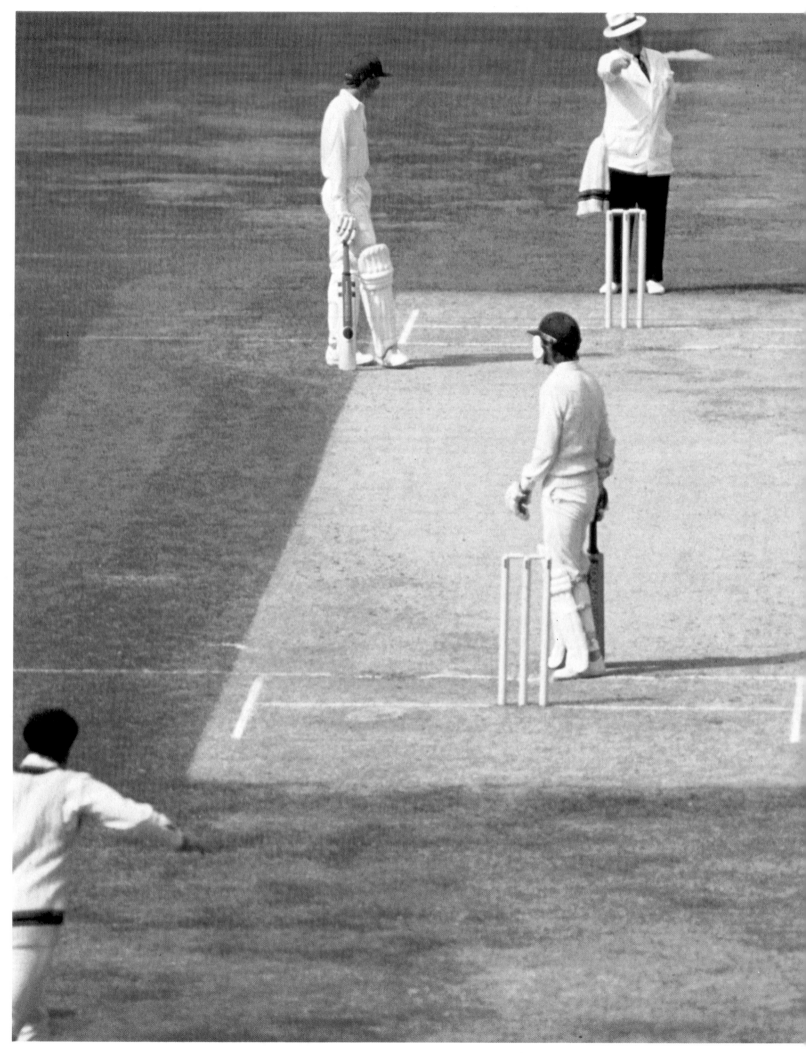

Terry Alderman takes Russell's wicket at the Oval.

ENGLAND v AUSTRALIA SERIES

Captains

Season	England	Australia	T	E	A	D
1876–77	James Lillywhite	D. W. Gregory	2	1	1	0
1878–79	Lord Harris	D. W. Gregory	1	0	1	0
1880	Lord Harris	W. L. Murdoch	1	1	0	0
1881–82	A. Shaw	W. L. Murdoch	4	0	2	2
1882	A. N. Hornby	W. L. Murdoch	1	0	1	0

THE ASHES
Captains

Season	England	Australia	T	E	A	D	Held by
1882–83	Hon. Ivo Bligh	W. L. Murdoch	4*	2	2	0	E
1884	Lord Harris[1]	W. L. Murdoch	3	1	0	2	E
1884–85	A. Shrewsbury	T. Horan[2]	5	3	2	0	E
1886	A. G. Steel	H. J. H. Scott	3	3	0	0	E
1886–87	A. Shrewsbury	P. S. McDonnell	2	2	0	0	E
1887–88	W. W. Read	P. S. McDonnell	1	1	0	0	E
1888	W. G. Grace[3]	P. S. McDonnell	3	2	1	0	E
1890†	W. G. Grace	W. L. Murdoch	2	2	0	0	E
1891–92	W. G. Grace	J. McC. Blackham	3	1	2	0	A
1893	W. G. Grace[4]	J. McC. Blackham	3	1	0	2	E
1894–95	A. E. Stoddart	G. Giffen[5]	5	3	2	0	E
1896	W. G. Grace	G. H. S. Trott	3	2	1	0	E
1897–98	A. E. Stoddart[6]	G. H. S. Trott	5	1	4	0	A
1899	A. C. MacLaren[7]	J. Darling	5	0	1	4	A

Cowdrey, Michael Colin

Cowdrey was born on Christmas Eve, 1932, at Ootacamund, India. A schoolboy prodigy, he played for Tonbridge School at Lord's when he was 13, and made his debut for Kent in 1950. A middle-order right-hand batsman, his solid strength and timing sent the ball to the boundary effortlessly. He played for England from 1954–55. His total of 114 Test appearances was a world record until passed by Gavaskar. On 27 of these he was captain. He scored 7,624 runs, average 44.06. He usually fielded at slip, and his 120 catches was also a Test record.

Previous pages: A record-breaking Test wicket. Neil Hawke looks round to see Colin Cowdrey catch him in the slips in the fifth Test at the Oval in 1964. It was Fred Trueman's 300th Test wicket.

Below: David Gower drives on his way to 136 in the second Australia v England Test at Perth in 1986–87.

THE ASHES
Captains

Season	England	Australia	T	E	A	D	Held by
1901–02	A. C. MacLaren	J. Darling[8]	5	1	4	0	A
1902	A. C. MacLaren	J. Darling	5	1	2	2	A
1903–04	P. F. Warner	M. A. Noble	5	3	2	0	E
1905	Hon. F. S. Jackson	J. Darling	5	2	0	3	E
1907–08	A. O. Jones[9]	M. A. Noble	5	1	4	0	A
1909	A. C. MacLaren	M. A. Noble	5	1	2	2	A
1911–12	J. W. H. T. Douglas	C. Hill	5	4	1	0	E
1912	C. B. Fry	S. E. Gregory	3	1	0	2	E
1920–21	J. W. H. T. Douglas	W. W. Armstrong	5	0	5	0	A
1921	Hon. L. H. Tennyson[10]	W. W. Armstrong	5	0	3	2	A
1924–25	A. E. R. Gilligan	H. L. Collins	5	1	4	0	A
1926	A. W. Carr[11]	H. L. Collins[12]	5	1	0	4	E
1928–29	A. P. F. Chapman[13]	J. Ryder	5	4	1	0	E
1930	A. P. F. Chapman[14]	W. M. Woodfull	5	1	2	2	A
1932–33	D. R. Jardine	W. M. Woodfull	5	4	1	0	E
1934	R. E. S. Wyatt[15]	W. M. Woodfull	5	1	2	2	A
1936–37	G. O. Allen	D. G. Bradman	5	2	3	0	A
1938†	W. R. Hammond	D. G. Bradman	4	1	1	2	A
1946–47	W. R. Hammond[16]	D. G. Bradman	5	0	3	2	A
1948	N. W. D. Yardley	D. G. Bradman	5	0	4	1	A
1950–51	F. R. Brown	A. L. Hassett	5	1	4	0	A
1953	L. Hutton	A. L. Hassett	5	1	0	4	E
1954–55	L. Hutton	I. W. Johnson[17]	5	3	1	1	E
1956	P. B. H. May	I. W. Johnson	5	2	1	2	E
1958–59	P. B. H. May	R. Benaud	5	0	4	1	A
1961	P. B. H. May[18]	R. Benaud[19]	5	1	2	2	A
1962–63	E. R. Dexter	R. Benaud	5	1	1	3	A
1964	E. R. Dexter	R. B. Simpson	5	0	1	4	A
1965–66	M. J. K. Smith	R. B. Simpson[20]	5	1	1	3	A
1968	M. C. Cowdrey[21]	W. M. Lawry[22]	5	1	1	3	A
1970–71†	R. Illingworth	W. M. Lawry[23]	6	2	0	4	E
1972	R. Illingworth	I. M. Chappell	5	2	2	1	E
1974–75	M. H. Denness[24]	I. M. Chappell	6	1	4	1	A
1975	A. W. Greig[25]	I. M. Chappell	4	0	1	3	A
1976–77‡	A. W. Greig	G. S. Chappell	1	0	1	0	—
1977	J. M. Brearley	G. S. Chappell	5	3	0	2	E
1978–79	J. M. Brearley	G. N. Yallop	6	5	1	0	E
1979–80‡	J. M. Brearley	G. S. Chappell	3	0	3	0	—
1980‡	I. T. Botham	G. S. Chappell	1	0	0	1	—
1981	J. M. Brearley[26]	K. J. Hughes	6	3	1	2	E
1982–83	R. G. D. Willis	G. S. Chappell	5	1	2	2	A
1985	D. I. Gower	A. R. Border	6	3	1	2	E
1986–87	M. W. Gatting	A. R. Border	5	2	1	2	E
1987–88‡	M. W. Gatting	A. R. Border	1	0	0	1	—
1989	D. I. Gower	A. R. Border	6	0	4	2	A

	T	E	A	D
In Australia	140	51	67	22
In England	129	37	34	58
TOTALS	**269**	**88**	**101**	**80**

* The Ashes were awarded in 1882–83 following a series of three matches which England won 2–1. A fourth unofficial match was won by Australia.

† The matches at Manchester in 1890 and 1938 and at Melborne (Third Test) in 1970–71 were abandoned without a ball being bowled and are therefore not included.

‡ The Ashes were not at stake.

Note: The following deputised for the official captain or were appointed captain for only part of the series:

[1] A. N. Hornby (First). [2] W. L. Murdoch (First), H. H. Massie (Third), J. McC. Blackham (Fourth). [3] A. G. Steel (First). [4] A. E. Stoddart (First). [5] J. McC. Blackham (First). [6] A. C. MacLaren (First, Second and Fifth). [7] W. G. Grace (First). [8] H. Trumble (Fourth and Fifth). [9] F. L. Lane (First, Second and Third). [10] J. W. H. T. Douglas (First and Second). [11] A. P. F. Chapman (Fifth). [12] W. Bardsley (Third and Fourth). [13] J. C. White (Fifth). [14] R. E. S. Wyatt (Fifth). [15] C. F. Walters (First). [16] N. W. D. Yardley (Fifth). [17] A. R. Morris (Second). [18] M. C. Cowdrey (First and Second). [19] R. N. Harvey (Second). [20] B. C. Booth (First and Third). [21] T. W. Graveney (Fourth). [22] B. N. Jarman (Fourth). [23] I. M. Chappell (Seventh). [24] J. H. Edrich (Fourth). [25] M. H. Denness (First). [26] I. T. Botham (First and Second).

Below: The first Ashes Test match after the Second World War. Sydney Barnes and George Tribe dive at a close catch offered by Hammond at Brisbane.

Sir Don Bradman at the match between the Prime Minister's XI and the MCC at Canberra in 1962–63. Sir Don had, of course, long since retired.

HIGHEST INNINGS TOTALS

For England in England: 903–7 dec. at The Oval, 1938
     in Australia: 636 at Sydney, 1928–29
For Australia in England: 729–6 dec. at Lord's, 1930
     in Australia: 659–8 dec. at Sydney, 1946–47

LOWEST INNINGS TOTALS

For England in England: 52 at The Oval, 1948
     in Australia: 45 at Sydney, 1886–87
For Australia in England: 36 at Birmingham, 1902
     in Australia: 42 at Sydney, 1887–88

Below: Walter Hammond leading his team out at Trent Bridge against Australia in 1938. The wicket-keeper is Leslie Ames. Kenneth Farnes and Hedley Verity, following, both lost their lives in the war which followed.

Above: Bradman's return to England after the Second World War was very much a question of carrying on where he had left off, by making a century in the first match at Worcester. Here he guides a ball through the slips.

Compton, Denis Charles Scott

Born on 23 May 1918, Compton became a leading cricketer and footballer, although his soccer caps were unofficial war-time ones. He was a brilliant right-hand batsman and occasional left-arm slow bowler. He made his debut for Middlesex in 1936, and his Test debut in 1937 as a 19-year-old. His cavalier style, and his speciality, the leg sweep, made him the most popular English batsman of the immediate post-war years. In the 1947 season he established a new record aggregate of runs (3,816) and centuries (18). His later career was handicapped by a knee injury. In 78 Tests he made 5,807 runs, average 50.06. He also took 25 wickets, average 56.40.

Rhodes, Wilfred

Rhodes was born on 29 October 1877 at Kirkheaton, Yorkshire, and first played for the county in 1898. He was a slow left-arm bowler and made such a quick impact that he played for England in 1899. During his career, his right-hand batting developed to such an extent that after beginning at number eleven for England he eventually opened with Hobbs and in 1911–12 at Melbourne they made the highest opening stand in Ashes Tests of 323. As a bowler, Rhodes took more first-class wickets than anybody else: 4,204. He is the only man over 4,000. His Test career lasted to 1929–30, when he played in the West Indies aged 52 years, 165 days, the oldest Test player. His Test career spanned 30 years, another record. In 58 Tests he scored 2,325 runs, average 30.19, and took 127 wickets, average 26.96. He died in Branksome, Dorset, on 8 July 1973, aged 95.

HIGHEST INDIVIDUAL SCORES

FOR ENGLAND

364	**L. Hutton,** The Oval, 1938
287	**R. E. Foster,** Sydney, 1903–04
256	**K. F. Barrington,** Manchester, 1964
251	**W. R. Hammond,** Sydney, 1928–29
240	**W. R. Hammond,** Lord's, 1938
231*	**W. R. Hammond,** Sydney, 1936–37
216*	**E. Paynter,** Nottingham,1938
215	**D. I. Gower,** Birmingham, 1985
200	**W. R. Hammond,** Melbourne, 1928–196 29
194	**G. A. Gooch,**The Oval, 1985
188	**H. Sutcliffe,**Sydney, 1932–33
187	**M. H. Denness,**Melbourne, 1974–75
187	**J. B. Hobbs,** Adelaide, 1911–12
185	**M. Leyland,** The Oval, 1938
184	**R. W. Barber,** Sydney, 1965–66
182*	**D. C. S. Compton,** Nottingham, 1948
180	**C. P. Mead,** The Oval, 1921
179	**E. R. Dexter,** Birmingham, 1961
178	**W. Rhodes,** Melbourne, 1911–12
177	**J. B. Hobbs,** Melbourne, 1911–12
176	**W. R. Hammond,** Adelaide, 1928-29
175	**H. Sutcliffe,** Melbourne, 1924–25
175	**K. S. Ranjitsinhji,** Sydney, 1897–98
175	**J. H. Edrich,** Lord's, 1975
	R. T. Robinson, Leeds, 1985

FOR AUSTRALIA

334	**D. G. Bradman,** Leeds, 1930
311	**R. B. Simpson,** Manchester, 1964
307	**R. M. Cowper,** Melbourne, 1956–66
304	**D. G. Bradman,** Leeds, 1934
270	**D. G. Bradman,** Melbourne, 1936–37
266	**W. H. Ponsford,** The Oval, 1934
254	**D. G. Bradman,** Lord's 1930
244	**D. G. Bradman,** The Oval, 1934
234	**S. G. Barnes,** Sydney, 1946–47
234	**D. G. Bradman,** Sydney, 1946–47
232	**D. G. Bradman,** The Oval, 1930
232	**S. J. McCabe,** Nottingham, 1938
225	**R. B. Simpson,** Adelaide, 1965–66
219	**M. A. Taylor,** Nottingham, 1989
212	**D. G. Bradman,** Adelaide, 1936–37
211	**W. L. Murdoch,** The Oval, 1884
207	**K. R. Stackpole,** Brisbane, 1970–71
206*	**W. A. Brown,** Lord's, 1938
206	**A. R. Morris,** Adelaide, 1950–51
201	**S. E. Gregory,** Sydney, 1894–95
201*	**J. Ryder,** Adelaide, 1924–25
196	**A. R. Morris,**The Oval, 1948
196	**A. R. Border,** Lord's, 1985
193*	**W. Bardsley,** Lord's, 1926
192	**I. M. Chappell,** The Oval, 1975
188	**C. Hill,** Melbourne, 1897–98
187*	**S. J. McCabe,** Sydney, 1932–33
187	**D. G. Bradman,** Brisbane, 1946–47
185*	**V. T. Trumper,** Sydney, 1903–04
184*	**D. M. Jones,** Sydney, 1986–87
184*	**D. C. Boon,** Sydney, 1987–88
182	**A. R. Morris,** Leeds, 1948
181	**W. H. Ponsford,** Leeds, 1934
181	**P. J. Burge,** The Oval, 1961
178	**J. Darling,** Adelaide, 1897–98
177*	**S. R. Waugh,** Leeds, 1989

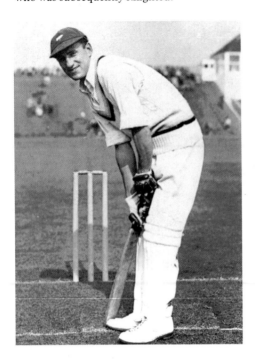

Below: Len Hutton, a great England opener who was subsequently knighted.

RECORD PARTNERSHIPS FOR EACH WICKET

For England

323 for 1st	J. B. Hobbs and W. Rhodes at Melbourne	1911–12
382 for 2nd†	L. Hutton and M. Leyland at The Oval	1938
262 for 3rd	W. R. Hammond and D. R. Jardine at Adelaide	1928–29
222 for 4th	W. R. Hammond and E. Paynter at Lord's	1938
206 for 5th	E. Paynter and D. C. S. Compton at Nottingham	1938
215 for 6th	L. Hutton and J. Hardstaff jun. at The Oval	1938
	G. Boycott and A. P. E. Knott at Nottingham	1977
143 for 7th	F. E. Woolley and J. Vine at Sydney	1911–12
124 for 8th	E. H. Hendren and H. Larwood at Brisbane	1928–29
151 for 9th	W. H. Scotton and W. W. Read at The Oval	1884
130 for 10th†	R. E. Foster and W. Rhodes at Sydney	1903–04

For Australia

329 for 1st	G. R. Marsh and M. A. Taylor at Nottingham	1989
451 for 2nd†	W. H. Ponsford and D. G. Bradman at The Oval	1934
276 for 3rd	D. G. Bradman and A. L. Hassett at Brisbane	1946–47
388 for 4th†	W. H. Ponsford and D. G. Bradman at Leeds	1934
405 for 5th‡	S. G. Barnes and D. G. Bradman at Sydney	1946–47
346 for 6th†	J. H. Fingleton and D. G. Bradman at Melbourne	1936–37
165 for 7th	C. Hill and H. Trumble at Melbourne	1897–98
243 for 8th†	R. J. Hartigan and C. Hill at Adelaide	1907–08
154 for 9th†	S. E. Gregory and J. McC. Blackham at Sydney	1894–95
127 for 10th†	J. M. Taylor and A. A. Mailey at Sydney	1924–25

† Denotes record partnership against all countries.
‡Record fifth-wicket partnership in first-class cricket.

MOST RUNS IN A SERIES

England in England	732 (average 81.33)	D. I. Gower	1985
England in Australia	905 (average 113.12)	W. R. Hammond	1928–29
Australia in England	974 (average 139.14)	D. G. Bradman	1930
Australia in Australia	810 (average 90.00)	D. G. Bradman	1936–37

Above: Colin Cowdrey at Trent Bridge in 1964 hooking a boundary. Until passed by Gavaskar, Cowdrey's 114 Test appearances was a record.

TEN WICKETS OR MORE IN A MATCH

For England

19–90 (9–37, 10–53)	**J. C. Laker,** Manchester	1956
15–104 (7–61, 8–43)	**H. Verity,** Lord's	1934
15–124 (7–56, 8–68)	**W. Rhodes,** Melbourne	1903–04
14–99 (7–55, 7–44)	**A. V. Bedser,** Nottingham	1953
14–102 (7–28, 7–74)	**W. Bates,** Melbourne	1882–83
13–163 (6–42, 7–121)	**S. F. Barnes,** Melbourne	1901–02
13–244 (7–168, 6–76)	**T. Richardson,** Manchester	1896
13–256 (5–130, 8–126)	**J. C. White,** Adelaide	1928–29
12–102 (6–50, 6–52)	**F. Martin,** The Oval	1890
12–104 (7–36, 5–68)	**G. A. Lohmann,** The Oval	1886
12–136 (6–49, 6–87)	**J. Briggs,** Adelaide	1891–92
11-68 (7–31, 4–37)	**R. Peel,** Manchester	1888
11–74 (5–29, 6–45)	**J. Briggs,** Lord's	1886
11–76 (6–48, 5–28)	**W. H. Lockwood,** Manchester	1902
11–88 (5–58, 6–30)	**F. S. Trueman,** Leeds	1961
11–107 (6–44, 5–58)	**C. Blyth,** Birmingham	1909
11–113 (5-58, 6–55)	**J. C. Laker,** Leeds	1956
11–173 (6–39, 5–134)	**T. Richardson,** Lord's	1896
11–176 (6–78, 5–98)	**I. T. Botham,** Perth	1979–80
11–215 (7–113, 4–102)	**D. L. Underwood,** Adelaide	1974–75
11–228 (6–130, 5–98)	**M. W. Tate,** Sydney	1924–25
10–49 (5–29, 5–20)	**F. E. Woolley,** The Oval	1912
10–57 (6–41, 4–16)	**W. Voce,** Brisbane	1936–37
10–58 (5–18, 5–40)	**R. Peel,** Sydney	1887–88
10–60 (6–41, 4–19)	**J. T. Hearne,** The Oval	1896
10–82 (4–37, 6–45)	**D. L. Underwood,** Leeds	1972
10–87 (8–35, 2–52)	**G. A. Lohmann,** Sydney	1886–87
10–104 (6–77, 4–27)	**R. M. Ellison,** Birmingham	1985
10–105 (5–46, 5–59)	**A. V. Bedser,** Melbourne	1950–51
10–124 (5–96, 5–28)	**H. Larwood,** Sydney	1932–33
10–130 (4–45, 6–85)	**F. H. Tyson,** Sydney	1954–55
10–142 (8–58, 2–84)	**G. A. Lohmann,** Sydney	1891–92
10–148 (5–34, 5–114)	**J. Briggs,** The Oval	1893
10–156 (5–49, 5–107)	**T. Richardson,** Manchester	1893
10–179 (5–102, 5–77)	**K. Farnes,** Nottingham	1934
10–204 (8–94, 2–110)	**T. Richardson,** Sydney	1897–98
10–253 (6–125, 4–128)	**I. T. Botham,** The Oval	1981

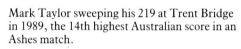

Mark Taylor sweeping his 219 at Trent Bridge in 1989, the 14th highest Australian score in an Ashes match.

For Australia

16–137 (8–84, 8–53)	**R. A. L. Massie,** Lords	1972
14–90 (7–46, 7–44)	**F. R. Spofforth,** The Oval	1882
13–77 (7–17, 6–60)	**M. A. Noble,** Melbourne	1901–02
13–110 (6–48, 7–62)	**F. R. Spofforth,** Melbourne	1878–79
13–236 (4–115, 9–121)	**A. A. Mailey,** Melbourne	1920–21
12–87 (5–44, 7–43)	**C. T. B. Turner,** Sydney	1887–88
12–89 (6–59, 6–30)	**H. Trumble,** The Oval	1896
12–173 (8–65, 4–108)	**H. Trumble,** The Oval	1902
12–175 (5–85, 7–90)	**H. V. Hordern,** Sydney	1911–12
11–82 (5–45, 6–37)	**C. V. Grimmett,** Sydney	1924–25
11–85 (7–58, 4–27)	**C. G. Macartney,** Leeds	1909
11–103 (5–51, 6–52)	**M. A. Noble,** Sheffield	1902
11–117 (4–73, 7–44)	**F. R. Spofforth,** Sydney	1882–83
11–129 (4–75, 7–54)	**W. J. O'Reilly,** Nottingham	1934
11–134 (6–47, 5–87)	**G. F. Lawson,** Brisbane	1982–83
11–138 (6–60, 5–78)	**D. K. Lillee,** Melbourne	1979–80
11–159 (7–89, 4–70)	**D. K. Lillee,** The Oval	1981
11–165 (7–68, 4–97)	**G. E. Palmer,** Sydney	1881–82
11–165 (6–26, 5–139)	**D. K. Lillee,** Melbourne	1976–77
10–63 (5–27, 5–36)	**C. T. B. Turner,** Lord's	1888
10–66 (5–30, 5–36)	**R. M. Hogg,** Melbourne	1978–79
10–122 (5–66, 5–56)	**W. J. O'Reilly,** Leeds	1938
10–122 (5–65, 5–57)	**R. M. Hogg,** Perth	1978–79
10–126 (7–65, 3–61)	**G. E. Palmer,** Melbourne	1882–83
10–128 (4–75, 6–53)	**H. Trumble,** Manchester	1902
10–129 (5–63, 5–66)	**W. J. O'Reilly,** Melbourne	1932–33
10–144 (4–54, 6–90)	**F. R. Spofforth,** Sydney	1884–85
10–151 (5–107, 5–44)	**T. M. Alderman,** Leeds	1989
10–152 (5–72, 5–80)	**K. R. Miller,** Lord's	1956
10–160 (4–88, 6–72)	**G. Giffen,** Sydney	1891–92
10–161 (5–95, 5–66)	**H. V. Hordern,** Sydney	1911–12
10–164 (7–88, 3–76)	**E. Jones,** Lord's	1889
10–181 (5–58, 5–123)	**D. K. Lillee,** The Oval	1972
10–201 (5–107, 5–94)	**C. V. Grimmett,** Nottingham	1930
10–239 (4–129, 6–110)	**L. O'B. Fleetwood-Smith,** Adelaide	1936–37
10–302 (5–160, 5–142)	**A. A. Mailey,** Adelaide	1920–21

Hammond, Walter Reginald

Hammond was born on 19 June 1903 at Dover, Kent, but played for Gloucestershire, making his debut in 1920. He became the leading English batsman of his day, particularly strong on the off-side. He was also a right-arm medium-pace bowler and a brilliant specialist slip fielder. He headed the English batting averages for eight successive seasons from 1933, a record. He made his Test debut in 1927–28. In 85 Tests he scored 7,249 runs, average 58.45, and took 83 wickets at 37.80. He also held 110 catches, at the time a record. In 1932–33 he scored 336 not out at Auckland against New Zealand, which set a new Test record. He turned amateur in 1938 and captained England in his last 20 Tests, but he was not the same player in his three post-war series. Had he not played after the war, his Test average would have been over 60. He died in Durban, South Africa, on 1 July 1965.

HAT-TRICKS

F. R. Spofforth (Australia), Melbourne, 1878–79
W. Bates (England), Melbourne, 1882–83
J. Briggs (England), Sydney, 1891–92
J. T. Hearne (England), Leeds, 1899
H. Trumble (Australia), Melbourne, 1901–02
H. Trumble (Australia), Melbourne, 1903–04

Left and below: Rodney Marsh, the great Australian wicket-keeper, announced his retirement after the Pakistan tour of Australia in 1983–84. He had a record number of Test victims.

TWO CENTURIES IN A MATCH

For England
176	127	**H. Sutcliffe,** Melbourne,	1924–25
119*	177	**W. R. Hammond,** Adelaide,	1928–29
147	103*	**D. C. S. Compton,** Adelaide,	1946–47

For Australia
136	130	**W. Bardsley,** The Oval, 1909	
122	124*	**A. R. Morris,** Adelaide,	1946–47

SCORERS OF OVER 2,000 RUNS

	T	I	NO	R	HI	Avge
D. G. Bradman	37	63	7	5,028	334	89.78
J. B. Hobbs	41	71	4	3,636	187	54.26
G. Boycott	38	71	9	2,945	191	47.50
D. I. Gower	37	67	3	2,862	215	44.71
W. R. Hammond	31	58	3	2,852	251	51.85
A. R. Border	36	66	17	2,834	196	57.83
H. Sutcliffe	27	46	5	2,741	194	66.85
C. Hill	41	76	1	2,660	188	35.46
J. H. Edrich	32	57	3	2,644	175	48.96
G. S. Chappell	35	65	8	2,619	144	45.94
M. C. Cowdrey	43	75	4	2,433	113	34.26
L. Hutton	27	49	6	2,428	364	56.46
R. N. Harvey	37	68	5	2,416	167	38.34
V. T. Trumper	40	74	5	2,263	185*	32.79
W. M. Lawry	29	51	5	2,233	166	48.54
S. E. Gregory	52	92	7	2,193	201	25.80
W. W. Armstrong	42	71	9	2,172	158	35.03
I. M. Chappell	30	56	4	2,138	192	41.11
K. F. Barrington	23	39	6	2,111	256	63.96
A. R. Morris	24	43	2	2,080	206	50.73

Statham, John Brian

Statham was born on 17 June 1930 at Gorton, Manchester. He got into the Lancashire team in 1950, as an accurate right-arm fast bowler. He was flown out to join the England tour party to Australia in 1950–51 and made his Test debut against New Zealand. He was the most consistent of England's fast bowlers for many years, although sometimes outshone by Trueman or Tyson. In 70 Tests he took 252 wickets, average 24.84, standing second in the all-time aggregates at the time.

Greg Chappell (below) captained Australia in 1980–81.

Davidson, Alan Keith

Davidson was born in Gosford, NSW, on 14 June 1929. He made his debut for his state as an all-rounder in 1949–50. A middle to lower left-hand batsman, his main value was as a left-arm fast-medium bowler. He was also a brilliant fielder. He made his first Test appearance in England in 1953. In 44 Tests he scored 1,328 runs, average 24.59, and took 186 wickets, average 20.53.

BOWLERS WITH 100 WICKETS

	T	Balls	R	W	5 W/i	Avge
D. K. Lillee	29	8,516	3,507	167	11	21.00
I. T. Botham	36	8,479	4,093	148	9	27.65
H. Trumble	31	7,895	2,945	141	9	20.88
R. G. D. Willis	35	7,294	3,346	128	7	26.14
M. A. Noble	39	6,845	2,860	115	9	24.86
R. R. Lindwall	29	6,728	2,559	114	6	22.44
W. Rhodes	41	5,791	2,616	109	6	24.00
S. F. Barnes	20	5,749	2,288	106	12	21.58
C. V. Grimmett	22	9,224	3,439	106	11	32.44
D. L. Underwood	29	8,000	2,770	105	4	26.38
A. V. Bedser	21	7,065	2,859	104	7	27.49
G. Giffen	31	6,325	2,791	103	7	27.09
W. J. O'Reilly	19	7,864	2,587	102	8	25.36
R. Peel	20	5,216	1,715	102	6	16.81
C. T. B. Turner	17	5,195	1,670	101	11	16.53
J. R. Thomson	21	4,951	2,418	100	5	24.18

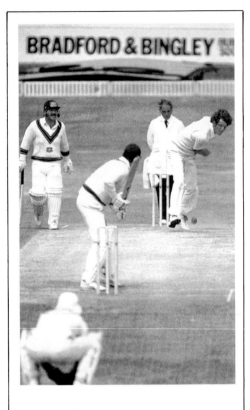

Willis, Robert George Dylan

Willis was born on 30 May 1949 at Sunderland. The Dylan in his name he added himself in admiration of the singer. He first played for Surrey in 1969, but moved to Warwickshire in 1972 for more opportunities. By then he had made his Test debut in 1970–71, when he was flown out as an addition to the party. He was a right-arm fast bowler. He played in 90 Tests, and was captain in 18. His best performance, eight for 43, helped England win the amazing Test match at Headingley in 1981. He took 325 Test wickets, average 25.20.

Opposite: Stump-grabbing for souvenirs as England beat Australia in the fifth Test at Edgbaston in 1985.

Lillee, Dennis Keith

Lillee was born in Subiaco, Western Australia, on 18 July 1949, and played for his state from 1969–70. An aggressive right-arm fast bowler, he made his Test debut a year later. He became the oustanding fast bowler of the 1970s. His name will be associated with Thomson, his fellow fast bowler who helped him demolish England in 1974–75, and with Marsh, who caught 95 of his Test victims. In 65 Tests he took 355 wickets, then the world record, average 23.92. He frequently attracted publicity, some of it of the worst kind.

Doug Walters, who topped the 1973–74 averages in Australia.

MOST WICKETS
IN A SERIES

England in England	46 (average 9.60)	J. C. Laker	1956
England in Australia	38 (average 23.18)	M. W. Tate	1924–25
Australia in England	42 (average 21.26)	T. M. Alderman (6 Tests)	1981
Australia in Australia	41 (average 12.85)	R. M. Hogg (6 Tests)	1978–79

WICKET-KEEPING —
MOST DISMISSALS

	M	Ct	St	Total
R. W. Marsh (Australia)	42	141	7	148
A. P. E. Knott (England)	34	97	8	105
W. A. Oldfield (Australia)	38	59	31	90
A. A. Lilley (England)	32	65	19	84
A. T. W. Grout (Australia)	22	69	7	76
T. G. Evans (England)	31	63	12	75

Don Bradman in the nets. He led Australia to victory in 19 Ashes Tests.

Bedser, Alec Victor

Bedser is one of twin brothers, born on 4 July 1918 at Reading, who both became part of the Surrey side which won the Championship in seven successive years in the 1950s, having made appearances in 1939. Alec was an outstanding medium-paced bowler who made his Test debut in 1946, taking 11 wickets in each of his first two Tests. He was England's leading bowler for eight years and especially successful against Australia and Bradman. In all he played in 51 Tests and took 236 wickets at 24.89 each. His aggregate was the world record at the time.

Right: Richie Benaud batting in England. Benaud captained Australia in Ashes series between 1958 and 1963.

May, Peter Barker Howard

Born on 31 December 1929 at Reading, May was a brilliant schoolboy batsman and made his debut for Surrey on vacation from Cambridge University in 1950. He made his Test debut the following year. He was a correct and polished right-hand bat,

the most talented English batsman of the 1950s. He played for Surrey throughout their seven successive championships. He played in 66 Tests, captaining England 41 times, an English record. He scored 4,537 runs, average 46.77. Ill-health caused him to give up Test cricket in 1961.

Picture Credits

All colour photographs in pages 1–80 are by Patrick Eagar, except for those on pages 7 and 10, which are by Allsport UK Ltd.

All the photographs in pages 81–107 are by Allsport UK Ltd.

All other illustrations have been supplied by The Keystone Collection, with the exception of the following, which are from the archive of Nottinghamshire County Cricket Club:
page 13; page 14, bottom left; 16, both; 22/23, both; 25; 26; 27; 28/29, both; 31, top; 33, both; 35, bottom right; 36; 37, both; 38; 39, bottom; 40; 42, top; 43; 47, top left; 48, top left and centre; 49, top right; 52, top left; 59, bottom; 60, bottom right; 111, bottom left.

AUTHORS' ACKNOWLEDGMENT

The authors would like to thank Dickie Bird for his contribution to this book, and hope that he will be in the middle for a few more Ashes series. The authors would also like to thank Jim Ledbeater for his help in supplying most of the series-by-series averages, for which the cut-off point is 250 runs or 12 wickets for series of five or more matches, 200 runs or 10 wickets for three or four-match series. All England–Australia Test series up to that in 1989 are included. Statistics conform to those of the Association of Cricket Statisticians.

Overleaf: The latest in a long line of Ashes-winning skippers. Let's hope he remembers to drink out of his right hand and not his left!